Picture This!

Learning English Through Pictures

Tim Harris   Allan Rowe

TEACHER'S EDITION

Ellen Kisslinger

PEARSON
Longman

Picture This! Learning English Through Pictures 1
Teacher's Edition

Pearson Education, 10 Bank Street, White Plains, NY 10606

Cover illustration: Allan Rowe
Text design: Tim Harris
Text composition: Jacqueline Tobin, Rainbow Graphics
Text font: 13/15 Times Roman, 13/15 Helvetica
Text art: Allan Rowe

ISBN 0-13-170337-4

Printed in the United States of America
1 2 3 4 5 6 7 8 9 10-ML-10 09 08 07 06

CONTENTS

PREFACE

Picture This! is a two-level multi-skills course for beginning students of English. This innovative course enables students to master the basics, so they can use English effectively for everyday situations.

APPROACH AND METHODOLOGY

The ability of our students to communicate in English involves two tasks at the same time: (1) deciding what they want to say and (2) using the appropriate language to express their thoughts. It's much easier for them to do both things at once if the second task can be done automatically. Our first priority, therefore, is to help students "automatize" basic structures and high-frequency vocabulary, the "core language" they need for communication.

Automatization is the ability of students to remember information and perform tasks without having to stop and think about what they are doing. When information or tasks are automatized, using this information and performing these tasks is almost as effortless as breathing. To help beginning students automatize the core language, *Picture This!* provides intensive practice based on principles of learning that promote memory.

Memory – central to all types of learning – is especially important in language learning because it determines how well students are able to use the language after they leave the classroom. If we understand how memory can be made stronger – for example, by visualization, by rehearsal, by transformation, or by writing – we can design lessons that will help our students improve their memory for the material they must learn. To enhance memory, *Picture This!* uses a range of picture-based lessons in an integrated skills approach to learning.

PICTURE-BASED LESSONS: It is all too easy for students to forget language or concepts that are "explained" in class. It is much easier to remember concepts that are shown or demonstrated, and pictures, by their very nature, show instead of tell. The lively and engaging illustrations in *Picture This!* make it easy for students to learn and remember the words for people, places, objects, and characteristics. The artwork also provides effective and meaningful practice with basic structures and language functions. Learning experts tell us an excellent way to remember something is to change it, to transform it in some way. To help students remember new grammar and vocabulary, *Picture This!* asks students to express in words the instructional information contained in the pictures. By taking something *visual* and making it *verbal*, the students are transforming information and filing it in their active working memory.

INTEGRATED SKILLS: In *Picture This!* the four skills of language learning (listening, speaking, reading, and writing) are usually combined in the same lesson. A typical lesson contains several pictures demonstrating a particular grammatical structure or language function. The students hear the target structure as they listen to conversations about the pictures, and they repeat the questions and answers they hear on the recordings. The students are encouraged to recreate the conversations with information provided by the pictures. They also write the sentences containing the target structure, which they then read aloud. By the end of the lesson, all four skills have been applied to learning a single structure, and when this happens, student retention increases dramatically.

Picture This! offers a true integrated skills approach to learning, with lessons designed in such a way that one skill improves another. Particular attention is given to integrating the writing skill, as writing can do so much to foster acquisition of the other skills. For example, it's a great advantage when students get in the habit of writing down their "talk" because this makes their thinking – and their mistakes – visible. So we suggest having students go to the board and write the language forms they have been practicing orally. With a little assistance, students are able to correct their own mistakes in grammar and spelling. This opportunity enables students to take risks, to monitor their progress, and to improve their ability to communicate – both orally and in writing.

LEARNING ENGLISH THROUGH PICTURES: The detailed illustrations in *Picture This!* make key vocabulary easily comprehensible to students, so they can perform a range of meaningful tasks from the first day of class. Packed with visual information, the illustrations provide frequent opportunities to go beyond the lesson on the page and engage in more spontaneous, less-structured activities. The illustrations present a cast of colorful characters in all kinds of situations, often humorous, for students to talk about. Having conversations about fictional characters paves the way for students to talk about their own life experiences. The warm, evocative illustrations in *Picture This!* make learning English more personal and enjoyable for the students.

WHAT EACH CHAPTER CONTAINS

Cartoon Story   The grammar of each chapter is introduced in an entertaining cartoon story that demonstrates the use of natural speech and conversational expressions. The stories personalize the themes and functions covered in the curriculum.

Grammar   Picture-based lessons provide thorough, systematic, and meaningful practice with the grammatical structures introduced in each chapter.

Listening   The listening activities are integrated with oral activities and writing exercises to develop students' ability to understand, reproduce, and remember what they hear.

Speaking   Students develop their speaking ability through a variety of activities including guided conversations, role plays, and free response questions that allow students to talk about themselves. Imaginative illustrations suggest many opportunities for creative language practice.

Reading   Various types of texts enable students to steadily develop their reading skills as they learn new grammar and vocabulary. Stimulating topics create motivated readers and opportunities for discussion.

Writing   The writing exercises reinforce core language and help students develop their listening, speaking, and reading skills.

Pronunciation   Each chapter includes a section with exercises that focus on pronunciation points, such as vowel and consonant sounds, plurals, stress and intonation.

Life Skills   Everyday life situations provide contexts for learning basic competencies in the areas that are most important to students: food, clothing, transportation, work, housing, and health care.

COURSE COMPONENTS:

The text of *Picture This!* is recorded on three CDs. An interleaved Teacher's Edition provides practical teaching tips, expansion activities, and answer keys.

CONTENTS

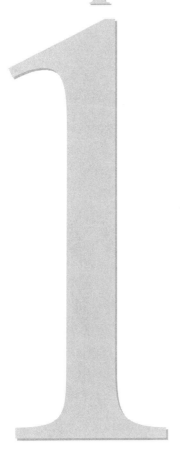

Chapter

1

MEETING AND GREETING PEOPLE

▶ **CONVERSATION 1**

🎧 *Listen. Listen and practice.*

▶ **PAIR WORK 1** • *Introduce yourself to other students.*

A: Hello. My name is _____.

B: I'm _____.

A: Nice to meet you, _____.

B: Nice to meet you, too.

▶ **CONVERSATION 2**

🎧 *Listen. Listen and practice.*

MARIA: Hi. How are you?

CARLOS: I'm fine. And you?

MARIA: Fine, thank you.

▶ **PAIR WORK 2** • *Have similar conversations.*

MEETING and GREETING

Page Summary

Grammar Present tense of *be*
Function Introducing yourself

Warm-up

Introduce yourself, *My name is . . . .* Point to a student and ask, *What's your name?* Go around the room and ask the question of several more students.

▶ CONVERSATION 1

🎧 *Listen. Listen and practice.*

1. Have students look at the illustrations.
2. Set the scene: Jack is meeting Jill for the first time.
3. Play the recording (CD track 2) as students listen.
4. Explain the use of contractions. Write on the board, *I am.* Cross out the *a* and replace it with an apostrophe.
5. Play the recording (CD track 3) for students to repeat.

❗ *Pronunciation Tip*

The stress shifts in the response: A: *Nice to MEET you.* B: *Nice to meet YOU, TOO.*

▶ PAIR WORK 1

1. Call on a student to practice the conversation with you. Switch parts and repeat.
2. Pair students. Call on a pair to model the conversation.
3. Have pairs practice the conversation. Have partners switch parts.
4. Call on pairs to present the conversation to the class.

Option: Model how to shake hands during an introduction.

Culture Note

In many English-speaking countries, it is important to give a firm handshake. For students unaccustomed to shaking hands, demonstrate three handshakes with a student partner: too weak, too firm, and in the middle. Explain that in a casual setting people don't always shake hands, but in a business or formal setting they do.

Expansion Activity

Have students go around the room and introduce themselves to other classmates. Either set a time limit (2 minutes) or tell them to introduce themselves to five other classmates.

▶ CONVERSATION 2

🎧 *Listen. Listen and practice.*

1. Have students look at the illustration.
2. Set the scene: Maria is greeting Carlos. Point out how she gives a casual wave.
3. Play the recording (CD track 4) as students listen.
4. Play the recording (CD track 5) for students to repeat.

❗ *Pronunciation Tip*

The stress in the response is: And YOU? In rapid speech And YOU? is reduced to andJU?

▶ PAIR WORK 2

1. Call on a student to practice the conversation with you. Point out that in this greeting exchange, people are expected to say *Fine* even if they are not.
2. Pair students. Call on a pair to model the conversation.
3. Have pairs practice the conversation. Have partners switch parts. Circulate to check pronunciation and stress.
4. Call on pairs to present the conversation to the class.

Expansion Activity

Have students greet other classmates seated near them. Have students stand up and shake hands as they greet each other. Encourage them to move around and speak to students in all parts of the room.

INTRODUCING SOMEONE

Page Summary

Grammar Present tense of *be*
Function Asking about and identifying people

Warm-up

Go around the room. Stop at a student and say the student's name, *Her name is . . . .* Turn to another student and ask, *Who's that?* (indicate the first student). After the second student answers, continue around the room with other students.

Grammar Note

- *Who's* is a contraction for *who is.* Some students might be confused if they are already familiar with the possessive *whose.* Write on the board *who is.* Erase the *i* and replace it with an apostrophe.
- Explain: *name's = name is* and *She's = She is.*

▶ CONVERSATION 1

🎧 *Listen. Listen and practice.*

1. Have students look at the illustrations.
2. Set the scene: Alice and Dallas are at a party. They're talking about Alice's friend, Daisy. Point to each character in the top picture. Explain that they will see Dallas and Daisy many times in the book.
3. Play the recording (CD track 6) as students listen.
4. Play the recording (CD track 7) for students to repeat.

Option: Explain that single = unmarried. Alice is making small talk. She is trying to get Dallas interested in Daisy by adding this information.

❗ *Pronunciation Tip*

Stress is on the stressed syllable of content words: *WOman, DAIsy, NICE, SINgle, COOK.* Read Alice's lines about Daisy, emphasizing the stress on the content words. Have students repeat.

Expansion Activity 1

Use the illustration for more speaking practice. Point to the illustration and have students describe what they see, for example, *Dallas is a cowboy.* Ask students to speculate what else might be true about Dallas and Daisy.

Expansion Activity 2

Have students each write down two things about themselves on a piece of paper. *(I like music. I am a terrific singer.)* Form groups of three. Students exchange papers. Have them practice the conversation, substituting their own names and each other's information.

▶ CONVERSATION 2

🎧 *Listen. Listen and practice.*

1. Have students look at the illustration.
2. Set the scene: Alice is introducing Daisy to her friend Dallas. Point out how Alice gestures toward Dallas during the introduction.
3. Play the recording (CD track 8) as students listen.
4. Play the recording (CD track 9) for students to repeat.

▶ GROUP WORK

1. Call on two students to practice the introduction with you, using their own names.
2. Form groups of three. Call on one group to model the introduction.
3. Have groups practice the conversation, switching parts.
4. Call on groups to present the introduction to the class.

Expansion Activity

Practice more introductions. Have students form groups of three, and tell them to introduce themselves using the model in the book. Tell that when you clap your hands, they should form a new group of three. Repeat several times to give students the opportunity to meet many classmates.

INTRODUCING SOMEONE

▶ **CONVERSATION 1**

🎧 *Listen. Listen and practice.*

Hey, Alice. Who's that woman over there?

Her name's Daisy. She's very nice...and she's single.

That's interesting.

She's a terrific cook.

That's very interesting.

▶ **CONVERSATION 2**

🎧 *Listen. Listen and practice.*

DAISY: Hi, Alice. Who's your friend?

ALICE: Daisy, this is Dallas.

DAISY: Nice to meet you.

DALLAS: Nice to meet you, too.

▶ **GROUP WORK** • *Have similar conversations with two other students. Use your own names.*

OCCUPATIONS

▶ 🎧 *Look and listen. Listen and repeat.*

1. This is John Denby.
   He's a teacher.

2. This is Susan Chen.
   She's a doctor.

3. This is Carlos Bravo.
   He's a mechanic.

4. This is Daisy Miller.
   She's a chef.

5. This is Mike Kelly.
   He's a pilot.

6. This is Betty Jones.
   She's a banker.

7. This is Peter Gamble.
   He's a businessman.

8. This is Maria Lopez.
   She's a carpenter.

9. This is Grover Muldoon.
   He's a police officer.

OCCUPATIONS

Page Summary

Grammar Present tense of *be*
Function Identifying people and occupations

Warm-up

Say, *I'm a teacher*. Write it on the board. Say the names of famous people the students will be familiar with, and help them identify their occupations, for example, *Madonna. She's a singer.*

NOTE

The term *businesswoman* is used as well as *businessman* (item 7).

▶ 🎧 *Look and listen. Listen and repeat.*

1. Have students look at the illustrations and listen as you play the recording (CD track 10).
2. Play the recording (CD track 11) and have the students repeat.
3. Call on various students to read one sentence each.

Option: Pair students. Have students take turns reading the sentences aloud.

❗ *Pronunciation Tip*

Point out that the content words are stressed: She's a CHEF, He's a meCHANnic, He's a poLICE officer, She's a CARpenter.

Expansion Activity 1

Practice introductions using the illustrations. Have students form groups of three. Have each student choose an identity from the page and write it down. Students show each other the information as it's needed in the conversation. Model an introduction with two student partners.

T: *Hi, (Susan). Who's your friend?*
Susan: *This is (Mike). He's (a pilot).*

Expansion Activity 2

Pair students. One student closes his or her eyes. The other points to the page and moves his or her finger until the partner says *Stop*. The student opens his or her eyes, and reads the information about the person in the picture closest to his or her finger. Students take turns. This can be done as a timed activity. Challenge the students to see how many turns they can take in a set time (3 minutes).

Page Summary

Grammar *Yes/no* questions and responses
Function Asking about occupations of people

Warm-up

Ask a few *yes/no* questions about famous people. Model the question and the response: *Is Brad Pitt an actor? Yes, he is./Is Venus Williams a pilot? No, she isn't. She's a tennis player.*

Grammar Notes

- Short answers are common when the information is clear from the context.
- Some students may be familiar with the other, equally common possibilities for negative short answers: *No, he's not./No, she's not.*

▶ 🎧 *Listen. Listen and repeat.*

1. Have students look at the illustrations and listen as you play the recording (CD track 12).
2. Play the recording (CD track 13) for students to repeat.

▶ WRITING

1. Have students work alone to fill in the answers using the responses at the top of the page and adding additional information for the negative responses.
2. Play the recording (CD track 12) again so that students can check their answers.
3. Go over the answers with the class by calling on pairs of students to read the conversations. Point out that the short answer is enough because it is clear what is being talked about.

Answer Key

1. No, she isn't. She's a police officer.
2. Yes, he is.
3. No, he isn't. He's a doctor.
4. Yes, she is.
5. No, she isn't. She's a mechanic.
6. Yes, he is.
7. No, he isn't. He's a carpenter.
8. Yes, she is.

❗ *Pronunciation Tip*

There is rising intonation on a *yes/no* question. Before students practice in pairs, model the intonation for students to repeat.

▶ PAIR WORK

1. Pair students. Have them practice the conversations.
2. Call on different pairs to read each conversation to the class.

Option: Call on one pair to say the first conversation. Have that pair choose another pair to say the next conversation.

Expansion Activity

Use the illustrations for more practice. Pair students. One partner reads one of the questions on the page, but then points to a different illustration. The other partner responds, answering the question correctly. For example, one partner points to the chef and asks, *Is he a mechanic?* The other partner responds, *No, he isn't. He's a chef.* Before having the students proceed, model the activity with a student partner. Have students take turns.

| Is | he / she | a pilot? / a doctor? | Yes, | he / she | is. | No, | he / she | isn't. |

| Is | he
she | a pilot?
a doctor? | | Yes, | he
she | is. | | No, | he
she | isn't. |

▶ 🎧 *Listen. Listen and repeat.*　　　▶ **PAIR WORK** • *Practice the conversations.*

1.
Is she a pilot?
No, she isn't. She's a police officer.

2.
Is he a firefighter?
Yes, he is.

3.
Is he a mechanic?

4.
Is she a teacher?

5.
Is she a banker?

6.
Is he a chef?

7.
Is he a doctor?

8.
Is she a pilot?

▶ **WRITING** • *Fill in the answers. Then read the conversations aloud.*

Chapter 1　**5**

LOCATIONS

Where	's (is)	Jimmy? Alice?

He She	's (is)	at the park. at the office.

▶ 🎧 *Listen. Listen and practice.*

1. **Where's Alice?** — **She's at the office.**

2. **Where's Jimmy?** — **He's at the park.**

3. **Where's Carlos?** — **He's at the bank.**

4. **Where's Maria?** — **She's at the library.**

5. **Where's Betty?** — **She's at the supermarket.**

6. **Where's Mike?** — **He's at the beach.**

7. **Where's Grover?** — **He's at the post office.**

8. **Where's Susan?** — **She's at the hospital.**

LOCATIONS

Page Summary

Grammar Prepositions
Function Asking about where people are

Grammar Notes

- To explain contractions, review *She's = She is*. Then write on the board, *Where is*. Erase the *i* and replace it with an apostrophe.
- In all of the responses, the definite article *the* is used. This is because the person is at a specific place, even if the name of the location is not given.

❗ *Pronunciation Tip*
Native speakers of English often link sounds, and the *s* in *where's* is pronounced like a *z*:

> *Where's Alice = Wherz Alice?*
> *She's at the bank = Shezat the bank.*

🎧 *Listen. Listen and practice.*

1. Have students look at the illustrations and listen as you play the recording (CD track 14).

2. Play the recording (CD track 15) and have the students repeat.

Option: Pair students. Have pairs practice the conversations.

Expansion Activity
Pair students. Have them use the illustrations to take turns asking and answering questions with *Where*. Student 1 says a name *(Maria)*. Student 2 asks the question *(Where is Maria?)*. Student 1 responds, *She's at the library.* Students switch parts.

Page Summary

Grammar *Yes/no* questions and responses; prepositions
Function Talking about where people are

▶ 🎧 *Listen. Listen and repeat.*

1. Have students look at the illustrations and listen, without writing anything, as you play the recording (CD track 16).
2. Play the recording (CD track 17) for students to repeat.

▶ **PAIR WORK**

1. Pair students. Have them practice the conversations.
2. Call on different pairs to say each conversation to the class.

▶ **WRITING**

1. Have students work alone to fill in the answers.
2. Play the recording (CD track 16) again so that students can check their answers.
3. Go over the answers with the class by calling on pairs of students to read the conversations.

Answer Key

1. No, he isn't. He's at the library.
2. Yes, she is.
3. No, she isn't. She's at the bank.
4. Yes, he is.
5. Yes, he is.
6. No, she isn't. She's at the park.
7. Yes, she is.
8. No, he isn't. He's at the beach.

Expansion Activity

Have students use the illustrations to practice more conversations. Pair students. Have them take turns asking each other more questions about the people on the page. First model an example with a student partner: *Is Jimmy at the beach? No, he isn't. He's at the library.* After students practice, call on a few pairs to present their conversations to the class.

Is	Jimmy / Alice	at the park? / at work?		Yes,	he / she	is.		No,	he / she	isn't.

▶ 🎧 *Listen. Listen and repeat.*　　　▶ **PAIR WORK** • *Practice the conversations.*

1. Is Jimmy home? — No, he isn't. He's at the library. (LIBRARY)

2. Is Alice at work? — Yes, she is. (Smith Real Estate)

3. Is Susan at the post office? (CITY BANK)

4. Is Carlos at the garage? (GARAGE)

5. Is Grover at the supermarket? (SUPERMARKET)

6. Is Maria home? (CITY PARK)

7. Is Betty at the post office? (POST OFFICE)

8. Is Mike at work?

▶ **WRITING** • *Fill in the answers. Then read the conversations aloud.*

NUMBERS

▶ 🎧 *Listen and repeat.*

0	1	2	3	4	5	6	7	8	9	10
zero (oh)	one	two	three	four	five	six	seven	eight	nine	ten

▶ **CONVERSATION**

🎧 *Listen.*

> What's your name?

> Ken Honda.

▶ **WRITING** • *Write your name, address and phone number.*

LIBRARY CARD

Name: ___Ken Honda___

Address: ___529 Maple Street___

___Portland, Oregon___

Phone Number: ___(503) 825-3906___

LIBRARY CARD

Name:_____

Address:_____

_____

Phone Number:_____

▶ **PAIR WORK** • *Ask the person next to you:*

• What's your name?

• What's your address?

• What's your phone number?

NUMBERS

Page Summary

Grammar *Wh-* questions
Function Asking for personal information

▶ 🎧 *Listen and repeat.*

1. Have students look at the numbers.
2. Play the recording (CD track 18) as students listen and repeat.

▶ CONVERSATION

🎧 *Listen.*

1. Have students look at the illustration.
2. Set the scene: Ken Honda is a student. He's at the library. He's talking with the librarian.
3. Play the recording (CD track 19) as students listen.
4. Play the recording (CD track 19) again for students to repeat.

▶ WRITING

NOTE

Some students may not feel comfortable sharing personal information in class. Make sure that students understand that it is OK to make up addresses or phone numbers if they would prefer not to give out their real ones.

1. Have students read aloud the information on the first library card.
2. Point to the illustration of Ken Honda and ask, *Who's this? What's his address? What's his phone number?* Point out that the zero in telephone numbers is often pronounced "oh," for example, 503 = five-oh-three.

Option: Pair students. Have them take turns asking and answering the questions.

3. Have students work alone to write their own information on the library card on the right.
4. Indicate a student. Ask, *What's your name? What's your address? What's your phone number?*

▶ PAIR WORK

1. Pair students. Have them practice asking and answering the questions.
2. Call on a couple of pairs to present for the class.

Expansion Activity 1

Have students walk around the room and ask two other people the questions at the bottom of the page.

Expansion Activity 2

Repeat the activity, but have students add the question, *What's your e-mail address?* Remind students that they do not have to give out their real e-mail addresses if they don't want to.

TIME

Page Summary

Grammar Present tense of *be*
Function Asking for and telling the time

▶ 🎧 *Listen. Listen and repeat.*
1. Have students look at the clocks.
2. Play the recording (CD track 20) as students listen.
3. Play the recording (CD track 21) for students to repeat.

▶ **PAIR WORK**
1. Read the example to the class.
2. Model the example with a student partner. Switch parts and repeat.
3. Have students look at the second clock. Ask a student, *What time is it?* Have the whole class repeat the response, *It's five o'clock.*
4. Call on a pair of students to present the same conversation in item 3.
5. Pair students. Have them take turns asking and answering questions about the time on the clocks.

Option: Call on different pairs to present each time for the class.

Expansion Activity 1
Review times in a chain ask-and-answer activity. Say a number and then a student's name, for example, *3. Ana.* Ana asks the question of another student, adding his or her name at the end of her question: *What time is it, (Alex)?* Alex responds, *It's ten o'clock.* Alex calls on another student: *5. Tomas.* Tomas continues by asking another student about the time for number 5 *(9:00).* Remind students to say the name after the question. This will keep everyone listening actively.

Expansion Activity 2
Have students use the clocks as a board for playing Tic-Tac-Toe. Pair students. Students take turns. To occupy a clock, a student must say the time first *(It's eleven o'clock)*, then place a piece of paper on the empty clock. When there are three clocks in a row covered, the student says, *Time.* To win, a student must occupy three clocks in a row in any direction. Have students repeat as time permits.

▶ **WRITING**
1. Have students work alone to write the time under each clock.
2. Pair students to compare answers.
3. Write or have students write the times on the board for the class to check answers.

Expansion Activity
Write five times on the board (8:00, 6:00, 5:00, 2:00, 1:00). Have students write out the times in complete sentences *(It's eight o'clock)*, and raise their hands when they are finished. Have volunteers write the sentences on the board for the class to check answers.

TIME

▶ 🎧 *Listen. Listen and repeat.*

What time is it?   What time is it?   What time is it?
It's seven o'clock.   It's twelve o'clock.   It's four o'clock.

▶ **PAIR WORK** • *Ask and answer questions.*

A: **What time is it?**
B: **It's eleven o'clock.**

1. <u>It's eleven o'clock.</u> 2. _____ 3. _____

4. _____ 5. _____ 6. _____

7. _____ 8. _____ 9. _____

▶ **WRITING** • *Write the time under each clock.*

GRAMMAR • This/That

What	's (is)	this? that?		It	's (is)	a cat. a dog.

🎧 *This is an English class for international students. Listen. Listen and practice.*

What's this? It's a chair.

What's that? It's a table.

What's this? It's an umbrella.

What's that? It's a coat.

What's this? It's a cat.

What's that? It's a dog.

What's this? It's a ball.

What's that? It's a bicycle.

GRAMMAR • This/That

Grammar *This/that*
Function Asking about and identifying objects

Warm-up

Point to an object near you, for example, a chair, and ask, *What's this?* Model the response, *It's a chair.* Have students repeat. Then identify another chair on the other side of the room and ask, *What's that?* Model the response, *It's a chair.*

Grammar Note

Explain the contractions. Write on the board:

> *What's this? = What is this?*
> *It's a (dog) = It is a (dog).*

▶ 🎧 *Listen. Listen and practice.*

1. Have students look at the illustrations.
2. Play the recording (CD track 22) as students listen.
3. Play the recording (CD track 23) for students to repeat.

4. Pair students. Have them practice the conversations. Tell them to use gestures. First model pointing close to you for *this*, and then far away for *that*.
5. Call on different pairs to present each conversation to the class.

Expansion Activity

Have students use the illustrations to practice more conversations. Pair students. Have one student in each pair cover an entire column of responses with a piece of paper. Have the other student point to the objects in the drawings at random and ask, *What's this?* First model an example with a student partner. After students practice, call on a few pairs to present to the class.

Page Summary

Grammar *Yes/no* questions; *this/that*
Function Asking about and identifying (singular) objects

Grammar Note

An alternative to *No, it isn't* is *No, it's not.*

⚠ *Pronunciation Tip*
The voice rises at the end of a *yes/no* question.

▶ 🎧 *Listen. Listen and repeat.*

1. Have students look at the illustrations and listen, without writing anything, as you play the recording (CD track 24).
2. Play the recording (CD track 25) for students to repeat.

▶ PAIR WORK

1. Pair students. Have them practice the conversations.
2. Call on different pairs to say each conversation to the class. Remind them to use rising intonation with the questions.

▶ WRITING

1. Have students work alone to fill in the answers using the responses at the top of the page. Circulate and check their work.
2. Play the recording (CD track 24) again so that students can check their answers.
3. Go over the answers with the class by calling on pairs of students to read the conversations.

Option: Divide the class into two groups. Have one group read the questions and the other group give the responses.

Expansion Activity 1

Have students practice more conversations using objects in the room. Pair students. Have them take turns asking each other more questions. First present or review the names of classroom objects: *desk, window, door,* and so on, as needed. Model an example with a student partner. Point to something close to you. Ask, *Is this a (desk)?* After the student responds, point to something farther away. Ask, *Is that a (door)?* Then switch parts. This can be done as a timed activity. Challenge students to see how many objects they can ask about in a set time (5 minutes).

Expansion Activity 2

Form two teams of students. Give one team member a paper with the word for an object familiar to the students written on it, such as *(book)*. The team member goes to board and starts to draw. The first person to say *Is that a book?* gets a point. Continue giving words to students, alternating teams, as time permits. The team with the most points wins.

Is	this that	a table? a chair?	Yes, it is.	No, it isn't.

▶ 🎧 *Listen. Listen and repeat.*　　　▶ **PAIR WORK** • *Practice the conversations.*

1. Is this a magazine? — No, it isn't. It's a newspaper.

2. Is that a magazine? — Yes, it is.

3. Is that a ball?

4. Is this a ball?

5. Is this a cat?

6. Is that a table?

7. Is that a book?

8. Is this a coat?

▶ **WRITING** • *Fill in the answers. Then read the conversations aloud.*

GRAMMAR • These/Those

What	are	these? those?

They	're (are)	apples. pears.

▶ 🎧 *Listen. Listen and practice.*

GRAMMAR • These/Those

Page Summary

Grammar *Wh-* questions; *these/those*
Function Asking about and identifying plural objects

Grammar Note

An alternative to *No, they aren't* is *No, they're not.*

Warm-up

Ask about a few objects in the classroom. Point to some chairs near you and ask, *What are these?* Model the response, *They're chairs.* Have students repeat. Then ask about a couple of objects far from you. Ask, *What are those?* Model the response, *They're (books).* Repeat with a few more objects to make the meaning of these and those clear.

❗ *Pronunciation Tip*

In the book, the questions use the full, noncontracted form *What are.* Both *are* and the contraction *'re* are used in the responses. However, in rapid speech the contracted form is often used in questions *(What're these?).*

▶ 🎧 *Listen. Listen and practice.*

1. Have students look at the illustrations.
2. Play the recording (CD track 26) as students listen.
3. Play the recording (CD track 27) for students to repeat.
4. Pair students. Have them practice the conversations.
5. Call on different pairs to present each conversation to the class.

Page Summary

Grammar *Yes/no* questions; *these/those*
Function Asking about and identifying plural objects

! *Pronunciation Tip*

The strongest stress is placed on the content words:
Are these *GLASSES? No, they aren't. They're CUPS,*
because the most important information is what the
object is.

🎧 *Listen. Listen and repeat.*

1. Have students look at the illustrations and listen,
   without writing anything, as you play the recording
   (CD track 28).
2. Play the recording (CD track 29) for students to
   repeat.

▶ PAIR WORK

1. Pair students. Have them practice the conversations.
2. Call on different pairs to say each conversation to
   the class.

▶ WRITING

1. Have students work alone to fill in the answers
   using the responses at the top of the page.
2. Play the recording (CD track 28) again so that
   students can check their answers.

Expansion Activity

Have students practice more conversations using the
objects in the room. Model an example using pens
near you. Ask, *Are these pencils?* Elicit, *No, they
aren't* (or *No, they're not*). *They're pens.* Ask about
some books across the room, *Are those books?* Elicit,
Yes, they are. Pair students. Have them take turns
asking and answering about objects in the room.
Circulate and help with vocabulary as needed.

Are	these	flowers?	Yes, they are.	No, they aren't.
	those	trees?		

▶ 🎧 *Listen. Listen and repeat.*　　　　▶ **PAIR WORK** • *Practice the conversations.*

▶ **WRITING** • *Fill in the answers. Then read the conversations aloud.*

GRAMMAR • Prepositions

▶ 🎧 *Look and listen. Listen and repeat.*

The bird is **in** the cage.

The cat is **under** the cage.

The cat is **on** the table.

The cat is **next to** the cage.

The bird is **in front of** the cat.

The man is **behind** the cat.

▶ **PAIR WORK** • *Ask and answer questions. Choose the correct preposition.*

Example: **Where are the birds?**
They're in the tree.

1. Where's Billy?
   He's (under/on) the tree.

2. Where's the ball?
   It's (behind/in front of) Billy.

3. Where's the bicycle?
   It's (next to/in) the tree.

4. Where's the dog?
   It's (in front of/behind) the tree.

5. Where are the apples?
   They're (in/under) the basket.

6. Where's the basket?
   It's (next to/on) the table.

GRAMMAR • Prepositions

Page Summary

Grammar Prepositions
Function Indicating location

🎧 *Look and listen. Listen and repeat.*

1. Have students look at the illustrations and listen as you play the recording (CD track 30). Tell students to point to each picture as they listen to help them understand the preposition.
2. Play the recording (CD track 31) and have the students repeat.
3. Call on individual students to read the sentences about each picture.

Option: Pair students. Have students take turns reading the sentences aloud.

▶ PAIR WORK

1. Read the example to the class.
2. Call on a student to answer the first question (*Where's Billy? He's under the tree*).
3. Call on a pair of students to answer question 2.
4. Pair students. Have them take turns asking the questions.

Option: First have students work alone to choose the correct prepositions, and then go over the answers as a class before students practice the conversations.

5. Call on different pairs to read each conversation to the class.

Answer Key

1. He's under the tree.
2. It's in front of Billy.
3. It's next to the tree.
4. It's behind the tree.
5. They're in the basket.
6. It's on the table.

Expansion Activity 1

Use the illustrations at the top of the page to play a game. Say two objects, for example, *cat*, then *table*. Students make the sentence: *The cat is on the table.* Have students respond first chorally, and then individually. Alternatively, say a preposition *(on)*; students make the sentence: *The cat is on the table.* Choose illustrations at random.

Expansion Activity 2

Use the illustration at the bottom of the page to ask more questions. Ask, *Where's Billy?* Elicit, *He's under the tree. Where's the bicycle? (It's next to the tree.).* Ask, *Where's the table?* Elicit, *It's under the tree. It's next to the dog.* Also ask, *What's on the table? (the basket). What's in the basket? (the apples).*

GRAMMAR • Prepositions

Page Summary

Grammar Prepositions
Function Indicating location

Warm-up

Quickly review the prepositions. Hold two classroom objects, such as a pen and a book, in different positions and have the students make sentences, for example, *The pen is on the book. The pen is under the book. The book is next to the pen.*

▶ WRITING

1. Read the example to the class.

Option: First, give students a minute or two to look at the illustration and to think about where the people and different objects are located.

2. Have students work alone to fill in the missing prepositions.
3. Go over the answers with the class by calling on individual students to read the sentences aloud.

Answer Key

1. behind	6. behind
2. in front of	7. next to
3. on	8. on
4. in	9. under
5. next to	10. in

▶ PAIR WORK

1. Read the examples or have pairs of students read the examples to the class.
2. Pair students. Have them take turns asking about the other items in the illustration.
3. Call on different pairs to present each conversation to the class.

Option: Divide the class into two groups. Group A asks the questions; Group B responds. Have groups switch parts and repeat.

Expansion Activity 1

Play a chain ask-and-answer game. Say an object *(chair)*, and then a student's name *(Teresa)*. Teresa asks the question of another student, *Where's the chair, (Raoul)?* (Raoul) responds, *The chair is behind the desk.* Then (Raoul) says another object *(vase)*, and another student's name *(Marta)*. (Marta) asks the next question, *Where's the vase, (Tony)?* (Tony) responds, then says a new object and a different student's name. Remind students to say the name after the question to keep everyone involved. This can be done in groups or as a whole class.

Expansion Activity 2

Review. Point to the illustration and ask questions. For example, *Is he a teacher? / Is she a student? / Is he a student? / Is this a (vase)? What's this? / What are these? What's that? / What are those?* (Hold up the book and point to different objects in the illustration.) Have the class respond chorally or call on individual students. Continue with *yes / no* questions about the objects, for example, *Is the coat on the chair? (Yes, it is). Are the books in the wastebasket? (No, they aren't. They're on the desk.)*

GRAMMAR • Prepositions

▶ **WRITING** • *Complete the sentences using these prepositions:*
in, on, under, next to, behind, in front of.

Example: The wastebasket is **in front of** the desk.

1. Mr. Denby is _____ the desk.

2. Becky is _____ Mr. Denby.

3. The books are _____ the desk.

4. The flowers are _____ the vase.

5. The vase is _____ the books.

6. The cat is _____ the door.

7. The chair is _____ the desk.

8. The coat is _____ the chair.

9. The umbrella is _____ the chair.

10. The paper cups are _____ the wastebasket.

▶ **PAIR WORK** • *Ask and answer questions.*

paper cups

A: **Where are the paper cups?**
B: **They're in the wastebasket.**

wastebasket

A: **Where is the wastebasket?**
B: **It's in front of the desk.**

1. cat
2. books
3. umbrella
4. Mr. Denby
5. Becky
6. flowers
7. coat
8. chair
9. paper cups

Where are you from?

▶ **CONVERSATION 1**

🎧 *Listen. Listen and practice.*

PIERRE: Hello. My name is Pierre.

HIROKO: Hi, I'm Hiroko.

PIERRE: Where are you from?

HIROKO: Japan. And you?

PIERRE: I'm from France.

▶ **PAIR WORK** • *Have similar conversations. Use your own information.*

A: Hello. My name is _____.

B: Hi. I'm _____.

A: Where are you from?

B: _____. And you?

A: I'm from _____.

▶ **CONVERSATION 2**

🎧 *Listen. Listen and practice.*

MARINA: Who's that?

HIROKO: His name's Pierre.

MARINA: Where's he from?

HIROKO: He's from France.

▶ **CONVERSATION 3**

🎧 *Listen. Listen and practice.*

OMAR: Who's that?

LUIS: Her name's Hiroko.

OMAR: Where's she from?

LUIS: She's from Japan.

▶ **PAIR WORK** • *Have similar conversations about other students in your class.*

Where are you from?

Page Summary

Grammar Present tense of *be*
Function Greeting people

Warm-up
If a map of the world is available, point to and identify a few countries. Then point to and say the country that you are from.

❗ *Pronunciation Tip*
The primary stress is on *from* in the first question: *Where are you FROM?* In the second question, the stress is on *you: And YOU?*

▶ CONVERSATION 1
🎧 *Listen. Listen and practice.*

1. Have students look at the illustration at the top of the page.
2. Set the scene: Pierre is starting a conversation with Hiroko.
3. Play the recording (CD track 32) as students listen.
4. Ask the students: *Where is Hiroko from?* (Japan) *Where is Pierre from?* (France)
5. Play the recording (CD track 33) for students to repeat.

❗ *Pronunciation Tip*
The main stress is on the most important content word, the country: *I'm from (FRANCE).*

▶ PAIR WORK
1. Call on a student to practice the conversation with you. Use your own information.
2. Pair students. Call on a pair to model the conversation with their own information.
3. Have pairs practice the conversation. Tell partners to switch parts.
4. Call on several pairs to present the conversation to the class.

Option: To encourage active listening by the entire class, tell students to write down the names and the countries they hear as pairs present the conversation.

Expansion Activity
Use the world map in the book to compile a list of the names of countries the students know in English. For each continent (except Australia), see if students can name three countries. Review spelling and pronunciation of the names.

▶ CONVERSATION 2
🎧 *Listen. Listen and practice.*

1. Have students look at the illustration.
2. Set the scene: Marina is talking to Hiroko about Pierre.
3. Play the recording (CD track 34) as students listen.
4. Play the recording (CD track 35) for students to repeat.

Option: Remind students that *he* and *his* are used with a man or a boy.

▶ CONVERSATION 3
🎧 *Listen. Listen and practice.*

1. Have students look at the illustration.
2. Set the scene: Omar is talking to Luis about Hiroko.
3. Play the recording (CD track 36) as students listen.
4. Play the recording (CD track 37) for students to repeat.

Option: Remind students that *she* and *her* are used with a girl or a woman.

▶ PAIR WORK
1. Call on a student to practice the conversation with you. Model how to gesture to indicate the person in question. (Gesture toward the person as you say *His/her name is. . . .*)
2. Pair students. Have pairs practice the conversation about at least three other students.
3. Call on pairs to present their conversations to the class.

Page Summary

Grammar *Wh-* questions
Function Asking about people and objects

! *Pronunciation Tip*
The intonation falls at the end of *Wh-* questions.

▶ 🎧 *Listen. Listen and repeat.*

1. Have students look at the illustrations and listen as you play the recording (CD track 38).
2. Play the recording (CD track 39) for students to repeat.

▶ PAIR WORK

1. Pair students. Have them practice the conversations.
2. Call on different pairs to say each conversation to the class.

▶ WRITING

1. Have students work alone to fill in the questions.

Option: For students needing more support, pair students to write the questions.

2. Play the recording (CD track 38) again so that students can check their answers.
3. Go over the answers with the class by calling on pairs of students to read the conversations.

Answer Key

1. How much is this hat?	6. Where's the ball?
2. What's your name?	7. What's your address?
3. What time is it?	8. Where are you from?
4. How are you?	9. What's that?
5. Who's that?	

Expansion Activity 1
Students work in pairs. One student's book is closed, the other open. The student whose book is open picks at random one of the answers given in the book, and reads it to the other student. The other student then supplies the question, and the first student says, *That's right* or, if necessary, corrects the question.

Expansion Activity 2
Write on the board *Where's the . . . ?* Ask the question about a classroom object, then say a student's name. The student answers, and then asks another student about a different classroom object. Students continue in a chain response. Remind students about falling intonation at the end of the question.

GRAMMAR • Wh- Questions

▶ 🎧 *Listen. Listen and repeat.* ▶ **PAIR WORK** • *Practice the conversations.*

▶ **WRITING** • *Write a question for each answer. Then read the conversations aloud.*

VOCABULARY

NOUNS

Occupations
banker
businessman
carpenter
chef
doctor
firefighter
mechanic
pilot
police officer
teacher

Places
bank
beach
garage
hospital
library
office
park
post office
supermarket

Other
apple	chair	man
ball	coat	newspaper
banana	cup	pear
basket	desk	table
bicycle	dog	tree
bird	door	umbrella
book	flower	vase
bottle	friend	wastebasket
cage	glass	woman
cat	magazine	

SUBJECT PRONOUNS
I
you
he
she
it
they

POSSESSIVE ADJECTIVES
my
your
his
her

PREPOSITIONS
in
on
under
next to
in front of
behind

VERB
be

ADVERB
(over) there

ADJECTIVES
interesting
terrific

ARTICLES
a/an
the

WH-WORDS
who
what
where

CONJUNCTION
and

INTERJECTION
Hey.

EXPRESSIONS

Greeting people
Hi. How are you?
    I'm fine. And you?
Fine, thank you.

Introducing yourself
Hello. My name is…
    I'm…
Nice to meet you.
    Nice to meet you, too.

Introducing someone
…, this is…
    Hi. It's nice to meet you.

Asking about people
Who's that?
    His/Her name's…
Where's he/she from?
    He/She's from…

Exchanging personal information
What's your name?
    I'm…/My name's…
What's your phone number?
    It's…
What's your address?
    It's…

Asking for the time
What time is it?
    It's two o'clock.

Other
She's single.
That's interesting.

VOCABULARY

The games below provide additional opportunities for students to use the vocabulary, grammar, and expressions presented in the unit. Before students play any of the games, have them individually review the lists of words and circle any words they don't know. Then put students into small groups and have them review the circled words together. Circulate so you can help in case no one in the group knows a particular word.

1. Spelling Game

Students' books are closed. Choose two words from the top three columns on the page (Occupations, Places, Other). Write the words on the board and leave out some letters, for example: *ap_ _le* and *l_br_ary*. Have students work in pairs to spell the words on a piece of paper (one piece of paper for each pair of students). Tell them to raise their hands when they are finished, and notice which pair finishes first. When all students have finished, call on the pair that finished first to write the words on the board. If the words are correct, the pair gets a point. Continue with other sets of words until you have done about 10 rounds. Leave out only a few letters, so that the students can spell the words easily and the main focus stays on vocabulary review. After ten rounds, do a couple of bonus rounds, where you leave out more letters.

2. Occupations Game

Write on the board the names of the characters on page 4 (*John, Susan, Carlos . . .*). Tell students that these will be important for the game they are about to play. Have students open their books to page 4 and study it for 60 seconds. Then have them close their books, and put them into teams (three students per team). When you point to a name on the board *(Susan)*, the first team to say that person's occupation *(She's a doctor)* gets a point. Check that students remember to include the *'s*, and that they pronounce it as a *z*.

3. Party Time

Divide students into groups of five or six. Tell them to imagine they are at a party. They can choose any identity they want: they can be themselves or a celebrity, such as a sports personality or movie star. Have them introduce themselves to the others in the group, exchanging personal information as they do so. (If they choose to be celebrities they can make up any information they don't know.) After they have finished their introductions, tell them to ask each other about someone else in the group, for example, *Who's that? What's his/her job?*, and so on.

STRESS

Page Summary

Focus Primary stress

▶ **A** 🎧 *Listen to the stressed vowels. Listen and repeat.*

1. Have students look at the words and listen as you play the recording (CD track 40).
2. Play the recording (CD track 41) and have the students repeat. Play again as needed.

Option: Read each word aloud as you clap your hands on the stressed vowel; pause for students to repeat.

▶ **B** 🎧 *Listen and mark the stressed vowels.*

1. Have students mark the stressed vowels as you play the recording (CD track 42).
2. Play the recording (CD track 42) again for the students to check their work.
3. Have students read the words out loud as a class or in pairs.

Option: Play the recording (CD track 42) again for a final check.

▶ **C** 🎧 *Listen. Listen and practice.*

1. Have students listen as you play the recording (CD track 43).
2. Play the recording (CD track 44) and have the students repeat.

3. Pair students. Have them practice the conversation, switching parts. Circulate and check their pronunciation.

Option: Before pair practice, divide the class into two groups to do the conversation chorally.

▶ **D** 🎧 *Listen and mark the main stress in these sentences.*

1. Have students listen only as you play the recording (CD track 45) once through.
2. Play the recording (CD track 45) again and have the students mark the main stress.

Option: Play the recording (CD track 45) again for the students to repeat, as needed.

3. Pair students. Have them practice the conversation, switching parts. Circulate and check their pronunciation.

Expansion Activity

Pair students. Have them do the conversation in Exercise D again, substituting their own information. Tell them to pay attention to the main stress.

STRESS

► **A** 🎧 *Listen to the stressed vowels. Listen and repeat.*

dóctor	ban**án**a	guit**ár**
stúdent	Am**ér**ica	hell**ó**
líbrary	loc**á**tion	intro**dúce**
ínteresting	ter**ríf**ic	com**pléte**

► **B** 🎧 *Listen and mark the stressed vowels. Then read these words out loud.*

example	garage	bicycle
number	mechanic	police
Japan	address	hospital
umbrella	behind	conversation

► **C** 🎧 *Listen. Notice the main stress in these sentences. Listen and practice.*

A: **Héy**, **Ál**ice. **Whó's** that **wó**man over **thére**?

B: Her **náme** is **Dái**sy. She's very **níce**…and she's **sín**gle.

A: **Thát's** interesting.

B: She's a ter**ríf**ic **cóok**.

A: That's **vér**y interesting.

► **D** 🎧 *Listen and mark the main stress in these sentences. Then practice the conversation with a partner.*

A: Hello. My name is Omar.

B: Hi. I'm Hiroko.

A: Where are you from?

B: Japan. And you?

A: I'm from Somalia.

GRAMMAR SUMMARY

TO BE Affirmative		
He She It	's (is)	
I	'm (am)	in the library.
You We They	're (are)	

Negative		
He She It	isn't (is not) 's not	
I	'm not (am not)	in the library.
You We They	aren't (are not) 're not	

Interrogative		
Is	he she it	
Am	I	in the library?
Are	you we they	

Short Answers						
Yes,	he she it	is.	No,	he she it	isn't.
	I	am.		I	'm not.
	you we they	are.		you we they	aren't.

Question with WHAT		
What	's (is)	this? that?
	are	these? those?

SINGULAR AND PLURAL NOUNS		
It	's (is)	a chair. a table.
They	're (are)	flowers. trees.

Question with WHERE		
Where	's (is)	Mr. Gamble?
	's (is)	the newspaper?
	are	the books?

PREPOSITIONS			
He	's (is)	at in	the post office.
It	's (is)	on under next to behind in front of	the table.
They	are		

CONTENTS

Chapter

2

GRAMMAR • Adjectives

▶ 🎧 *Listen. Listen and practice.*

▶ **PAIR WORK** • *Ask each other the same questions.*

A: **Are you hungry?**

B: **Yes, I am.** OR **No, I'm not.**

2Chapter 2

Page Summary

Grammar Adjectives
Function Describing people

Warm-up

Ask a few questions based on the current weather or time of day, for example, if it's winter, say, *It's cold today. Are you cold?* If it's early in the morning, say, *I'm tired. Are you tired?* Pantomime *cold, hungry, tired* in order to give the class a model for the expansion activity to come. Ask the questions of the whole class or of individual students.

Grammar Note

The contraction *'m* can be used in the negative response *(No, I'm not)*, but there is no contraction for the affirmative response. Only *Yes, I am* is possible.

! *Pronunciation Tip*

In the positive short answer response, the stress is on the verb to be: *Yes, I AM.* In the negative response, the stress is *No, I'm NOT.*

▶ 🎧 *Listen. Listen and practice.*

1. Have students look at the illustrations.
2. Have students listen as you play the recording (CD track 46).
3. Play the recording (CD track 47) again and have the students repeat.

▶ PAIR WORK

1. Call on a student to practice the first conversation with you. Switch parts and repeat.
2. Pair students. Call on a pair to model the second conversation.
3. Have pairs practice the conversations. Have partners switch parts.
4. Call on pairs to present the conversations to the class.

Expansion Activity

Have students form pairs. Tell students to make slips of paper with the adjectives on them. Student A takes a slip *(cold)* and pantomimes feeling cold. Student B guesses: *Are you cold?* Student A responds, *Yes, I am* for a correct guess or *No, I'm not* for an incorrect guess. For added challenge have students ask questions that will elicit the negative response, *No, I'm not;* for example, if Student A pantomimes *cold,* Student B asks, *Are you hungry?*

Page Summary

Grammar Adjectives
Function Describing people

🎧 Look and listen. Listen and repeat.

1. Have students look at the illustrations.
2. Play the recording (CD track 48) as students listen.
3. Play the recording (CD track 49) again for students to repeat.

Option: Have students read the sentences out loud. Then play the recording (CD track 49) again for students to repeat.

Grammar Note

Point out the phrases *interested in* and *afraid of*. Explain that these adjectives often require these prepositions.

❗ *Pronunciation Tip*

The main stress in two-syllable adjectives is often on the first syllable: HAPpy, NERvous. However, if the adjective is followed by a noun, the noun is stressed: She's a good SINGer.

▶ PAIR WORK

1. Present the example to the class with a student partner. Encourage the students to personalize the conversation by using information about themselves.
2. Call on a pair of students to do item 1. Have them switch parts and repeat.
3. Pair students. Have them take turns asking each other the questions.
4. Call on pairs to present their conversations to the class.
5. Point out that in a conversation, it's common not to repeat words when the meaning is clear, for example,
   A: *Are you hungry?*
   B: *Yes, I am. Are you?*
   A: *Yes.* (OR *No, I'm not.*)

Expansion Activity 1

Write on the board, *Find someone who is . . . .* Set a time limit (10 minutes). Tell students to walk around the classroom and ask different partners the questions listed in Pair Work and write down names and answers, for example *3. Tony: No.* Tell them to talk to at least five classmates. At the end of 10 minutes, have the students form small groups. In the groups, students take turns saying what they learned about their classmates (for example, *Tony is interested in sports. He isn't afraid of spiders*) and then choose a representative from each group to summarize findings: *No one is nervous. Six students are interested in sports.* Have the rest of the class listen and then make some conclusions about the class as a whole: *We are interested in sports. We aren't good dancers. We're good drivers.*

Expansion Activity 2

Have students work alone to write a short description of a couple, real or imagined, using sentences from page 23. They can also make substitutions; for example, they can say *He's a good dancer* or *She's a good singer.* After they finish writing, have them form pairs and read their descriptions out loud.

She's happy.

He's nervous.

She's married.

He's rich.

He's a good singer.

He's a bad dancer.

She's a good cook.

She's a bad driver.

She's interested in the news.

He's interested in sports.

She's afraid of dogs.

He's afraid of spiders.

PAIR WORK • *Ask each other questions.*

A: **Are you hungry?**

B: **Yes, I am.** OR **No, I'm not.**

1. Are you happy?
2. Are you nervous?
3. Are you married?
4. Are you rich?
5. Are you a good singer?
6. Are you a good dancer?
7. Are you a good cook?
8. Are you a good driver?
9. Are you interested in the news?
10. Are you interested in sports?
11. Are you afraid of dogs?
12. Are you afraid of spiders?

GRAMMAR • Adjectives

Joe The car	is	married. new.

He's It's	a married man. a new car.

▶ 🎧 *Look and listen. Listen and repeat.*

1. Joe is married.   Carlos is single.

2. Sara is happy.   Linda is sad.

3. Mary is rich.   Jane is poor.

4. Ben is strong.   Fred is weak.

5. Snow White is beautiful.   The witch is ugly.

6. Peter is handsome.   The Wolfman is ugly.

7. Nick is hot.   Max is cold.

8. The car is new.   The truck is old.

GRAMMAR • Adjectives

Page Summary

Grammar Adjectives
Function Describing people and objects

Warm-up

Say a celebrity's name. Have students come up with an adjective that describes the person; for example, say *David Beckham.* Call on one student to describe him: *He's interested in sports.* Have the whole class repeat the student's response. Continue with several more celebrities students are familiar with.

Pronunciation Tip

In spoken English the contracted form is more common than the full form: *Joe's married.*

Culture Note

The term *single* is used both for someone who has never married and for someone who was married but is now divorced.

▶ 🎧 *Look and listen. Listen and repeat.*

1. Hold up a book and describe it in two ways: *The book is small. It's a small book.*
2. Have students look at the illustrations. Play the recording (CD track 50) as students listen.

3. Play the recording (CD track 51) for students to repeat.

Option: Have students read the sentences out loud. Then play the recording (CD track 51) again for students to repeat.

Expansion Activity 1

Use illustrations 1–6 for more practice. First make sure that students know the vocabulary *man* and *woman*; then have them form groups of three. One student in the group says one of the adjectives on the page as a cue. The other two students make sentences. For example, Student 1 says, *happy*; Student 2 says, *Sara is happy*; Student 3 says, *Sara's a happy woman.* Tell students to use the illustrations in random order. Alternatively, Student 1 can say the name (Sara) and Students 2 and 3 can describe her.

Page Summary

Grammar Adjectives; *yes/no* questions
Function Describing people

▶ 🎧 *Listen. Listen and repeat.*

1. Have students look at the illustrations and listen as you play the recording (CD track 52).
2. Play the recording (CD track 53) for students to repeat.

▶ PAIR WORK

1. Model the first conversation with a student partner. Switch parts and model the second conversation.
2. Pair students. Have them practice the conversations.

Option: Call on different pairs to present each conversation for the class.

Grammar Note

Remind students of the alternative to *No, he isn't* or *No, she isn't* (*No, he's not* or *No, she's not*).

❗ *Pronunciation Tip*

The voice rises at the end of *yes/no* questions.

▶ WRITING

1. Have students work alone to fill in the answers, referring to page 24 if they need to.
2. Play the recording (CD track 52) again and have the students check their answers.
3. Go over the answers with the class by calling on pairs of students to read the conversations. Point out that the short answer is enough because it is clear what is being talked about.

Answer Key

1. No, he isn't. He's married.	5. Yes, she is.
2. Yes, she is.	6. No, he isn't. He's ugly.
3. No, she isn't. She's rich.	7. No, he isn't. He's hot.
4. Yes, he is.	8. No, it isn't. It's old.

Expansion Activity 1

Have the students use the first illustration to write a short story (of three to five short sentences) about the brother who is married. Tell them to make up names for him, his wife, and his daughter. Students can also make up where he lives and what he and his wife each do for their jobs. Tell them to include any other details they can think of. Circulate and help them as they write. When they are finished, have students form small groups and take turns reading their stories. Then call on one or two students to present their stories to the class.

Expansion Activity 2

Do a spelling dictation. Tell students to close their books and to write the numbers 1–8 on a piece of paper. Spell the adjectives one at a time in random order and have students write them down. When students are done, call on volunteers to write the words on the board for the class to check their answers. Then have the students read the words aloud chorally.

Is your brother single?

No, he isn't. He's married.

①

Is your daughter happy?

Yes, she is.

②

Is the queen poor?

③

Is Superman strong?

④

Is Cinderella beautiful?

⑤

Is Rasputin handsome?

⑥

Is James cold?

⑦

Is the bicycle new?

⑧

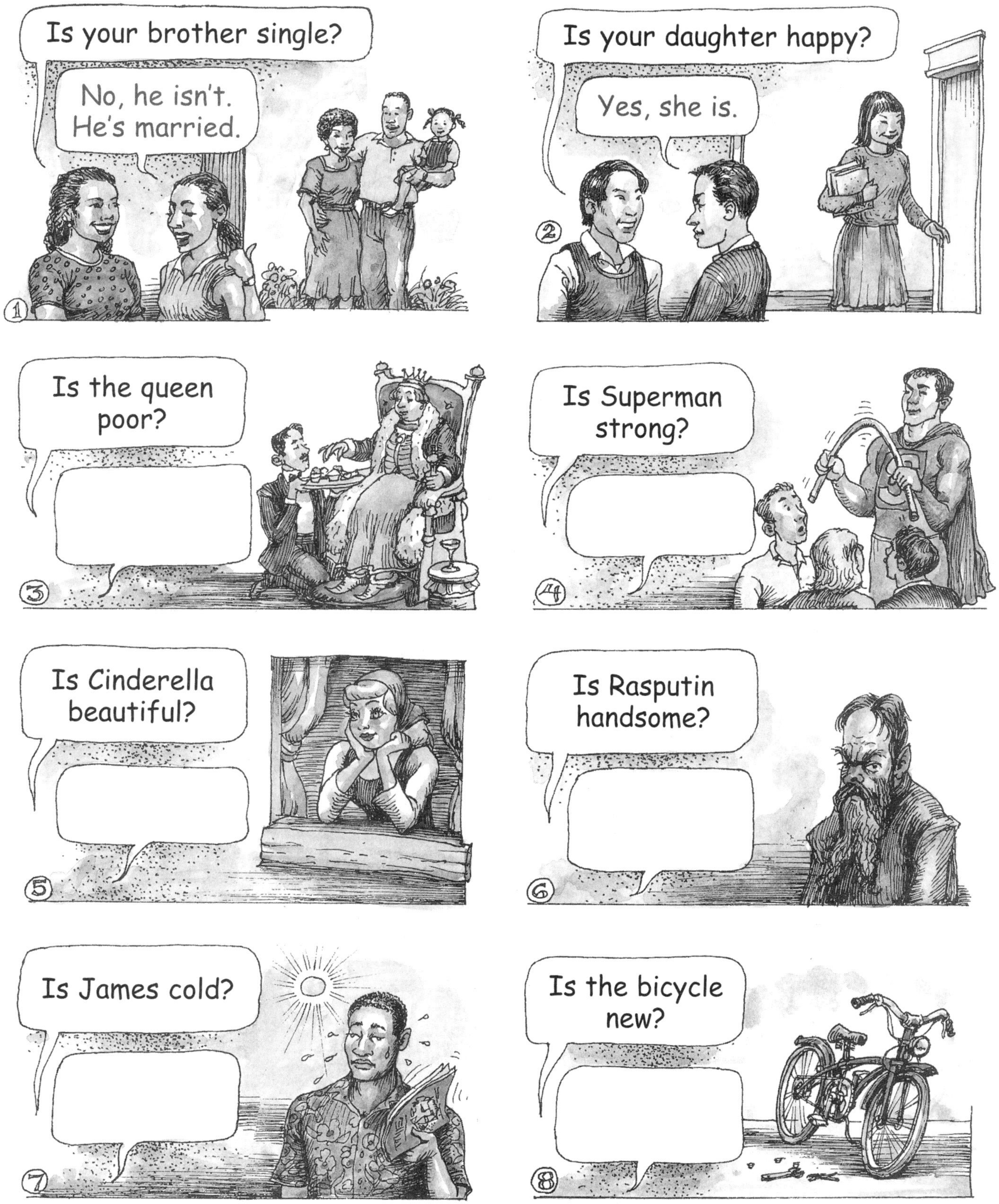

▶ **WRITING** • *Fill in the answers. Then read the conversations aloud.*

GRAMMAR • Adjectives

The students	are	young.
The apples		big.

They're	young students.
	big apples.

 *Look and listen. Listen and repeat.*

1. They're young.   They're old.

2. They're noisy.   They're quiet.

3. They're fat.   They're thin.

4. They're tall.   They're short.

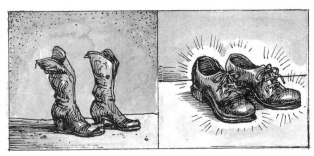

5. The boots are old.   The shoes are new.

6. The glasses are clean.   The dishes are dirty.

7. The apples are big.   The pears are small.

8. The bananas are cheap.   The oranges are expensive.

Page Summary

Grammar Adjectives
Function Describing people and objects

Culture Note

There are many adjectives in English to describe people's physical size. Because weight is an issue for some people, adjectives such as *heavy* or *big* are sometimes used instead of *fat*; likewise, *slender* or *small* are used instead of *thin*. At this level, students aren't expected to learn all of the synonyms and their nuances, but some students might be familiar with these words.

▶ 🎧 *Look and listen. Listen and repeat.*

1. Have students look at the illustrations.
2. Play the recording (CD track 54) as students listen.
3. Play the recording (CD track 55) again for students to repeat.

Expansion Activity 1

Direct students' attention to the boxes at the top of the page. Go over the examples. Have students talk about pictures 5–8, practicing the sentence construction that is *not* written under the illustrations. For example, say, *5. The boots are old.* Students respond: *They're old boots.* To expand the activity for the whole page, first teach some additional vocabulary for pictures 1–4 (*people, men, women, children*) since students may not be familiar with these words.

Expansion Activity 2

Play a matching game. Have each student write each adjective on the page on a small piece of paper. Pair students. Tell them to spread their pieces of paper upside down between them and to mix them up. Tell students to take turns turning over two slips of paper. If the words are opposites, it's a match. The student then says each word and takes another turn. If the two words are not opposites, the turn is over. Students continue until all the words are matched up. The student with the most matches wins.

Page Summary

Grammar Adjectives
Function Describing people and objects

Warm-up

Ask *yes/no* questions about various objects in the classroom: *Are the books big? Are the windows clean?* Students respond: *Yes, they are* or *No, they aren't.*

▶ 🎧 *Listen. Listen and repeat.*

1. Have students look at the pictures and listen as you play the recording (CD track 56).
2. Play the recording (CD track 57) for students to repeat.

▶ PAIR WORK

1. Have students form pairs and practice the conversations, switching parts.
2. Go over the conversations in a chain activity. Have one student start by asking question 1 of another student in the class: *Are your neighbors old, (Tony)?* Tony answers and then asks question 2 of a different student. Students continue until they finish the page.

▶ WRITING

1. Have students work alone to fill in the answers.
2. Play the recording (CD track 56) again, and have students check their answers.
3. Go over the answers with the class by calling on pairs of students to read each conversation. Remind students that the short answer is enough because the meaning is clear from the question.

Answer Key

1. Yes, they are.
2. No, they aren't. They're noisy.
3. Yes, they are.
4. No, they aren't. They're short.
5. No, they aren't. They're old.
6. Yes, they are.
7. No, they aren't. They're big.
8. Yes, they are.

Expansion Activity

Have students work in pairs to describe what they see in each picture. Encourage them to work together to say as many details as possible, for example, for picture 1: *They're talking on the phone. The man and woman are sitting. The man is reading the newspaper.* After pairs have finished, call on one student at a time to say a descriptive sentence, but not the picture number. Have the rest of the class guess which picture is being described.

▶ 🎧 *Listen. Listen and repeat.*   ▶ **PAIR WORK** • *Practice the conversations.*

1. Are your neighbors old?
   Yes, they are.

2. Are your neighbors quiet?
   No, they aren't. They're noisy.

3. Are the models thin?

4. Are the basketball players tall?

5. Are the books new?

6. Are the windows clean?

7. Are the carrots small?

8. Are the avocados expensive?
   Three dollars each.

▶ **WRITING** • *Fill in the answers. Then read the conversations aloud.*

NUMBERS and TELLING TIME

▶ 🎧 **NUMBERS** • *Listen and repeat.*

11	eleven	21	twenty-one	40	forty
12	twelve	22	twenty-two	50	fifty
13	thirteen	23	twenty-three	60	sixty
14	fourteen	24	twenty-four	70	seventy
15	fifteen	25	twenty-five	80	eighty
16	sixteen	26	twenty-six	90	ninety
17	seventeen	27	twenty-seven	100	one hundred
18	eighteen	28	twenty-eight	105	one hundred five
19	nineteen	29	twenty-nine	110	one hundred ten
20	twenty	30	thirty	125	one hundred twenty-five

▶ 🎧 **TELLING TIME** • *Listen and repeat.*

It's two o'clock.

It's two-oh-five.
It's five after two.

It's two fifteen.
It's a quarter past two.

It's two-thirty.
It's half past two.

It's two forty-five.
It's a quarter to three.

It's two fifty-five.
It's five to three.

NUMBERS AND TELLING TIME

Page Summary

Grammar Present tense of *be*
Function Telling time

NUMBERS

Listen and repeat.

1. Play the recording (CD track 58) as students listen and repeat.
2. Ask students to look at the numbers again. Point out the spelling change: *fourteen* / *forty*.

TELLING TIME

Listen and repeat.

1. Have students look at the clocks and read the times silently.
2. Play the recording (CD track 59) as students listen and repeat.

Expansion Activity

Dictate 10 numbers between 11 and 100. Say each number twice, pausing for students to write it down. Call on volunteers to write the numbers on the board. Give students time to check their answers. Read each number aloud; have the class repeat.

TIME

Page Summary

Grammar Present tense of *be*
Function Asking for and telling the time

! *Pronunciation Tip*

The main stress is as follows: *What TIME is it? It's three o' CLOCK.*

▶ PAIR WORK

1. Read the example to the class.
2. Model the example with a student partner. Switch parts and repeat.
3. Have students look at the second clock. Point at it and ask, *What time is it?* Have the whole class respond, *It's four thirty-five* or *It's twenty-five to five.*
4. Pair students. Have them take turns asking and answering the time on each clock. Remind them to say the time two ways. Circulate and help with the times, as needed.
5. Call on different pairs to ask and answer about each time for the class.

Option: As a recap, divide the class into three groups. Group A asks the question; Group B says the time one way; Group C says the time the other way. After two questions, have groups switch parts.

Answer Key

1. It's nine-twenty.
2. It's four thirty-five or twenty-five to five.
3. It's eleven ten or ten after eleven.
4. It's six-thirty.
5. It's ten to three or two-fifty.
6. It's eight-fifteen or a quarter after eight.
7. It's one forty-five or a quarter to two.
8. It's seven-oh-five or five after seven.

Culture Note

The divisions between afternoon, evening, and night vary somewhat from place to place. Generally it is *afternoon* from noon until about five o'clock; *evening* from five until about nine o'clock; and then *night* up until midnight. You can point out that students don't need to concern themselves about the exact division between *evening* and *night*. For example, they can say either *I get home at eight o'clock in the evening* or *I get home at eight o'clock at night.* It would sound odd to say *I go to sleep at eleven o'clock in the evening.* *Good evening* is a greeting, like *hello. Good night* is a way of saying *good-bye.*

▶ TIMES OF DAY

🎧 *Look, listen and read.*

1. Have students look at the illustrations and notice the clock in each picture.
2. Play the recording (CD track 60) as students listen and read silently.
3. Play the recording (CD track 60) again for students to listen and read.
4. Point out the prepositions: *in the (evening)* and *at night.*

Expansion Activity

Use the illustrations for more listening practice. In random order, read one of the sentences under each illustration. Have the students respond with the other sentence. For example, read: *It's time for breakfast.* Students say, *It's seven o'clock in the morning.* Read: *It's bedtime.* Students say, *It's ten o'clock at night.* For more challenge, have students cover the captions and repeat the exercise.

TIME

▶ **PAIR WORK** • *Ask and answer questions.*

A: **What time is it?**

B: **It's nine-twenty.** OR **It's twenty after nine.**

🎧 **TIMES OF DAY** • *Look, listen and read.*

It's seven o'clock **in the morning**.
It's time for breakfast.

It's one o'clock **in the afternoon**.
It's lunchtime.

It's seven o'clock **in the evening**.
It's dinnertime.

It's ten o'clock **at night**.
It's bedtime.

NOUNS

▶ **SINGULAR NOUNS** • *Complete the sentences with **a** or **an**.*

> • Use **a** before a consonant sound: b c k f l m p r
> • Use **an** before a vowel sound: a e i o u

1. It's __an__ apple.

2. It's __a__ peach.

3. It's _____ orange.

4. It's _____ pencil.

5. It's _____ eraser.

6. It's _____ watch.

7. It's _____ umbrella.

8. It's _____ letter.

9. It's _____ dictionary.

▶ **PLURAL NOUNS** • *Change the nouns from singular to plural.*

> • Add **s** to make a plural noun: students, books, chairs
> • Add **es** to words that end in -s, -ch, -sh: glasses, dishes
> • Change **y** to **i** and add **es**: cities
> • Irregular: man – men   woman – women   child – children

1. man __men__

2. car __cars__

3. watch _____

4. flower _____

5. tree _____

6. woman _____

7. dictionary _____

8. umbrella _____

9. peach_____

10. family _____

11. student _____

12. class _____

Family

NOUNS

Page Summary

Grammar Indefinite articles
Function Talking about singular and plural nouns

▶ SINGULAR NOUNS

1. Present the rules for article use at the top of the page. Point out that the first rule applies to all the consonant sounds, not just those listed in the box. In addition, emphasize that these rules apply to sounds, not letters. For example, *university* starts with the letter *u*, but not the sound. We say *a university*, not *an university.*

2. Go over the example. Ask students why the answer is *an* (*apple* starts with an *a*).

3. Have students work alone to complete the sentences.

Option: Have them first go through and underline the first letter of the noun in each sentence to help them focus on the article needed.

4. Go over the answers as a class by calling on different students to read the sentences aloud.

Option: Pair students. Have them practice reading sentences aloud.

Answer Key

1. It's an apple.	6. It's a watch.
2. It's a peach.	7. It's an umbrella.
3. It's an orange.	8. It's a letter.
4. It's a pencil.	9. It's a dictionary.
5. It's an eraser.	

▶ PLURAL NOUNS

1. Present the rules for how to change nouns from singular to plural. Explain that the irregular words have to be memorized; they don't follow the rules.

2. Go over the example.

3. Have students work alone to change the nouns from singular to plural.

4. Call on three students to each write a third of the answers on the board (Student 1 writes 1–4, and so on).

5. Go over the answers by having the class read the plural words aloud.

⚡ *Pronunciation Tip*

Women is irregular in its pronunciation as well as its spelling: the first vowel, *o* changes to an |I| sound for the plural form, even though it is still written as *o*.

Answer Key

1. men	7. dictionaries
2. cars	8. umbrellas
3. watches	9. peaches
4. flowers	10. families
5. trees	11. students
6. women	12. classes

Expansion Activity 1

Have students form the plural of the nouns at the top of the page that are not included at the bottom *(apple, orange, pencil, eraser, letter)*. Say one word at a time and have students write the plural on a piece of paper. Then ask students what they notice about the plurals (They all end in -*s*). Ask if they notice anything different about the sound of *books* (an *s* sound rather than a *z* sound) to prepare them for the Pronunciation page at the end of the chapter on page 39. Say the words, pausing for the class to repeat.

Expansion Activity 2

Ask students to think of other nouns they know. (If students have trouble, you can refer them to the vocabulary list at the end of Chapter 1.) Ask them to try to form the plurals. Write their ideas on the board. Have the class make corrections as needed.

COLORS • CLOTHES

Page Summary

Grammar Adjectives
Function Describing clothing

Warm-up

Ask students to look at the colors in the book. Then ask them to look around the room and notice the colors they see. Give them a minute or so to look around, but don't go over the names of the colors at this point. Then ask, *What colors do you see?* Call on several students.

Grammar Notes

- If students ask about the hyphens in *Those boots are good looking* and *Those are good-looking boots,* tell them that when the adjective phrase comes before the noun, the words are hyphenated.
- Remind students that *jeans*, *pants*, and *shorts* are all plural nouns in English and therefore need *are* instead of *is*.

▶ 🎧 *Look and listen. Listen and repeat.*

1. Have students look at the circles of color and the illustrations.
2. Play the recording (CD track 61) as students listen, and point to the colors.
3. Play the recording (CD track 62) again for students to repeat.
4. Have students point to the various colors as you read them, in random order.
5. Play the recording (CD track 63) as students listen and point to the illustrations of clothes.
6. Play the recording (CD track 64) again for students to repeat.
7. Have students point to the various articles of clothing as you read them in random order.

Option: Pair students. Have them take turns reading the names of the colors and the articles of clothing while their partner points at the correct place on the page.

▶ **PRACTICE**

1. Go over the example.
2. Pair students. Have them practice making sentences about the people in the illustrations.
3. Call on different students to say each sentence for the class.

Answer Key

1. Her dress is red. Her shoes are black.
2. His jacket is brown. His belt is black. His pants are beige.
3. Her blouse is yellow. Her skirt is green.
4. His hat is beige. His tie is red. His coat is gray.
5. Her shirt is orange. Her jeans are blue. Her boots are brown.
6. His socks are white. His shorts are gray. His sweater is green.

Expansion Activity

Have students form pairs and play a guessing game. To play, they take turns describing what a classmate is wearing. Student 1 says one or two sentences. Student 2 listens to the description, looks around the room, and makes a guess: *Is it (Ana)?* If this is correct, Student 1 responds, *Yes, it is.* If it's incorrect, the response is, *No, it isn't.* Student 1 then continues making more sentences about what the classmate is wearing, until Student 2 guesses correctly. Students then switch parts.

Culture Note

Although giving compliments is often a way to strike up a conversation, it can be delicate for men and women to comment on each other's clothing. In this situation, Dallas and Daisy are getting to know each other, and perhaps flirting a bit.

▶ 🎧 *Listen. Listen and practice.*

1. Have students listen as you play the recording (CD track 65).
2. Play the recording (CD track 66) again and have the students repeat.

▶ **PAIR WORK**

1. Model the task by giving a compliment to one or two students.
2. Have students then practice the conversation, switching parts. Circulate to check their pronunciation and to watch for *are* where necessary.
3. Call on different pairs to present to the class.

COLORS • CLOTHES

▶ 🎧 *Look and listen. Listen and repeat.*

● red ● orange ● yellow ● green ● blue ○ white ● black ● gray ● brown ● beige

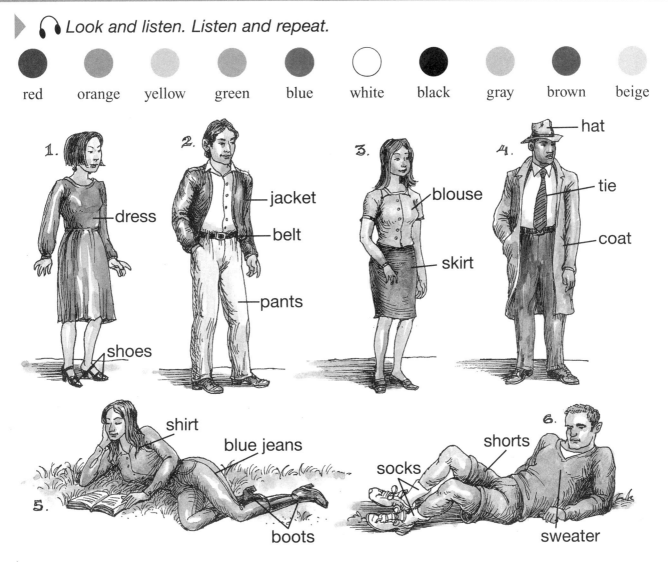

1. dress, shoes
2. jacket, belt, pants
3. blouse, skirt
4. hat, tie, coat
5. shirt, blue jeans, boots
6. socks, shorts, sweater

▶ **PRACTICE** • *What color are their clothes?*

1. Her dress is red. Her shoes are black.

▶ 🎧 *Listen. Listen and practice.*

1. Those are good-looking boots.
   Thank you.
2. And that's a beautiful hat!
   Thanks.

▶ **PAIR WORK** • *Give the people near you a compliment.*

LIFE SKILL • Shopping

▶ 🎧 **DICTATION** • *Listen to the conversations. Listen and fill in the answers.*

PAIR WORK • *Practice the conversations.*

Page Summary

Grammar Singular/plural questions
Function Asking about prices

Grammar Note

How much is used for both singular and plural nouns when we are asking about prices. The verb *(is/are)* and the determiner *(this/that/these/those)* change according to the quantity of the item(s) in question.

! *Pronunciation Tip*

In rapid speech, the sounds in the question are reduced and linked, and the stress is on the stressed syllable of the noun:

> *How much is this sweater? =*
> *HowmuchizthisSWEATer?*

Culture Note

In picture 4, the girl asks the price of a *handbag*. The words *purse* and *pocketbook* are also used for this type of bag. Within the United States, all of these words are used; there are regional differences as to which word is more common.

▶ DICTATION

🎧 *Listen to the conversations. Listen and fill in the answers.*

1. Have students look at the illustrations.
2. Play the recording (CD track 67) once through for students to listen. Tell them not to write.
3. Play the recording (CD track 68) again for students to fill in the answers.
4. Play the recording (CD track 67) again for students to check their work.
5. Go over the answers by calling on pairs to present the conversations.

Answer Key

1. Eighty-five dollars	4. Sixty-four dollars
2. Thirty-five dollars	5. Forty-five dollars
3. Seven dollars	6. Twenty-nine dollars

▶ PAIR WORK

1. Pair students. Have them practice the conversations, switching parts.
2. Call on different pairs to present each conversation to the class.

Expansion Activity

Set up a store situation by asking two volunteers to bring six to eight items of clothing or their backpacks to the front of the class. One student is the store clerk who decides the prices, and the other is the shopper who asks how much things cost. For added challenge, have the shopper first decide how much money he or she has. After asking all the prices, the shopper tells the clerk what he or she wants. Model on the board, *I want (that jacket). I want (this backpack).* After the volunteer pair has modeled several exchanges, have the whole class practice this in pairs. Note: Although students haven't yet been taught *I want*, it is simple and useful in this life skills practice.

LIFE SKILL • Shopping

Page Summary

Grammar Review of *this/that, these/those*; plural nouns
Function Asking about prices

Warm-up

Point to an item near you in the classroom that students will probably know the price of, such as a newspaper or a magazine. Ask the price, *How much is this?* Point to an item farther away and ask, *How much is that?* Then repeat with plural items to review *these* and *those*. If you are outside of the United States, students can answer in their own currency.

▶ DICTATION

🎧 *Listen to the conversations. Listen and fill in the questions.*

1. Have students look at the illustrations and identify the items being sold.
2. Play the recording (CD track 69) as students listen.
3. Play the recording (CD track 70) again for students to fill in the questions.
4. Play the recording (CD track 69) again for students to check their work.
5. Go over the answers by calling on different pairs to present the conversations.

Answer Key

1. How much are these sunglasses?
2. How much is that jacket?
3. How much is this dress?
4. How much are those pants?
5. How much are those shoes?
6. How much is that shirt?

▶ PAIR WORK

1. Pair students. Have them practice the conversations, switching parts.
2. Call on different pairs to present each conversation to the class.

Expansion Activity

Have students expand the conversations. Tell the clerk to greet the customer, and the customer to say *Thank you* at the end. Model an example with a student partner. Then model again, pausing for students to repeat.
T: *Hello!*
S: *How much are these sunglasses?*
T: *They're sixty-nine dollars.*
S: *Thank you.*

| this | that | these | those | | dress | jacket | pants | shirt | shoes | sunglasses |

1. How much are these sunglasses? — Sixty-nine dollars.
2. — One hundred fifty dollars.
3. — Ninety-eight dollars.
4. — One hundred and ten dollars.
5. — Seventy-five dollars.
6. — Thirty-nine dollars.

▶ **PAIR WORK** • *Practice the conversations.*

GRAMMAR • Commands

▶ 🎧 *Look and listen. Listen and repeat.*

Note: Use *please* to be more polite. ➡ Please wait for me.

Page Summary

Grammar Commands
Function Giving and understanding commands

Grammar Notes

- The verb here is always in the base form and is the same whether the command is made to one person or to more than one person.
- The subject is *you*, but it isn't spoken or written: *Close the door.*
- On this page the command form has several meanings: "Commands" 1 and 3 are invitations, 5 and 6 are orders, and 9 is a suggestion.
- *Please* is not usually used with suggestions such as 9.

▶ *Look and listen. Listen and repeat.*

1. Play the recording (CD track 71) as students listen.
2. Play the recording (CD track 72) again for students to repeat.
3. Go over the note at the bottom of the page.

Expansion Activity 1

Elicit from students other examples in which someone might use *please* with the command form, for example, *Please close the window.* Write these on the board for students to practice.

Expansion Activity 2

Play a "polite" version of Simon Says. Give students commands starting with the phrase *Simon Says*, for example, *Simon Says: "Sit down."* Tell students to follow the command only if it includes *please*, for example, *Simon Says: "Please sit down."* After a few rounds, tell students they are "out" if they follow a command given without *please*.

Page Summary

Grammar Commands
Function Giving and understanding commands

▶ **DICTATION**

🎧 *Listen. Listen and write a command for each picture.*

1. Have students look at the illustrations and try to guess what command might be used in each situation.
2. Play the recording (CD track 73) as students listen, without writing.
3. Play the recording (CD track 74) again for students to write the commands.
4. Play the recording (CD track 73) again for students to check their answers.
5. Go over the answers by calling on different students to read aloud.

Option: Supply a situation (*The dishes are dirty.* or *The phone is ringing.*) and have students supply the appropriate command.

Answer Key

1. Please answer the phone!
2. Listen to me!
3. Wait for Becky!
4. Look at the dog!
5. Take your umbrella!
6. Wear your red dress!
7. Wash the dishes!
8. Open your mouth!
9. Eat your dinner!

▶ **PRACTICE**

1. Pair students. Have them practice reading the commands.
2. Read the commands aloud with the class chorally.

Expansion Activity 1

Pantomime some gestures for the commands on this page: picking up a phone receiver for *Answer the phone,* cupping a hand to your ear for *Listen to me,* pointing to your mouth and opening a hand for *Open your mouth,* pointing first to your eye and then to an object in the classroom for *Look at the (clock).* First, have students say the commands in response to your gesture, then reverse the order: You say the command and the entire class pantomimes it. You can gradually increase the speed and see if the class can keep up with you.

Expansion Activity 2

Pair students. Tell them to give each other advice on how to improve their English, for example, *Try to speak! Listen to TV in English! Read English books! Study hard!*

▶ **PRACTICE** • *Read the commands out loud.*

GRAMMAR • Negative Commands

▶ 🎧 *Look and listen. Listen and repeat.*

▶ **PRACTICE** • *Read the commands out loud.*

GRAMMAR • Negative Commands

Page Summary

Grammar Commands
Function Giving and understanding negative commands

Grammar Notes

All the sentences on this page are the same grammatically. However, the negative command form conveys different functions. For example, command 1 is a warning, 3 is a suggestion, 9 is advice.

! Pronunciation Tip

This page is an opportunity to demonstrate the importance of tone of voice in conveying different possible meanings of grammatically identical commands. Command 1, for example, would be said in a firm voice, while 3 would be said more gently. After students have listened to the recording, choose a few of the commands and say them with different tones of voice to demonstrate this.

Option: Write *warning, suggestion, advice* on the board. Turn your back to the class and say, *Don't do that!* in several tones of voice. Students call out *suggestion, warning,* or *advice.*

▶ ∩ Look and listen. Listen and repeat.

1. Play the recording (CD track 75) as students listen only.
2. Play the recording (CD track 76) again for students to repeat.

Expansion Activity

To review the vocabulary as well as the grammar on this page, write on the board: *sofa, dress, dictionary, tie, cookies, keys.* Say one of the words *(sofa),* then call on a student who says, *Don't sleep on the sofa.* That student then says another word *(keys)* and says another student's name, who, in turn, says, *Don't forget your keys.*

Page Summary

Grammar Negative commands
Function Giving and understanding negative commands

▶ DICTATION

🎧 *Listen. Listen and write a negative command for each picture.*

1. Have students look at the illustrations and try to predict the negative command for each situation.
2. Play the recording (CD track 77) as students listen without writing or repeating.
3. Play the recording (CD track 78) again for students to write the commands.
4. Play the recording (CD track 77) again for students to check their answers.
5. Go over the answers by calling on different students to read aloud.

Answer Key

1. Don't forget your umbrella.
2. Don't sleep on the bus!
3. Don't be afraid!
4. Don't talk in the library!
5. Don't eat that cake!
6. Don't play with my umbrella!
7. Don't wear that hat!
8. Don't buy those shoes!
9. Don't take that watch!

▶ PRACTICE

1. Say the number of the pictures one at a time; pause for the class to read the command chorally.
2. Call on individual students to read each command aloud.

Option: Pair students. Have them practice reading the commands.

Expansion Activity

Drawing on the commands presented on pages 35 and 36, write several situations on the board. Have students tell you the appropriate command for each. For example, write:

It's raining outside. (to elicit, *Don't forget your umbrella.*)
It's cold today. (to elicit, *Don't forget your coat.*)
You need your pencil. (to elicit, *Don't take my pencil.*)

PRACTICE • *Read the commands out loud.*

VOCABULARY

NOUNS

Clothes
belt
blouse
boots
coat
dress
gloves
hat
jacket
jeans
pants
shirt
shoes
shorts
skirt
socks
sweater
tie

Colors
beige
black
blue
brown
gray
green
orange
red
white
yellow

Meals
breakfast
lunch
dinner

Other
avocados
basketball player
brother
bus
cake
carrots
class
cookies
dancer
daughter
dictionary
dishes
driver
eraser
hand
keys
kitchen
letter
man
money
mouth
neighbor
oranges
peaches
pencil
singer
sofa
spinach
student
sunglasses
watch
window

VERBS
answer
buy
come
eat
forget
listen to
look at
open
play
relax
sit down
sleep
take
talk
wait for
wash
wear

ADJECTIVES

happy ≠ sad
rich ≠ poor
strong ≠ weak
big ≠ small
tall ≠ short
fat ≠ thin
young ≠ old
married ≠ single

hot ≠ cold
new ≠ old
clean ≠ dirty
noisy ≠ quiet
cheap ≠ expensive
beautiful ≠ ugly
handsome ≠ ugly
good-looking ≠ ugly

good
bad
hungry
thirsty
tired
afraid
nervous
comfortable

ADVERBS

Time Expressions

in the morning
in the afternoon
in the evening
at night

EXPRESSIONS

Telling the time

It's five after two.
It's two-fifteen.
It's a quarter past two.
It's two-thirty.
It's a quarter to three.
It's five to three.

Using time expressions

It's lunchtime.
It's dinnertime.
It's bedtime.

Giving a compliment

That's a beautiful hat.
Those are good-looking boots.

Describing clothing

Her dress is red.
His pants are brown.

Other

He's interested in…
She's afraid of…

VOCABULARY

The games below provide additional opportunities to use the vocabulary, grammar, and expressions presented in the unit. Before students play any of the games, have them review the lists of words and circle any words they don't know. Then have students form small groups and review the circled words together. Circulate so you can help in case no one in the group knows a particular word.

Game 1: Opposites

Books are closed. Use the Adjectives list. Choose an adjective *(happy)* and ask the question, *Are you (happy)?* Shake your head and pantomime *No* until the the students respond chorally with the opposite adjective: *No, I'm (sad)*. Do a couple of examples, supplying the adjective and the pantomimed response yourself and having the entire class respond. Then have students continue in pairs. Be sure to model a few examples with subjects other than *you* or *I* in order to cover *new, old, expensive.*

Student 1: *Are you (sad)?*
Student 2: *No, I'm (happy).*
Student 2: *Is the teacher's car (expensive)?*
Student 1: *No, it's (cheap).*

Encourage students to exaggerate any possible gestures that could go with the adjectives, for example, weight-lifting for *strong*. This can also be done in small groups as a chain activity. Student 1 starts by asking a question of the student on the left. That student answers, and asks a question of the next student. They continue around the group.

Game 2: Numbers and Times

Books are closed. Say the following numbers one at a time: *45, 30, 15, 16, 20, 50, 11, 5, 22, 25.* Have students work individually to write the words for the numbers on a piece of paper. Then call on two students to write the words on the board. After students check their spelling, have the class read the words aloud. Alternatively, say the number and have students write the numerals, not the words.

Then divide the class into teams. Have each team stand in line at the board. Say a time and have the first member of each team write the time on the board, for example, *2:15*, and then go to the end of the line. Each team that writes it correctly gets a point.

Game 3: Describing Someone

Books are open. Students work individually. Have them imagine a person and describe how the person is dressed. Tell them to write at least five sentences, for example, *Her shoes are black.* Circulate and help them as needed. When the students are finished writing, tell them to form pairs. Have them take turns describing the person they have imagined. If students are comfortable drawing, you can also have them draw what their partner tells them. They can make a simple drawing and write the word for the color of each article of clothing if colors aren't available. Have students turn their backs to each other. While one student describes, the other student draws. Then they can look at the drawing together. If there are errors, tell the student to repeat that part of the description.

PRONUNCIATION

Page Summary

Focus Plural ending of nouns

A 🎧 *Listen to these plural nouns. Notice the pronunciation of the s endings.*

1. Have students look at the words and listen as you play the recording (CD track 79).
2. Play the recording (CD track 79) again and have the students close their books and listen only.

B 🎧 *Listen and repeat.*

1. Play the recording (CD track 80) again and have the students repeat.
2. Have students read the words out loud as a class or in pairs.

C 🎧 *Listen to the plural forms of these nouns. Listen and repeat.*

1. Have students listen as you play the recording (CD track 81).
2. Play the recording (CD track 82) and have the students repeat. Play again, as needed.

D 🎧 *Complete the chart with the plural forms of the nouns in Part C.*

1. Write the endings on the board. Do item 1 with the class. Write *roses* under /**iz**/.
2. Do item 2 with the class. Write *dogs* under /**z**/.
3. Call on a student to do item 3, writing *cats* under /**s**/.
4. Have students work alone to write the words in the correct columns.

Option: Pair students needing support. Have them work together to complete the chart.

E 🎧 *Listen and check your answers.*

1. Have students listen as you play the recording (CD track 83) through.
2. As a final check, have students read the words out loud chorally.

Option: Pair students. Have them practice saying the words. Circulate and check their pronunciation.

Answer Key

/**s**/	/**z**/	/**iz**/
cats	dogs	roses
trucks	birds	dishes
maps	cameras	watches
stamps	radios	glasses

Expansion Activity

With books closed, dictate the words from Part C. Have students write down the plural forms. Then call on individual students to read the words aloud.

PRONUNCIATION

▶ **A** 🎧 *Listen to these plural nouns. Notice the pronunciation of the* **s** *endings.*

/**s**/	/**z**/	/**iz**/
book**s**	key**s**	dish**es**
student**s**	door**s**	glass**es**
desk**s**	window**s**	peach**es**

▶ **B** 🎧 *Listen and repeat.*

▶ **C** 🎧 *Listen to the plural forms of these nouns. Listen and repeat.*

1. rose	2. dog	3. cat	4. dish

5. bird	6. watch	7. truck	8. camera

9. map	10. radio	11. glass	12. stamp

▶ **D** *Complete the chart with the plural forms of the nouns in Part C.*

/**s**/	/**z**/	/**iz**/
cats	_____	_____
_____	_____	_____
_____	_____	_____
_____	_____	_____

▶ **E** 🎧 *Listen and check your answers.*

GRAMMAR SUMMARY

ADJECTIVES AND WORD ORDER

The bicycle is new. The flowers are beautiful.	It's a new bicycle. They're beautiful flowers.

IMPERATIVE

Close the door!
Open the window!

NEGATIVE IMPERATIVE

Don't	close the door! open the window!

INDEFINITE ARTICLE

It's	a	pear. banana.		It's	an	apple. orange.

Question with HOW MUCH

How much	is the watch? are the books?	It's ninety-five dollars. They're twenty dollars.

CONTENTS

Chapter

3

CARTOON STORY

▶ 🎧 *Dallas is calling his new girlfriend, Daisy. Listen. Listen and practice.*

CARTOON STORY

Page Summary

Grammar Present continuous
Function Talking on the phone

The Teacher's Notes for the Cartoon Story continue on page T43.

The Teacher's Notes for the Cartoon Story continue on page T43.

Culture Note

In the cartoon story, Dallas is calling his new girlfriend, Daisy. Dallas is also the name of a city in Texas in the southwestern part of the United States. There are many ranches and cowboys in Texas. Dallas and Daisy are in a new relationship and they are flirting with each other a bit. His response to her compliment "You look so handsome" is "Aw shucks." "Aw shucks" is a way to deflect the compliment. A more common response would be a simple "Thanks" or "Thank you."

To show he cares about her, Dallas uses the phrase "my little angel." Similar terms of endearment in English are, "honey," "sweetie," and "sweetheart." Discuss with students other terms they might be familiar with from American movies and TV.

Warm-up

Walk toward the classroom door and say, *I'm walking to the door.* Walk to the board and say, *I'm walking to the board.* Then indicate a student and give the command, *Walk to the door.* As the student walks, ask *What are you doing?* Elicit from the student, *I'm walking to the door.* Give two more students other commands, and ask them what they're doing.

! *Pronunciation Tip*

In rapid speech, the contraction *I'm* is linked to the next sound and is barely pronounced *(ImBRINGing)*.

▶ 🎧 *Listen. Listen and practice.*

1. Direct students' attention to the illustrations.
2. Set the scene: Dallas is calling his new girlfriend, Daisy.

Option: Review that Dallas met Daisy at a party. Alice introduced them. (See page 3.)

3. Play the recording (CD2, track 1) as students listen.
4. Use the illustrations to go over key vocabulary and expressions.

   cell phone
   downtown
   heavy traffic
   That's terrible.
   I'm okay.
   Are you busy?
   Not really.
   I'm on my way.
   That's very sweet of you.

5. Play the recording (CD2, track 2) for students to practice the conversation.

▶ QUESTIONS

1. Have students form pairs. Tell them to take turns asking and answering the questions on page 43.
2. Check answers as a class by asking the questions of different students.
3. Pair students. Have students practice the conversation by reading and looking up after every sentence.
4. Call on pairs to present the conversation to the class.

Answer Key

1. He is downtown. He's driving in heavy traffic.
2. He's calling Daisy.
3. No, she isn't busy.
4. She's watching a dumb movie.
5. Yes, he is.
6. Dallas is bringing Daisy flowers.
7. Yes, she is. He's bringing her flowers. OR She's happy because Dallas is coming to see her.

CARTOON STORY

Expansion Activity 1

Use the illustrations for more speaking practice. Point to each illustration and discuss it. For example, ask *What is he wearing? (He's wearing a hat.) What is she drinking? (She's drinking coffee.) Is she smiling? What is she wearing?* Then pair students. Have them continue asking each other questions about the illustrations. Call on pairs to present for the class.

Expansion Activity 2

Discuss gifts with your students. In the United States it is appropriate to give candy, flowers, or other small, inexpensive gifts to a new girlfriend. Write *OK gifts* and *Not OK gifts* on the board. Under *OK gifts* write *flowers*. Under *Not OK gifts* write *expensive jewelry*. Ask students to give examples of gifts for both categories. Write them on the board.

▶ QUESTIONS

1. Where is Dallas?
2. Who's he calling?
3. Is Daisy busy now?
4. What's she doing?

5. Is Dallas coming to see Daisy?
6. What's he bringing?
7. Is Daisy happy? Why?

GRAMMAR • Present Continuous

▶ 🎧 *Listen. Listen and practice.*

Page Summary

Grammar Present continuous; *Wh-* questions
Function Describing actions

Warm-up

Books are closed. Carry out various actions (write on board, walk, look at the clock) while saying what you are doing: *I'm writing on the board. I'm walking.* Write the verbs on the board. As you do each action, ask students, *What am I doing?* Students respond, *You're (walking).* Then call on several students, one at a time, to demonstrate an action as they say what they are doing, for example, *I'm looking at the board.*

Grammar Note

The present continuous is used here to describe actions that are taking place now. Remind students of the inverted word order in *Wh-* questions. Write an example on the board, and draw an arrow from the object to the *Wh-* word, for example,

I'm thinking about the weekend.

What are you thinking about?

Pronunciation Tips

- In these *Wh-* questions, the strongest stress is on the stressed syllable of the verb *(THINKing, GOing). What are you THINKing about? Where are you GOing?*
- The voice falls at the end of a *Wh-* question.

Culture Note

In picture 5, the man is calling from a barbershop. In the United States, traditionally a barbershop is a place where men go to get their hair cut, while women go to a beauty shop. Nowadays, both men and women also go to *hair salons, beauty salons,* and *hairdressers.* People who work in these places are *hair stylists* or *hairdressers.*

▶ Listen. Listen and practice.

1. Set the scene: They are asking about what is happening now.
2. Play the recording (CD2, track 3) as students listen only.
3. Play the recording (CD2, track 4) for students to practice the conversations.
4. Pair students. Have students practice the conversations, switching parts.
5. Call on different pairs to present each conversation to the class.

Expansion Activity

Use the illustrations for more speaking practice. Point to each illustration and discuss it. For example, picture 1, point to the thought bubble. Ask, *Where is she sitting?* (On the beach.) *What is she doing?* (Sitting, relaxing, looking at the water.) *What is she wearing?* (A swimming suit.) In preparation for the material presented on page 45, ask *yes/no* questions; for example, ask about picture 2: *Is he sitting?* Continue with questions about the other pictures.

Page Summary

Grammar Present continuous
Function Describing actions

Warm-up

Point to a book and say, *I'm pointing to the book.*
Point to a table and say, *I'm pointing to the table.*
Then point to the door and ask, *Am I pointing to the window?* Shake your head "no," and say, *No, I'm not. I'm pointing to the door.* Then ask, *Am I pointing to the desk?* Shake your head, and say, *No, I'm not.* Then ask, *Am I pointing to the door?* Nod and say, *Yes, I am.*

Grammar Note

Remind students what they learned in Chapter 2: A contraction isn't used with a short answer in the affirmative. We cannot say, *Yes, I'm.*

! *Pronunciation Tip*

The voice rises at the end of *yes/no* questions.

▶ ⌒ *Listen to the conversations.*

Have students look at the illustrations and listen as you play the recording (CD2, track 5). Play it again, as needed.

▶ WRITING

1. Have students work alone to write a question for each picture using the questions in the box at the top of the page.
2. Play the recording (CD2, track 5) again and have students check their answers.
3. Go over the answers with the class by calling on different pairs to read each conversation, mixing up the order of the pictures.

Option: Pair students. Have them practice the conversations.

Answer Key

1. Are you learning a lot in school?
2. Are you wearing new shoes?
3. Are you thinking about the weekend?
4. Are you enjoying this class?
5. Are you eating something?
6. Are you listening to me?

▶ PAIR WORK

1. Model the example with a student partner. Make sure students understand they should use their own information.
2. Pair students. Have them take turns asking each other the questions.
3. Call on different pairs to present each conversation for the class.

Expansion Activity

Have students form pairs. Write on the board: *eating, enjoying, listening, wearing.* Ask students to take turns asking their partners questions using these verbs. Students can answer with true or made-up information.

GRAMMAR • Present Continuous

▶ 🎧 *Listen to the conversations.*

▶ **WRITING** • *Write a question for each picture using the questions in the box.*

Are you thinking about the weekend? Are you enjoying this class? Are you listening to me?
Are you learning a lot in school?   Are you wearing new shoes? Are you eating something?

▶ **PAIR WORK** • *Ask each other the same questions.*

A: **Are you learning a lot in school?**
B: **Yes, I am. My classes are very interesting. OR No, I'm not. My classes are boring.**

GRAMMAR • Present Continuous

What	's (is)	he she	doing?

He She	's (is)	listening to the radio.

▶ 🎧 *Listen. Listen and repeat.*

▶ **PAIR WORK** • *Practice the conversations.*

▶ **WRITING** • *Fill in the answers. Then read the conversations aloud.*

Who's Maria dancing with?

She's dancing with Carlos.

1.

Where's Billy going?

2.

What's Daisy reading?

3.

Who's Becky talking to?

4.

Page Summary

Grammar Present Continuous; *Wh-* questions and answers
Function Describing actions

The Teacher's Notes for this activity continue on page T47.

Warm-up

Write *He's* and *She's* on the board. Ask students to look around the room at their classmates. Ask one student about another student: *What's (Teresa) doing?* Point to *She's* on the board to cue the student to use it in the response. Ask several more students about other classmates to elicit both *He's* and *She's*. Note: Encourage them to make different sentences, for example, *He's sitting at his desk. She's looking at the book. He's holding a pen. She's listening to you.*

Listen. Listen and repeat.

1. Have students look at the illustrations on pages 46 and 47.
2. Play the recording (CD2, track 6) as students listen, without writing.
3. Play the recording (CD2, track 7) for students to repeat.

PAIR WORK

Have students form pairs and practice the conversation, switching parts.

WRITING

1. Have students work alone to write the answer to the question about each picture.

2. Play the recording (CD2, track 6) again and have the students check their answers.
3. Go over the answers with the class by calling on different pairs to read each conversation.

Option: Divide the class into two groups. One group reads the questions, and the other reads the answers.

Answer Key

1. She's dancing with Carlos.
2. He's going to the park.
3. She's reading a letter.
4. She's talking to the teacher.
5. He's looking at a bird.
6. She's studying at the library.
7. He's drinking coffee.
8. He's writing to his family.
9. She's having lunch at Al's Café.

Expansion Activity 1

Books are closed. Say a name from one of the pictures on pages 46 and 47. Call on a student to ask the question. For example, say *Billy*. The student asks, *Where's Billy going?* Call on another student to answer the question: *He's going to the park.* Say the name cues in random order. Call on different students each time.

Expansion Activity 2

Use the illustrations to review Chapter 2 vocabulary. Ask the class questions, for example: *1. What is Maria wearing? (She's wearing a dress.) 2. Where is the woman sitting? (She's sitting* in front *of the house.) 3. Where is Daisy standing? (She's standing in the* kitchen.)

GRAMMAR • Present Continuous

Affirmative		
He She	's (is)	listening to the radio.

Negative		
He She	isn't (is not)	watching TV.

▶ **WRITING** • *Write affirmative and negative sentences about the people in the pictures. After you finish, read the sentences out loud.*

Jill

1. (sit on the sofa) <u>She's sitting on the sofa.</u>

2. (watch television) <u>She isn't watching television.</u>

3. (talk on the phone) _____

4. (read the newspaper) _____

Carlos

5. (listen to the radio) _____

6. (play the guitar) _____

7. (stand) _____

8. (sit) _____

Jane

9. (read a book) _____

10. (write a letter) _____

11. (drink coffee) _____

12. (eat candy) _____

Milton

13. (wait for the bus) _____

14. (wear a coat) _____

15. (look at his watch) _____

16. (look at the dog) _____

GRAMMAR • Present Continuous

Page Summary

Grammar Present continuous; affirmative and negative statements
Function Describing actions

Warm-up

Talk about what people in the class are currently doing. Name a student and say what he or she is doing. For example, *Yasuo is wearing a blue shirt. Maria is looking at the board.* Elicit similar sentences from a couple of students. Try to elicit a few negative sentences as well: *Yasuo is wearing a blue shirt. She isn't wearing a red shirt. Maria is looking at the board. She isn't looking at her watch.*

Grammar Note

Remind students of the alternate form: *No, he's not. / No, she's not.*

WRITING

1. Go over the examples in the boxes at the top of the page, making sure that students notice *not* or *n't*.
2. Have students look at the first illustration. Read the first two sentences about Jill to the class.
3. Call on a student for the answer to item 3. *(She's talking on the phone.)* Call on another student for item 4. *(She isn't reading the newspaper.)*
4. Have students work alone to write the sentences for the other pictures.
5. Go over the answers with the class by calling on different students to read each sentence.
6. Have students read the sentences out loud chorally or in pairs.

Answer Key

1. She's sitting on the sofa.
2. She isn't watching television.
3. She's talking on the phone.
4. She isn't reading the newspaper.
5. He isn't listening to the radio.
6. He's playing the guitar.
7. He isn't standing.
8. He's sitting.
9. She's reading a book.
10. She isn't writing a letter.
11. She's drinking coffee.
12. She isn't eating candy.
13. He's waiting for the bus.
14. He isn't wearing a coat.
15. He's looking at his watch.
16. He isn't looking at the dog.

Expansion Activity

Have students look around the room and then write two affirmative sentences and two negative sentences about what their classmates are doing. When they are finished, have them form groups and take turns reading their sentences out loud. Then call on individual students to write their sentences on the board.

GRAMMAR • Present Continuous

Page Summary

Grammar Present continuous; *yes/no* questions
Function Asking about and describing actions

Warm-up

Ask a few questions about what students in the class are doing. For example, *Is Alex reading?* Model the response, *Yes, he is* or *No, he isn't. Is Cara standing? Yes, she is* or *No, she isn't.* Elicit questions from several students. Have the whole class respond to their questions.

! *Pronunciation Note*

Remind students about the rising intonation for the *yes / no* question, and the falling intonation for the short answer.

Culture Note

In item 5, the question is: *Is Daisy going to the market?* Another common expression is *going to the store.*

▶ PAIR WORK

1. Go over the examples in the boxes at the top of the page.
2. Model item 1 with a student partner, switching parts. Repeat with item 2. Make sure students understand that if the answer is negative, they also need to say what the person is doing.
3. Have students form pairs. Tell them to take turns asking and answering the questions. Circulate and help, as needed, checking for correct intonation.
4. Call on different pairs to present each conversation for the class.

Answer Key

1. B: Yes, he is.
2. B: No, she isn't.
   She's buying a computer.
3. B: Yes, he is.
4. B: No, he isn't.
   He's studying at the library.
5. B: No, she isn't.
   She's going to the post office.
6. B: Yes, he is.
7. B: Yes, she is.
8. B: No, he isn't.
   He's playing the guitar.
9. B. No, she isn't.
   She's wearing a red dress.

Expansion Activity 1

Use the illustrations for more listening practice. Ask other questions, for example: *4. Is Ken studying at the library? 5. Is Daisy going to the post office? 6. Is Milton waiting for his friend? 7. Is Becky standing by the door? 8. Is Carlos playing the guitar?* Have students respond chorally or individually.

Expansion Activity 2

Have students write original questions for several of the pictures, and then ask their questions of other students.

GRAMMAR • Present Continuous

Yes/No Question		
Is	he she	working?

Short Answers					
Yes,	he she	is.	No,	he she	isn't.

▶ **PAIR WORK** • *Ask and answer questions.*

1. A: **Is Mario singing?**
   B: **Yes, he is.**

2. A: **Is Jane buying a television?**
   B: **No, she isn't. She's buying a computer.**

3. Is Jimmy playing basketball?

4. Is Ken studying at home?

5. Is Daisy going to the market?

6. Is Milton waiting for the bus?

7. Is Becky standing by the window?

8. Is Carlos playing the piano?

9. Is Maria wearing a green dress?

GRAMMAR • Present Continuous

What are they doing?	They	're (are)	making dinner.

▶ 🎧 *Listen. Listen and repeat.*

▶ **PAIR WORK** • *Practice the conversations.*

▶ **WRITING** • *Fill in the answers. Then read the conversations aloud.*

Who are the neighbors talking to?

They're talking to a police officer.

1.

Where are Ken and Suzi having lunch?

2.

What are the men drinking?

3.

Who are the students waiting for?

4.

Page Summary

Grammar Present continuous; answers to *Wh-* questions
Function Describing actions

The Teacher's Notes for this activity continue page T51.

Warm-up

Ask students to cover the speech bubbles on pages 50–51. Have students form pairs. Tell them to choose three pictures and make a sentence about each picture. Give an example: *In picture 1 the man and woman are standing.* Call on pairs to say their sentences for the class.

🎧 Listen. Listen and repeat.

1. Have students look at the illustrations on both pages 50 and 51.
2. Play the recording (CD2, track 8) as students listen.
3. Play the recording (CD2, track 9) for students to repeat.

▶ PAIR WORK

1. Read the picture 1 conversation with a student partner. Switch parts and repeat.
2. Have students form pairs. Tell them to practice the conversations, switching parts.
3. Call on different pairs to present each conversation for the class.

▶ WRITING

1. Have students work alone to write the answer to the question for each picture.

2. Play the recording (CD2, track 8) again and have the students check their work.
3. Go over the answers with the class by calling on different pairs to read each conversation.

Option: Divide the class into two groups: Have one group read the questions and the other group read the answers. Halfway through, have the groups switch parts.

Answer Key

1. They're talking to a police officer.
2. They're having lunch in the park.
3. They're drinking coffee.
4. They're waiting for the teacher.
5. They're going to the beach.
6. They're eating hot dogs.
7. They're looking at Bruno.
8. They're shopping at Gold's Department Store.
9. They're buying a television.

Expansion Activity 1

Students' books are closed. Choose five questions from pages 50 and 51. Write each on the board in scrambled word order. Have students work individually to unscramble the words and write them in the correct order to make the questions. Have volunteers write the questions on the board. Review the word order in questions. Then have the students read the questions chorally.

Expansion Activity 2

For each picture, have students in pairs take turns asking what the people are doing. This requires them to manipulate the same information from the activity on pages 50 and 51, but in a different way. Model an example first. For example, for picture 1: *What are the neighbors doing?* A: *They're talking to a police officer.*

Where are your friends going?

5. _____

What are Jimmy and Becky eating?

6. _____

Who are the people looking at?

7. _____

Where are Lucy and Grover shopping?

8. _____

What are they buying?

9. _____

Affirmative		
They	're (are)	listening to music.

Negative		
They	aren't (are not)	watching TV.

▶ **CLASS ACTIVITY** • *Look at the picture of Grover and Lucy. Where are they? What are they doing? Are they happy? Are they having a good time?*

▶ **WRITING** • *Write affirmative and negative sentences about Grover and Lucy. After you finish, read the sentences out loud.*

1. (sit in front of the fire) <u>They're sitting in front of the fire.</u>

2. (stand by the window) <u>They aren't standing by the window.</u>

3. (drink coffee)_____

4. (listen to music)_____

5. (watch television) _____

6. (play the piano) _____

7. (smile) _____

8. (have a good time)_____

9. (look at the clock) _____

10. (read the newspaper)_____

GRAMMAR • Present Continuous

Page Summary

Grammar Present Continuous
Function Describing actions

Warm-up

Say the names of two students in the class and say what they're doing, for example, *They're looking at their books.* Then say what they aren't doing, for example, *They aren't listening to the radio.*

Grammar Notes

- Both *they are* and *they're* are presented here. The contracted form is much more common in spoken English.
- Remind students of the alternate form for the negative contraction *(they're not).*

► CLASS ACTIVITY

Have students look at the picture of Grover and Lucy. Ask the questions to set the scene.

Option: Have the students form pairs and ask each other the questions instead.

► WRITING

1. Go over the examples in the boxes at the top of the page.
2. Read the examples of affirmative and negative sentences (items 1 and 2).
3. Ask students to write the sentence for item 3. Call on a student for the answer. *(They're drinking coffee.)* Tell students to use contractions in their answers.
4. Have students work alone to write the other sentences about Grover and Lucy.
5. Go over the answers with the class by calling on different students to read each sentence.
6. Have the students read the sentences out loud chorally or in pairs.

Answer Key

1. They're sitting in front of the fire.
2. They aren't standing by the window.
3. They're drinking coffee.
4. They're listening to music.
5. They aren't watching television.
6. They aren't playing the piano.
7. They're smiling.
8. They're having a good time.
9. They aren't looking at the clock.
10. They aren't reading the newspaper.

Expansion Activity 1

Have students rewrite the affirmative sentences as negative sentences, and the negative sentences as affirmative sentences, for example, *They aren't sitting by the fire. They're standing by the window.* Have students check their work in pairs. Then call on students to read the new sentences for the class. Tell the rest of the class to listen carefully to see if they agree with the new sentences.

Expansion Activity 2

Go over the spelling rules for the main verb of the present continuous. Write on the board: *smile/smiling have/having.* Explain that the *e* is dropped. Next write *sit/sitting*, and go over the rule that if the verb ends in vowel + consonant, double the consonant. Next write, *drink drinking* Explain that if the verb ends in two consonants, only add *-ing*. Write a few more verbs on the board and have students write the *-ing* form, for example, *walk, eat, dance, read.*

GRAMMAR • Present Continuous

Page Summary

Grammar Present continuous; *yes/no* questions
Function Asking about and describing actions of more than one person

Warm-up

Ask the class about what two students in the class are doing, for example, *Are (Tomas and Tony) looking out the window?* Model the response, *No, they aren't. They're looking at the teacher.* Then ask a question to get an affirmative response: *Are (Sonya and Katy) sitting at their desks?* Model the response, *Yes, they are.* Then ask a few more questions about what other pairs of students are doing. Call on individual students to respond.

▶ PAIR WORK

1. Go over the *Yes/No* Question and Short Answers at the top of the page.
2. Call on a pair to model the first conversation. Then divide the class into two groups to model item 2. One group is A; the other is B. Have them switch parts and repeat.
3. Have students form pairs. Tell them to take turns asking and answering the questions about the pictures.
4. Call on different pairs to present each conversation for the class.

Answer Key

1. B: No, they aren't. They're taking the bus.
2. B: Yes, they are.
3. B: No, they aren't. They're watching television.
4. B: Yes, they are.
5. B: No, they aren't. They're playing basketball.
6. B: Yes, they are.
7. B: No, they aren't. They're dancing.
8. B: Yes, they are.
9. B: No, they aren't. They're talking.

Expansion Activity 1

Set the scene: it is 6:00 P.M. at Lucy and Grover's home. There are at least three activities going on; for example, Lucy and Grover are cooking dinner while their children, Tim and Suzi, are talking on the phone, studying, playing basketball, or reading the newspaper. Have students form pairs and sit back to back. The students take turns describing what is happening. Student 1 describes what is happening right now and Student 2 makes a simple drawing. Student 2 then shows the drawing to Student 1. Then they switch parts and repeat (Student 2 should say different activities). When pairs are finished, have them form groups of four with another pair. Have them take turns explaining what is happening.

Expansion Activity 2

Books closed. Use the illustrations for more listening practice. Divide the class into two groups. In random order, read the names only from an illustration, for example, *Maria and Carlos.* Group A forms a question: *Are Maria and Carlos singing?* Group B answers: *No, they aren't. They're dancing.*

GRAMMAR • Present Continuous

Yes/No Question	Short Answers	
Are they working?	Yes, they are.	No, they aren't.

▶ **PAIR WORK** • *Ask and answer questions.*

1. A: **Are the girls walking to school?**
   B: **No, they aren't. They're taking the bus.**

2. A: **Are the men singing?**
   B: **Yes, they are.**

3. Are Mr. and Mrs. Lee listening to the radio?

4. Are Lucy and Grover making dinner?

5. Are the boys studying?

6. Are Jack and Jill talking on the phone?

7. Are Maria and Carlos singing?

8. Are the children smiling?

9. Are Becky and Jimmy listening to the teacher?

| Look at | Mike.
Diana.
Jack and Jill.
Lisa and me.
the clock. | Look at | him.
her.
them.
us.
it. |

▶ 🎧 *Look and listen. Listen and repeat.*

1. **Look at him. He's really strong.**

2. **She's a good dancer. Look at her.**

3. **Look at me. I'm beautiful.**

4. **We're clowns. Look at us.**

5. **Look at them. They're acrobats.**

6. **This is a real diamond. Look at it.**

Page Summary

Grammar Object Pronouns
Function Talking about people and objects

Grammar Notes

• In order to understand object pronouns, students need to know the difference between *subject* and *object*. Use the information in the box at the top of the page and some nouns in the illustrations to present this. Write three column headings on board:

subject/noun   subject/pronoun   object/pronoun

Then add the words from the exercise under the headings:

subject/noun	subject/pronoun	object/pronoun
Mike	*he*	*him*
Diana	*she*	*her*
diamond	*it*	*it*
clowns	*they*	*them*

Point out to students that sometimes the pronoun looks the same in subject and object position *(it/it)* and sometimes it doesn't *(she/her)*.

• Some students might get confused with the third-person pronouns *him/her. Her* is used for both the object pronoun and the possessive *(I see her, This is her handbag)*, while *him* is used for the object pronoun, but *his* for the possessive *(his car)*. It isn't necessary to present this now, but students who have already studied English might ask about it.

Culture Note

The illustrations are about a circus. Picture 6 shows a magician who has performed a magic trick and is suddenly holding a real diamond. This is a good opportunity for students to use their prior knowledge about circuses to expand their vocabulary. Encourage them to use dictionaries, as needed, to talk about circus acts they have seen or heard about.

▶ 🎧 *Look and listen. Listen and repeat.*

1. Play the recording (CD2, track 10) as students listen.
2. Play the recording (CD2, track 11) again for students to repeat.

Option: Have students read the sentences out loud in pairs.

Expansion Activity

Say a subject noun or pronoun. Have students say the object pronoun, for example, *he/him, Daisy/her, clowns/them, they/them.* Do this as a rapid drill.

Expansion Activity 2

The illustrations are all about a circus. Talk about other activities they might see at the circus. Help with vocabulary as needed. Compile a list of activities on the board. Have students form pairs. Tell students to imagine that one of them is at the circus. The other student is at home. Student 1 calls Student 2 on a cellular phone (mobile phone) and tells him/her what is going on, for example, *I'm looking at a man. He's really strong. Oh, the clowns are smiling. They're saying, "Look at us!"* Encourage students to use the activities in the illustrations and the list on the board.

Page Summary

Grammar Object pronouns
Function Giving and understanding commands

Warm-up

Give students a few simple commands to follow:
Please open your books. Please turn to page 55.
Don't read it. Look at the pictures. Just look at them.

▶ ⌂ Listen.

Have students look at the illustrations and listen as you play the recording (CD2, track 12). Play it again, as needed.

▶ WRITING

1. Have students work alone to fill in the blanks using the pronouns at the top of the page.
2. Play the recording (CD2, track 12) again and have the students check their answers.

Option: Have students check their answers in pairs before playing the recording again.

3. Go over the answers with the class by calling on different students to read the sentences.
4. Have students form pairs. Have them take turns reading the sentences aloud.

Answer Key

1. him	7. us
2. us	8. it
3. it	9. me
4. me	10. her
5. them	11. them
6. her	12. him

Expansion Activity

Rewrite some of the sentences on the board, changing them slightly. Have the students fill in the blanks with the appropriate object pronouns. For example,

5. *That jacket is ugly. Don't buy _____.* (it)
6. *Sally and Alice are good students. Ask _____ for help.* (them).
7. *We're hungry. Bring _____ something to eat.* (us)
11. *That is my apple. Don't eat _____.* (it)
12. *Don't be afraid of _____.* (them) *They're very friendly.*

GRAMMAR • Object Pronouns

 Listen. ▶ **WRITING** • *Fill in the blanks with* **her, him, me, us, it, them**.

1. Call the waiter. Ask <u>him</u> for the menu.

2. Waiter! Please bring ____ the menu.

3. How's your dinner? Are you enjoying ____?

4. Here's my phone number. Call ____ next week.

5. Those glasses are ugly. Don't buy _____.

6. Fern's a good student. Ask ____ for help.

7. We're leaving now. Please wait for ____.

8. Where's the newspaper? You're sitting on ____.

9. I'm hungry. Bring ____ something to eat.

10. Look! There's Annie! That's ____ over there.

11. Those are my apples! Don't eat _____!

12. Don't be afraid of ____. He's very friendly.

Chapter 3   55

WEATHER

▶ 🎧 *Listen. Listen and practice.*

1. Rio de Janeiro

It's sunny.

And hot!

2. Hollywood

It's cloudy.

But it's warm.

3. London

It's raining.

And it's cool.

4. Moscow

It's snowing.

And it's very cold!

▶ **PAIR WORK** • *Talk about the weather in each city.*

1. Rio de Janeiro

    A: **How's the weather in Rio de Janeiro?**

    B: **It's sunny and hot.**

WEATHER

Page Summary

Grammar *It's* followed by adjective or by present continuous
Function Describing the weather

Grammar Notes

- *It's* can be used with the present continuous: *It's raining.* It can also followed by an adjective: *It's sunny.* Student might be confused by *It's raining* versus *It's rainy.* Both are correct.
- *Very* can go before the adjective, but not in the middle of the present continuous expression, for example, *It's very sunny,* but not *It's very raining.*

Culture Note

Hollywood is located in what is often described as "sunny California." In fact, the weather is not always perfect there, and in parts of California, especially around San Francisco and further north, the weather is often cloudy and cool. As you discuss the weather and the seasons in different cities around the world, remind students that the seasons between the Southern and Northern hemispheres are opposite; for example, when it's winter in New York, it's summer in Sidney, Australia.

▶ 🎧*Listen. Listen and practice.*

1. Play the recording (CD2, track 13) as students listen. (Have them cover the text the first time you play the recording.)
2. Play the recording (CD2, track 14) again for students to practice the sentences.

▶ PAIR WORK

1. Go over the example in the book about Rio de Janeiro.
2. Have students form pairs. Tell them to take turns asking and answering about the weather in each city.
3. Call on different pairs to present each conversation for the class.

Expansion Activity

Ask students to tell you what the weather is like in cities they know. Write the name of each city and its weather on the board. Then have students form pairs. Ask them to talk about the weather in each city on the board, modeling their conversations after the one in the book.

SEASONS

Page Summary

Grammar Present continuous; simple present of *be*
Function Describing the weather

Warm-up

Talk about the seasons where the class is. If there is a classroom calendar available, hold it up and point to the months of the year that correspond to each season *(winter, spring, summer, fall)*. Say the name of each season. Then ask, *What season is it now?* If students can't answer, tell them, *It's (spring)*. Then say, *I like (summer). I like walking in the park in summer.* Ask a few students which seasons they like and why.

NOTE

Some of the vocabulary on this page may need a little explanation. Check to be sure that students understand *cloudy, backyard, windy, favorite.*

▶ ⌂*Listen.*

1. Have students look at the illustrations.
2. Set the scene: Mary is showing some family photos to her friend, Alice. Tell students to listen to what Mary says about each photo.
3. Play the recording (CD2, track 15) as students listen. (They should cover the text the first time they listen to the recording.)
4. Play the recording (CD2, track 15) again as students follow along silently in their books.

▶ **QUESTIONS**

1. Read the questions out loud to the class. Make sure students understand they should use true information in their answers.

2. Pair students. Have them take turns asking each other the questions.
3. Call on different students to answer the questions for the class.

Answer Key

Answers will vary

Expansion Activity

Have students work alone to write a short description (one or two sentences) of each of the seasons where they live. Write on the board *It's. . . .* Tell them to start each description this way. Circulate and help as the students write. When they're finished, have them form groups. Tell them to take turns reading a description *without saying* which season they are describing. The rest of the group listens and then guesses the season. For extra challenge at the end of group work, write a season on the board, for example, *winter*. Call on volunteers to describe winter. Write their ideas on the board. Remind them to listen carefully and not to repeat what someone else has already said. To give students more practice with the present continuous, follow up with the prompt: *It's winter. What are you doing?* Possible responses: *I'm sitting in front of the fire, I'm making a snowman, I'm wearing warm clothes, I'm drinking hot chocolate.*

SEASONS

▶ 🎧 *Listen.*

Mary is showing some family photos to her friend, Alice. Listen to what Mary says about each photo. Then read her comments out loud.

It's **winter**. We're in the mountains. It's snowing, and it's very cold. But we're having fun. We're making a big snow man.

It's **spring**. We're enjoying the pretty flowers in our backyard. It's a cloudy day, but the weather is nice and warm.

It's **summer**. We're spending a day at the beach. The weather is sunny and hot. We're drinking ice-cold lemonade.

It's **fall**. We're taking a walk in the park. The weather is windy and cool, and the leaves are falling. It's a beautiful day.

▶ **QUESTIONS**

- How's the weather in your city today?
- What season is it now?
- What's your favorite season?
- What's your favorite place in the summer?

VOCABULARY

NOUNS

Seasons of the year
winter
spring
summer
fall

Other
acrobat
backyard
barbershop
bird
boyfriend
candy
cell phone
clown
cowboy
diamond
downtown
fire
friend
glasses
guitar
help
lemonade
menu
mountains
people
phone
photo
radio
spaghetti
television
waiter
weekend

VERBS
bring
call
dance
drink
drive
enjoy
fall
learn
look
shop
sing
smile
spend
stand
study
take
think (about)
walk
work

PRONOUNS

Object pronouns
you
me
him
her
us
them
it

Other
something

ADJECTIVES
boring
dumb
favorite
friendly
ice-cold

EXPRESSIONS

Talking about the weather
How's the weather?
    It's hot/warm/cool/cold.
    It's sunny/cloudy/windy.
    It's raining/snowing.

Talking on the phone
Hello there.
    Who's calling? Is that you, _____ ?
Yes, it's me. Are you busy?
    Not really.

Saying goodbye
Bye, bye.
See you soon.

Giving a compliment
You look so handsome.

Showing appreciation
That's very sweet of you.

Other
We're taking a walk.
We're having a good time.

I'm okay.
I'm on my way.

I'm driving in heavy traffic.
That's terrible.

Right now.
Aw, shucks.

VOCABULARY

The games below provide additional opportunities to use the vocabulary, grammar, and expressions presented in the unit. Before students play any of the games, have them review the lists of words and circle any words they don't know. Then put students into small groups and have them review the circled words together. Circulate so you can help in case no one in the group knows a particular word.

Game 1: Telephone Time

Books are open. Have students look at the conversation under **Talking on the phone**. Then form groups of six to eight students. Choose one student in each group to start. That student says *Hello there,* plus the name of another group member who is being called. The second student continues the conversation. After the line *Not really,* Student 2 describes what he or she is doing. Student 2 then starts the conversation again with another student (S3). Before the students begin, write the example below on the board, substituting names of students in your class. Model the example with two student partners. Have the groups continue until everyone has a chance to say what he or she is doing. Encourage the students to make things up; the information doesn't have to be real. For added challenge, have the students turn their chairs so that they can't see each others' faces.

(S1): Hello there, (S2 name).
(S2): Who's calling? Is that you, (S1 name)?
(S1): Yes, it's me. Are you busy?
(S2): Not really. I'm listening to music. Bye, bye.
(S2): Hello there, (S3 name).

Game 2: Word Scramble

Books are closed. Choose eight words from the column labeled **Other**. Write them on the board, but scramble the order of the letters in each word. Have students unscramble the letters and spell each word correctly. Tell students to compare answers with a partner when they are finished. Then call on volunteers to write the words on the board. Have the class read the words chorally.

Game 3: Seasons Game

Books are open. Have students form pairs. Tell each pair to take four slips of paper and to write one season on each: *summer, fall, winter, spring.* Have students turn the slips of paper face down between them. Tell Student 1 to draw a slip, read the season, and put the paper down again. The student then decides what the weather is like in that season (you can decide in advance if the students are talking about the local weather where the class is held, or the weather in another city with which they are familiar). Student 2 asks, *How's the weather?* S1 says, *It's (raining).* S2 then guesses the season. The question is repeated until S2 guesses correctly. Then S2 takes a slip. Students continue taking turns. Note: For extra challenge, use a world map and talk about the weather in a few cities around the world. Then have the student play the game. This time, they must guess the name of the city as well as the season.

INTONATION

Page Summary

Focus Intonation of questions

▶ 🎧 *Listen. Notice the rising and falling intonation of the questions. Listen and practice.*

1. Have students look at the conversations and listen as you play the recording (CD, track 16).
2. Go over the NOTE with the class.
3. Play the recording (CD, track 16) again and have the students close their books and listen only.
4. Play the recordings (CD, tracks 17 and 18) for students to listen and repeat.

▶ 🎧 *Listen and write the intonation.*

1. Have students look at the conversation and listen as you play the recording (CD, track 19).
2. Play the recording (CD, track 19) again and have the students mark the intonation at the end of the questions.
3. Write the conversation on the board, and mark the intonation.
4. Go over the conversation with the class, emphasizing the intonation.
5. Have students form pairs. Have them practice the conversation, switching parts. Circulate and check their pronunciation.

Answer Key

Rising intonation on: *Dallas, is that you? Are you busy? Are you coming to see me?*
Falling intonation on: *Where are you? What are you doing?*

Expansion Activity

Have students turn to other activities in the unit and mark the intonation. Then have them listen to the audio for that activity to check their work.

INTONATION

▶ 🎧 *Listen. Notice the rising and falling intonation of the questions. Listen and practice.*

CONVERSATION 1

A: Where's Suzi?↘

B: She's at the library.

A: Is she studying?↗

B: Yes, she is.

CONVERSATION 2

A: Is David working at the office?↗

B: No, he isn't. He's at home.

A: What's he doing?↘

B: He's playing the piano.

> **NOTE:** Yes/No questions have a rising intonation at the end.
> Wh- questions have a falling intonation at the end.

▶ 🎧 *Listen and write* ↗ *for the rising intonation and* ↘ *for the falling intonation at the end of the questions. After you finish, practice the conversation with a partner.*

A: Hello, there.

B: Dallas, is that you?

A: Yes, it's me. I'm calling you on my cell phone.

B: Where are you?

A: I'm nearby. Are you busy?

B: Not really.

A: What are you doing?

B: I'm making lunch. Are you coming to see me?

A: Yes…here I am!

GRAMMAR SUMMARY

PRESENT CONTINUOUS Affirmative

He She	's (is)	
I	'm (am)	working today.
You We They	're (are)	

Negative

He She	isn't (is not) 's not	
I	'm not (am not)	working today.
You We They	aren't (are not) 're not	

Interrogative

Is	he she	
Am	I	working today?
Are	you we they	

Short Answers

Yes,	he she	is.		No,	he she	isn't.
	I	am.			I	'm not.
	you we they	are.			you we they	aren't.

Questions with WHO, WHAT, WHERE

Who What Where	's (is)	Jill talking to? Jack looking at? Mr. Davis going?	Her friend. The clock. To the library.

OBJECT PRONOUNS

Look at	Mike. Diana. Jack and Jill. Lisa and me. the clock.	Look at	him. her. them. us. it.

CONTENTS

Chapter

4

CARTOON STORY

▶ 🎧 *Listen. Listen and practice.*

CARTOON STORY

Page Summary

Grammar Review
Function Talking on the phone

The Teacher's Notes for the Cartoon Story continue on page T63.

Culture Note

In the cartoon story, Jason is going to his first dance class. At this lesson, he is learning the cha-cha. For students unfamiliar with the cha-cha, it is a fast, rhythmic ballroom dance from Latin America. The basic pattern is three steps and a shuffle. In the United States in recent years there has been a surge of interest in ballroom dancing, especially in urban areas, but some people are still nervous about trying it. Jason is uncomfortable at his first lesson, and the teacher, Lola, tries to help him relax. Even by the last picture, picture 15, he doesn't seem to be having a good time.

Warm-up

Write on the board: *dance*. Pantomime dancing. Ask, *Do you like to dance?* Say, *Raise your hand if you like to dance.* Demonstrate raising your hand. If any students indicate that they like to dance, ask them, *Where do you like to dance?* Elicit the names of clubs or other places where they like to go. To review location, ask them to explain where the clubs are located.

Pronunciation Tip

The contraction *'s* is often reduced and linked to the next sound in the sentence, for example, *Itsacross the street, Thatsokay, Itseasy.*

▶ 🎧 *Listen. Listen and practice.*

1. Direct student's attention to the illustrations.
2. Set the scene: Jason is taking his first dance lesson from Lola, the dance teacher. Ask students to look at Jason and describe how he's feeling. Ask, *Is he happy? (No, he isn't. He's nervous.)*
3. Play the recording (CD2, track 20) as students listen.
4. Use the illustrations to go over key vocabulary and expressions.

   Excuse me. I'm looking for . . .
   It's across the street.
   Thank you.

You're welcome.
I'm a little nervous.
That's okay.
Are you ready?
Let's dance.
Don't worry. You're doing fine.

5. Play the recording (CD2, track 21) for students to practice the conversation.
6. Have students form pairs to continue practicing the conversation, changing parts.

▶ STORY QUESTIONS

1. Have students form pairs. Tell them to take turns asking and answering the questions.
2. Check answers as a class by asking the questions of different students. (Note: For question 6, It's easy for Lola, but not for Jason. For question 8, students need to infer that Jason isn't having a good time because he isn't smiling. In the last frame he's smiling, but only because Lola has asked him to.)

Option: To check answers, call on pairs to ask and answer each question instead of asking it yourself.

3. Pair students. Have students practice reading the conversation.
4. Call on pairs to present the conversation to the class.

Answer Key

1. The Rainbow Dance Studio is across the street.
2. Lola is Jason's dance teacher.
3. Yes, she is.
4. It's his first dance lesson.
5. Jason is learning the cha-cha.
6. It is easy (for Lola, not Jason).
7. Yes, he is.
8. No, he isn't. He isn't smiling.

Expansion Activity 1

Have students describe the illustrations Ask individual students: *In picture 1: What is he wearing? (He's wearing a jacket.) In picture 3: What is he doing? (He's walking.) In picture 6: What are they doing? (They're talking.)* Then pair students. Have them continue asking each other questions about the illustrations. Call on pairs to present for the class.

Expansion Activity 2

Find out if anyone in the class knows how to cha-cha. If so, invite the student to show the class how to do the dance. If there is another student willing to be a dance partner, have the two students demonstrate the dance together. Have the student who knows how to cha-cha say some of the lines from the story. Write the lines on the board for the student to refer to: *Take my hand. Let's dance. Don't look at your feet. Just move to the music. One, two, cha, cha, cha.*

STORY QUESTIONS

1. Where is the Rainbow Dance Studio?
2. Who is Jason's dance teacher?
3. Is she very friendly?
4. Why is Jason nervous?

5. What dance is Jason learning?
6. Is it easy or difficult?
7. Is Jason a good student?
8. Is he having a good time?

GRAMMAR REVIEW • Present Continuous

> I'm at the hospital. I'm visiting my aunt.

> We're at the zoo. We're looking at a gorilla.

1. Mike <u>is at the hospital.</u>

<u>He's visiting his aunt.</u>

2. Lois and her kids <u>are at the zoo.</u>

<u>They're looking at a gorilla.</u>

> I'm at the gas station. I'm putting some gas in my car.

> I'm at the flower shop. I'm getting roses for my girlfriend.

3. Jane _____

_____

4. Carlos _____

_____

> We're at the Rex Theater. We're watching a funny movie.

> I'm at the market. I'm buying some groceries.

5. Jack and Jill_____

_____

6. Lucy _____

_____

Page Summary

Grammar Present continuous
Function Describing actions

The Teacher's Notes for this Grammar Review continue on page T65.

Warm-up

Books are closed. Demonstrate an action as you say what you are doing, for example *I'm walking. I'm looking for my pencil.* Then call on several students, one at time, to demonstrate a different action as they describe it. Next, call on one or two students to pantomime an action. Have the class try to guess where they are and what they're doing.

❗ *Pronunciation Tips*

- The contraction *I'm* is often pronounced *um* in rapid conversation.
- The contractions *we're* and *you're* are only one syllable.

Grammar Note

- Point out that *their* and *they're* are written differently even though they are pronounced the same.
- Point out that in the verbs in pictures 2 and 12 *(look at, try on)* at and on cannot be left off.

Culture Notes

In picture 2, Lois is with her "kids." "Kids" is a casual way to say "children." Parents often refer to their children as "the kids." In picture 5, Jack is talking on his phone, ignoring the angry looks from the people around him. As phone use increases, situations like this become more and more common.

▶ 🎧 *Listen.*

Have students look at the illustrations and listen as you play the recording (CD2, track 22). Play it again, as needed.

▶ **WRITING**

1. Have students work alone to write where the people are and what they are doing in each picture.
2. Play the recording (CD2, track 22) again and have the students check their sentences.
3. Go over them with the class by calling on different students to read the sentences for each picture.

Option: Have students form pairs and compare answers before going over the answers with the class.

Answer Key

1. Mike is at the hospital. He's visiting his aunt.

2. Lois and her kids are at the zoo. They're looking at a gorilla.

3. Jane is at the gas station. She's putting some gas in her car.

4. Carlos is at the flower shop. He's getting roses for his girlfriend.

5. Jack and Jill are at the Rex Theater. They're watching a funny movie.

6. Lucy is at the market. She's buying some groceries.

7. Grover is at Al's Cafe. He's having a cup of coffee and a donut.

8. Mr. and Mrs. Lee are at the laundromat. They're washing their clothes.

9. Maria is at home. She's cleaning the living room.

10. Dallas is at the barbershop. He's getting a haircut.

11. Ken and Suzi are at the library. They're doing their homework.

12. Mr. Gamble is at the department store. He's trying on a pair of shoes.

▶ PRACTICE

Have students read out loud the sentences they wrote. This can be done in pairs, chorally, or by calling on individual students to read an answer for the class.

Expansion Activity

Have students use the illustrations to practice *I* and *you* forms of the present continuous. One partner chooses a picture at random and says what he or she is doing, for example, *I'm buying some groceries.* The other partner says the location, *You're at the market.* Have students take turns. (Note: When there are two people in the illustration (pictures 8 and 11), have the students change *we* to *I*.)

7. Grover _____

_____

8. Mr. and Mrs. Lee _____

_____

9. Maria _____

_____

10. Dallas _____

_____

11. Ken and Suzi _____

_____

12. Mr. Gamble _____

_____

▶ **PRACTICE** • *Read out loud the sentences you wrote about the pictures.*

▶ **WHAT'S WRONG?** • *Correct the sentences about the pictures.*

1. A: Maynard is taking a bath.

   B: <u>He isn't taking a bath.</u>

   <u>He's taking a shower.</u>

2. A: The girls are playing basketball.

   B: <u>They aren't playing basketball.</u>

   <u>They're playing volleyball.</u>

3. A: Daisy is trying on a coat.

   B: _____

   _____

4. A: Lucy and Grover are buying a radio.

   B: _____

   _____

5. A: The men are having breakfast.

   B: _____

   _____

6. A: Dallas is talking with Maria.

   B: _____

   _____

Page Summary

Grammar Present continuous
Function Describing actions

The Teacher's Notes for this activity continue on page 67.

▶ WHAT'S WRONG?

1. Go over the conversation about picture 1 to make sure students understand that they should identify the mistake in part A, and correct it in part B. Point out the contractions: *isn't, aren't, He's, They're, She's.*

2. Have students work alone to correct the sentences about the pictures.

3. Go over the answers with the class by calling on different pairs to read each conversation.

Option: For each conversation, call on one student to read the sentence (part A). Have that student choose someone to read the correction (part B). This will keep the whole class listening actively.

Answer Key

1. He isn't taking a bath. He's taking a shower.
2. They aren't playing basketball. They're playing volleyball.
3. She isn't trying on a coat. She's trying on a hat.
4. They aren't buying a radio. They're buying a computer.
5. They aren't having breakfast. They're having lunch.
6. He isn't talking with Maria. He's talking with Daisy.
7. She isn't reading a book. She's reading a newspaper.
8. They aren't going to the bank. They're going to the library.
9. He isn't eating an orange. He's eating an apple.
10. She isn't wearing a blue dress. She's wearing a yellow dress.
11. They aren't looking at a dog. They're looking at a cat.
12. He isn't repairing a car. He's repairing a motorcycle.

▶ PAIR WORK

Have students form pairs. Tell them take to practice the conversation, switching parts.

Expansion Activity 1

Choose one of the pictures at random. Ask *yes/no* questions, for example, *Is Daisy trying on a hat?* Call on a student to answer, *Yes, she is*. Or ask, *Is Daisy taking, a shower?* Call on a student to answer, *No, she isn't. She's trying on a hat*. Model how you want the students to respond. Call on different students each time.

Expansion Activity 2

Have each student write one untrue sentence about what the people are wearing in each picture, for example, for picture 2, *The girls are wearing brown jackets*. After they finish, have students form pairs and exchange papers. Then have them take turns reading their partner's sentences and correcting them. Demonstrate with a student partner how to do this. Read: *2. The girls are wearing brown jackets*. Then say, *No, they aren't. They're wearing white shirts*.

7. A: Maria is reading a book.

B: _____

_____

8. A: Jack and Jill are going to the bank.

B: _____

_____

9. A: Mr. Denby is eating an orange.

B: _____

_____

10. A: Suzi is wearing a blue dress.

B: _____

_____

11. A: The boys are looking at a dog.

B: _____

_____

12. A: Carlos is repairing a car.

B: _____

_____

▶ **PAIR WORK** • *Practice the conversations.*

GRAMMAR REVIEW • Present Continuous

▶ 🎧 *Listen. Listen and repeat.*   ▶ **PAIR WORK** • *Practice the conversations.*

▶ **WRITING** • *Complete the questions using these verbs:* **dance (with), drink, eat, go, make, read, sleep, wait (for), write (to)**.

Who <u>are they waiting for</u>?

Donna.

1.

Where _____?

On the sofa.

2.

What _____?

Lemonade.

3.

Where _____?

At Al's Cafe.

4.

Page Summary

Grammar Present Continuous
Function Describing actions

The Teacher's Notes for this Grammar Review continue on page T69.

Warm-up

Review verb + preposition combinations. Greet a student and ask how he or she is doing. Then ask the class, *Who am I talking to?* Elicit, *You're talking to (name).* Hold up a book. Look at it and ask, *What am I looking at?* Elicit, *You're looking at a book.*

Grammar Note

Questions 1, 5, and 9 require the preposition in the question: *Who are they waiting for? Who is she dancing with? Who is he writing to?* In question 8, however, the preposition *to* is not included in the question even though it must be present in the answer: *Where is she going? To school.*

! *Pronunciation Tip*

Remind students that stress is placed on the stem of the verb in the question: *Who are they WAITing for? Where is he SLEEPing?*

▶ ⌂ *Listen. Listen and repeat.*

1. Have students look at the illustrations and listen as you play the recording (CD2, track 23). Play it again, as needed.
2. Play the recording (CD2, track 24) for students to listen and repeat.

▶ PAIR WORK

1. Have students form pairs to practice the conversations.
2. Tell them to switch parts and repeat.

▶ WRITING

1. Have students work alone to complete the questions using the verbs listed.
2. Play the recording (CD2, track 23) again and have the students check their answers.
3. Have students form pairs and compare answers before going over the answers with the class.

Answer Key

1. Who are they waiting for?
2. Where is he sleeping?
3. What is she drinking?
4. Where are they eating?
5. Who is she dancing with?
6. What is he making?
7. What are they reading?
8. Where is she going?
9. Who is he writing to?

Expansion Activity 1

Use the illustrations for more speaking practice. Point to each illustration and discuss it. For example, for picture 2 ask, *Is he sleeping?* (A: *Yes, he is.*) *Is he eating lunch?* (A: *No, he isn't.*) Continue with questions about the other pictures.

Expansion Activity 2

Ask students to form pairs and talk about the details in each picture. Review time expressions: *in the morning, afternoon/evening, at night.* For additional practice, write on the board only _____ *morning,* _____ *night* so that students have to come up with *in the* and *at.* Tell students to include the time of day in their descriptions. They may need to make guesses in some cases. See, for example, picture 8, where a logical guess is that it is in the morning because the girl is going to school. Call on a few students to present details about one of the pictures to the class.

Who _____?

Her boyfriend.

5.

What _____?

A sandwich.

6.

What _____?

The newspaper.

7.

Where _____?

To school.

8.

Who _____?

His family.

9.

GRAMMAR REVIEW • Adjectives

▶ 🎧 *Listen. Listen and repeat.*

▶ **PAIR WORK** • *Practice the conversations.*

1. A: Where's Alice?

   B: <u>She's in the kitchen.</u>

   A: Is she married or single?

   B: <u>She's married.</u>

   A: Is she busy?

   B: <u>Yes, she is.</u>

2. A: Where are the children?

   B: <u>They're at the park.</u>

   A: Are they quiet or noisy?

   B: <u>They're noisy.</u>

   A: Are they sad?

   B: <u>No, they aren't. They're happy.</u>

3. A: Where's Bruno?

   B: _____

   A: Is he handsome or ugly?

   B: _____

   A: Is he strong?

   B: _____

4. A: Where are the apples?

   B: _____

   A: Are they red or green?

   B: _____

   A: Are they small?

   B: _____

Page Summary

Grammar Adjectives
Function Describing locations, people, and objects

The Teacher's Notes for this Grammar Review continue on page 71.

Warm-up

Ask a few questions about classroom objects, for example, several books. Ask, *Where are the books? Are they (red) or (blue)? Are they big? Are they small?* Continue with a few more objects. Elicit answers from the whole class or from individual students.

! Pronunciation Tip

Remind students that the voice falls at the end of a *Wh-* question and rises at the end of a *yes/no* question. On a "choice" question, the voice goes up on the first choice and down on the second, for example, *Is he rich* (up) *or poor* (down)*?*

Listen. Listen and repeat.

1. Have students look at the illustrations and listen as you play the recording (CD2, track 25) of the conversations.
2. Play it again as students follow along in their books.
3. Play the recording (CD2, track 26) for students to repeat.

PAIR WORK

Have pairs practice the conversations, switching parts.

▶ WRITING

1. Have students work alone to answer the questions about the people in each picture. Remind them to use contractions.
2. Play the recording (CD2, track 25) again and have students check their answers.
3. Have students form pairs and compare answers before going over the answers with the class.

Option: Call on several students to write the answers on the board. Then divide the class into two groups. For 1–4, have Group A ask the questions and Group B respond. For 5–8, have groups switch parts.

Answer Key

1. B: She's in the kitchen.
   B: She's married.
   B: Yes, she is.
2. B: They're at the park.
   B: They're noisy.
   B: No, they aren't. They're happy.
3. B: He's at the beach.
   B: He's ugly.
   B: Yes, he is.
4. B: They're on the table.
   B: They're red.
   B: No, they aren't. They're big.

5. B: She's in the library.
   B: She's young.
   B: No, she isn't. She's a student.
6. B: It's on Pine Street.
   B: It's small.
   B: Yes, it is.
7. B: They're at the bus stop.
   B: They're hot.
   B: Yes, they are.
8. B: He's at home.
   B: He's rich.
   B: No, he isn't. He's short.

Expansion Activity 1
Do a rapid drill to practice the three types of questions (*yes/no* questions, questions with *or*, and questions with *where*). Say an adjective and then one question cue (*yes/no*, *where*, or *or*) and call on a student to make the question. For example, say *married, yes/no.* Call on a student to ask, *Is she married?* or *Are Bruno and Alice married?*

Expansion Activity 2
Have students work alone to write five sentences about what they see in any of the pictures. They can describe what people are wearing, what they are doing, or where people and objects are located. Write an example of each on the board. Circulate and help students as needed. Then call on students to present their sentences to the class. For added challenge, ask a student to read a sentence, and have the class guess the picture. For example, the student reads, *The book is on the table.* The class responds, *number 5.* The student reads, *The tree is next to the library.* The class responds, *number 6.* Note: If students are going to play the guessing game, tell them not to use names in their sentences; they should use pronouns instead. For example, instead of saying *Vanessa is wearing . . . ,* they write *She is wearing. . . .*

5. A: Where's Vanessa?

   B: _____

   A: Is she young or old?

   B: _____

   A: Is she a teacher?

   B: _____

6. A: Where's the library?

   B: _____

   A: Is it big or small?

   B: _____

   A: Is it old?

   B: _____

7. A: Where are the boys?

   B: _____

   A: Are they hot or cold?

   B: _____

   A: Are they thirsty?

   B: _____

8. A: Where's Mr. Grand?

   B: _____

   A: Is he rich or poor?

   B: _____

   A: Is he tall?

   B: _____

▶ **WRITING** • *Fill in the answers. Then read the conversations aloud.*

GRAMMAR REVIEW • Giving Commands

▶ 🎧 *Look and listen. Listen and repeat.*

▶ **PRACTICE** • *Give commands to other students in your class. Use the verbs* **(1) open, (2) close, (3) show, (4) give, (5) bring, (6) put** *and the nouns in the box.*

Example: (1) open   **Open the door.** OR **Open your dictionary.**

pen	ruler	book	magazine	table	door	watch
pencil	eraser	notebook	dictionary	bookcase	window	ring

Note: Use *please* to be more polite. ⟶ Please open the door.

Page Summary

Grammar Commands
Function Giving Commands

Warm-up

To review commands, play a few rounds of Simon Says. Remind students to carry out the command only if you say *Simon Says.*

> *Simon says look at the board.*
> *Simon says stand up.*
> *Sit down. (Any student who sits down is out.)*

🎧 Look and listen. Listen and repeat.

1. Play the recording (CD2, track 27) as students listen.
2. Play the recording (CD2, track 28) again for students to repeat.
3. Have students form pairs to read the sentences out loud.

▶ PRACTICE

1. Go over the directions. Read aloud the items in the box.
2. Go over the example.
3. Have students form pairs. Tell them to take turns giving each other commands. The partner should follow the command.

Option: Have students change partners after each has a turn giving a command.

Expansion Activity 1

Play a command board game. Have students work in small groups to make a board. Tell them to draw 12 squares in a grid of three rows and four columns. There should be a START square in the upper left corner and a FINISH square in the lower right corner. Students write a command in each square: *stand up, walk to the window, look at the clock,* etc. (All commands must be something that can actually be done in the classroom.) Circulate while they write to check for accuracy. When the boards are ready, one player in each group flips a coin: heads = move one space; tails = move two spaces. The student must carry out the command written in the space he or she lands on, and the first team to reach FINISH wins. Note: explain to students they move down the first column, up the second column, and down the third column to FINISH.

Expansion Activity 2

Play more rounds of Simon Says. This time, tell the students to carry out the command only if you say *Simon says please.* For example, *Simon says please turn left. Simon Says please sit down. Simon Says point to the door.* (Any student who points to the door is out.)

Page Summary

Grammar Present continuous; *yes/no* questions
Function Asking about and describing actions

Warm-up

Put a few word cues on the board to remind students of some of the vocabulary they've just been learning: *sandwich (I'm making a sandwich), breakfast (I'm having breakfast), newspaper (I'm reading the newspaper)*. Pantomime telephoning a student, and say, *Hi, (Juan), This is (your name). What are you doing?* Point at *sandwich* on the board; (Juan) answers, *I'm making a sandwich*. Do a few more examples with other students and activities, then have the students continue on their own.

Listen. Listen and practice.

1. Play the recording (CD2, track 29) as students listen.
2. Explain that *just* indicates that while the person is in fact doing something, the activity is not so important, and can be either interrupted or continued during the phone conversation.
3. Play the recording (CD2, track 30) again for students to practice the conversations.
4. Have students form pairs to practice the conversations.

WRITING

1. Have students work alone to complete the sentences using the expressions in the box.
2. Have students check their answers in pairs.
3. Go over the answers with the class by calling on different students to read the sentences.

Answer Key

1. No, I'm just relaxing in the backyard.
2. Yes, I'm making dinner.
3. No, I'm just playing with the dog.
4. Yes, I'm doing my homework.
5. No, I'm just listening to some CDs.
6. Yes, I'm cleaning my kitchen.

▶ PAIR WORK

1. Make sure students understand to use their own names.
2. Have students form pairs. Tell them to take turns asking the questions.

Expansion Activity 1

Together with the class compile a list of about eight to ten other activities. Put these on the board, but in an abbreviated form, for example, *TV* for *watching TV*. Encourage students to look back through Chapters 1–3 as needed to review vocabulary for activities they have learned. Have students continue the pair work conversation, substituting activities from the list. After students practice, call on several pairs to present for the class.

Expansion Activity 2

Tell students to do a role play based on the conversation between Daisy and Dallas in the Cartoon Story on pages 42 and 43, substituting the activities from page 73. In pairs, students can decide on which activities to substitute. For example, Daisy could be in her backyard relaxing, just listening to music. Dallas calls her. He could be making dinner, but decides to take a break and call Daisy to say hi. Emphasize to students they don't need to include all the lines from pages 42 and 43. Circulate and help as needed. After students finish, call on a few pairs to present to the class.

LIFE SKILL • Talking on the telephone

🎧 *Listen. Listen and practice.*

WRITING • *Complete the sentences using the expressions in the box.*

cleaning the kitchen	listening to some CDs	playing with the dog
doing my homework	making dinner	relaxing in the backyard

PAIR WORK • *Have conversations using the information in the pictures.*

A: **Hi, _____. Are you busy?**

B: **Yes, I'm _____. OR No, I'm just _____.**

READING

▶ 🎧 *Listen and read.*

This is Richard Garcia. I'm reporting to you from the corner of Main Street and Third Avenue. I'm standing in front of the Majestic Apartments on a beautiful spring day. Right here I see some children washing their dog in a large bucket of water. The children are only about eight years old, but they're doing a good job of washing their dog. And they're having fun!

Down the street a young woman is talking to her boyfriend. They're standing next to a big motorcycle. Both of them are wearing leather jackets and blue jeans. They're holding hands, and they look happy.

Right behind me an elderly gentleman is walking up the steps. He's carrying a large bag of groceries. His wife is standing at the top of the steps. She's waiting for her husband, and she's smiling. He's probably bringing home some food for their dinner.

Well, this gives you an idea of what's happening today at the corner of Main Street and Third Avenue. I'm Richard Garcia reporting for KWIC News.

▶ **STORY QUESTIONS**

1. Where is Richard Garcia?
2. Is he reporting for a news station?
3. What are the children doing?
4. Are they having a good time?

READING

Page Summary

Grammar Review present continuous
Function Talking about events as they are happening

🎧 Listen and read.

1. Have students look at the illustration. Ask them to describe what they see. Ask a few questions, such as: *What are the people doing? What is the dog doing? Is it morning? Is it evening? How do you know?* Also ask them to describe the clothes of the people, for example, *His shirt is. . . .*
2. Have the students cover the text and look at the illustrations as you play the recording (CD2, track 31).
3. Play the recording (CD2, track 31) again as students follow along silently.

▶ STORY QUESTIONS

1. Have students work alone to find the answers to the questions. They can underline the answers or they can write them out.
2. Have students form pairs. Tell them to take turns asking and answering the questions.
3. Go over the answers by asking the questions of individual students.

Expansion Activity

Ask students to go through the story and underline the verbs in the present continuous. Then have students form pairs. Tell them to work together to write their own short news story. The story should be two to three sentences about what is going on right now in the classroom, or outside the classroom. Remind them to use the present continuous. After students finish, have pairs form groups of four and read their stories to each other. Tell the students to listen carefully and to compare ideas.

PICTURE DICTATION

Page Summary

Grammar Review present continuous
Function Talking about events as they are happening

▶ WRITING

1. Have students work alone to write four questions about the other people from page 74: the young woman, her boyfriend, the elderly gentleman, and his wife.
2. Have students form pairs and read their questions.
3. Call on students to read their questions aloud for the class.
4. Have students form pairs. Have them take turns reading the sentences aloud.

Answers will vary. Sample answers:

1. What is the young woman doing? A: She's talking to her boyfriend.
2. What is her boyfriend doing? A: He's standing next to a motorcycle.
3. What is the elderly man doing? A: He's walking up the steps.
4. What is his wife doing? A: She's waiting for her husband. She's smiling.

▶ CLASS ACTIVITY

To review the present continuous, ask the class to say what is happening in the picture. Call on individual students. Compile a list on the board, for example, *The boy and girl are standing. The girl is smiling. The woman is reading. The reporter is talking.* Challenge students to make as many sentences as possible using the present continuous.

Grammar Note

In item 4, the construction is *What is she doing while she's waiting?* To help students understand that this means that two actions are simultaneous, write *at the same time* on the board and then present a couple of examples to the class. For example, walk to the door of the room as you talk. As you do this, say, *I'm talking while I'm walking to the door.* Hold a book. Say, *I'm holding a book while I'm standing here.*

▶ WARM-UP

Ask the questions one at a time. Call on individual students for each answer.

Option: Ask students to form pairs. Tell them to take turns asking the questions. Then go over the answers with the whole class.

Answers will vary. Sample answers:

1. The children are under the tree.
2. They're laughing at the cat.
3. The elderly woman is at the bus stop.
4. She's reading a book.
5. Yes, I do. / No, I don't. / Yes, she does. No, she doesn't.
6. No, he isn't.
7. He's bringing her flowers.

▶ 🎧 DICTATION

1. Have students listen and write as you play the recording (CD2, track 32).
2. Play the recording (CD2, track 32) again for students to check what they wrote.

Option: Read the audioscript one line at a time, pausing for students to write and make corrections.

3. Write the audioscript (see page T76) on the board. Have students check their work.
4. Read the paragraph aloud together.
5. In pairs have students practice presenting the news report. Demonstrate gesturing as you speak; for example, gesture to your right as you say *Over here. . . .*

PICTURE DICTATION

▶ **WRITING** • *Write 4 questions about the other people in the picture on page 74:
The young woman and her boyfriend, the elderly gentleman and his wife.*

1. _____
2. _____
3. _____
4. _____

▶ **CLASS ACTIVITY** • *What's happening in the picture?*

▶ **WARM UP**

1. Where are the children?
2. What are they laughing at?
3. Where is the elderly woman?
4. What is she doing while she's waiting for the bus?
5. Do you think she looks elegant in her red dress?
6. Is the young man waving to his girlfriend?
7. What is he bringing her?

▶ 🎧 **DICTATION** • *Listen and write what you hear on a separate piece of paper.*

VOCABULARY

NOUNS

Places

barbershop
department store
flower shop
gas station
laundromat
market
theater
zoo

Other

aunt
bath
bills
bookcase
donut
feet
food
gentleman
girlfriend
groceries
hand
haircut
homework
idea
leather jacket
living room
motorcycle
notebook
pair
pen
ring
roses
ruler
sandwich
shower
volleyball
water

VERBS

clean
close
give
hold
make
move
pay
put
repair
show
try on
visit
wave

ADJECTIVES

busy
easy
elderly
elegant
funny

ADVERB

probably

DETERMINER

some

EXPRESSIONS

Asking for and giving location

Excuse me. I'm looking for…
　　It's across the street.
　　　…down the street.
　　　…at the corner of…
　　　…right here.

Giving encouragement

I'm a little nervous.
　　That's okay.
I'm not a very good dancer.
　　Don't worry. You're doing fine.

Thanking someone

Thank you.
　　You're welcome.

Complimenting

They're doing a good job.

Other

Welcome…
Are you ready?
Let's dance.

Come on.
Do your homework.
See how easy it is?
Uh, huh.

Like this?
That's better.
That's perfect.

KEY VOCABULARY

The games below provide additional opportunities to use the vocabulary, grammar, and expressions presented in the unit. Before students play any of the games, have them review the lists of words and circle any words they don't know. Then put students into small groups and have them review the circled words together. Circulate so you can help in case no one in the group knows a particular word.

Game 1: Where am I? What am I doing?

Books are closed. Write the following words on the board:

barbershop
market
flower shop
department store
groceries
haircut
roses
leather jacket

Have students work alone to write four sentences, modeled after the one on page 64, in which they say where they are and what they are doing: *I'm at the gas station. I'm putting gas in my car.*

Game 2: Dictation

Books are closed. Dictate the following words from the key vocabulary. Say each word twice, pausing for students to write: *shower, water, close, try on, move,*

wave, volleyball, elegant, elderly, busy, repair, funny. To check answers, say a word, and call on a volunteer to spell the word out loud. After all the words are spelled, challenge students to make original sentences. Say one of the words. Tell students to think of a sentence using the word, and to raise their hands when they are ready. Give a student one point for each correct sentence.

Game 3: Directions

Books are open. Have students work in pairs to draw a simple map of the area near your school. Have them include street names and the names of five or six businesses or landmarks. Tell them to take turns asking for directions to different places. The student who is asking should start by saying where he or she is located and where he or she wants to go. Model an example: *I'm standing in front of the school. I'm looking for the library.* The partner gives directions. Remind them to say *Thank you* at the end.

🎧 DICTATION (continued)

Audioscript for DICTATION on page 75:

This is Richard Garcia. I'm reporting to you from the corner of High Street and Central Avenue. I'm standing in front of the Regal Apartments on a windy day in November. Over here, I see some children standing under a tree. They're looking at a big yellow cat. The cat is making a funny face, and the children are laughing. Down the street an elderly woman is sitting at the bus stop. She's about 75 years old. She's reading a book while she's waiting for the bus. The lady is wearing a beautiful red dress. She looks very elegant. Right behind me, a young man is walking up the steps to the Regal Apartments. He's bringing his girlfriend some flowers. She's at the top of the steps, smiling and waving to her boyfriend. She's very happy to see him.

PRONUNCIATION

▶ A 🎧 *Listen and repeat.*

1. Have students look at the words and listen as you play the recording (CD2, track 33).
2. Play the recording (CD2, track 33) again and have the students listen and repeat the words.
3. Have students form pairs to practice reading the words out loud.

▶ B 🎧 *Listen and repeat.*

1. Have students look at the words and listen as you play the recording (CD2, track 34).
2. Play the recording (CD2, track 34) again and have the students listen and repeat the words.

▶ C 🎧 *Listen to each pair of words. Listen and repeat.*

1. Have students look at each pair of words and listen as you play the recording (CD2, track 35).
2. Play the recording (CD2, track 36) again and have the students listen and repeat each word pair.
3. Say one of the words in each pair and have students point to the correct picture.

▶ D 🎧 *Look at the words in Part C. Listen and circle the words you hear.*

1. Have students look at the words in Part C. Tell them to listen and circle the words they hear as you play the recording (CD2, track 37).
2. Have students form pairs and compare their answers.
3. Play the recording (CD2, track 37) again as a final check.
4. Go over the answers with the class by saying the number of an item, for example, *number 1,* and have the class say the letter of the correct word (*a* or *b*).

Answer Key

1. b. sheep	4. b. heel
2. a. Tim	5. a. grin
3. a. rich	6. b. seat

▶ E 🎧 *Listen and practice.*

1. Have students listen and read the sentences silently as you play the recording (CD2, track 38).
2. Play the recording (CD2, track 38) again and have the students practice reading the sentences out loud.
3. Have students form pairs to practice reading the sentences out loud.

Expansion Activity

Play Bingo. First have students make their own cards using the words in Part C. The card should have three rows across and four columns. Have students write the 12 words in random order in the 12 spaces. (Each student also needs to have 12 coins.) Call out one word at a time. Tell students to cover the word as they hear it. Tell the students to say *Bingo* if they have three squares down or four across. Check the words to make sure they are the words you actually said. If the words are correct, then the student wins. Have students clear their boards and start a new game.

PRONUNCIATION

▶ **A** 🎧 *Listen and repeat.*

/ɪ/

1. this   4. give   7. sit
2. big   5. him   8. in
3. dish   6. dinner   9. kitchen

▶ **B** 🎧 *Listen and repeat.*

/i/

1. see   4. sweet   7. weak
2. clean   5. peach   8. green
3. feet   6. tree   9. tea

▶ **C** 🎧 *Listen to each pair of words. Listen and repeat.*

1. a. ship   b. sheep

2. a. Tim   b. team

3. a. rich   b. reach

4. a. hill   b. heel

5. a. grin   b. green

That's my seat!

6. a. sit   b. seat

▶ **D** 🎧 *Look at the words in Part C. Listen and* (circle) *the words you hear.*

▶ **E** 🎧 *Listen and practice.*

1. Jim is eating a big peach.
2. Please clean this window.
3. See how easy it is?
4. Nick is reading his magazine.
5. We live on Hill Street.
6. Please visit me this week.

TEST

1. a. Hello there.
   b. How are you?
   c. What's your name?
   d. What are you doing?

2. a. That's good.
   b. Thank you.
   c. You're welcome.
   d. Nice to meet you.

3. "Where is Mr. Denby?"
   "_____ in the classroom."

   a. He's   c. You're
   b. She's   d. It's

4. "Where are the pencils?"
   "_____ in the desk."

   a. It's   c. They're
   b. They   d. Those

5. "_____ is that man?"
   "His name is Mike Kelly."

   a. What   c. Who
   b. Where   d. How

6. "_____ is Ms. Adams?"
   "She's at the office."

   a. What   c. Who
   b. Where   d. How

7. "How much is that dress?"
   "It's _____."

   a. small   c. beautiful
   b. for sale   d. fifty dollars

8. "What time is it?"
   "It's ten _____."

   a. o'clock   c. hours
   b. minutes   d. years old

9. a. this   c. these
   b. that   d. those

10. a. This   c. These
    b. That   d. Those

TEST

11. Nick is standing _____ his car.

    a. on   c. behind

    b. next to   d. in front of

12. The bank is _____ the hotel.

    a. on   c. behind

    b. next to   d. in front of

13. The radio is _____ the living room.

    a. in   c. at

    b. on   d. of

14. What's the color _____ your kitchen?

    a. at   c. of

    b. on   d. to

15. "_____"

"It's sunny and warm."

    a. Are you comfortable?

    b. How's the weather?

    c. What's your favorite season?

    d. When is summer?

16. "_____ Where's the library?"

"It's on Central Avenue."

    a. Ask me.

    b. Listen to me.

    c. Talk to me.

    d. Excuse me.

17. My _____ is 673 Maple Street.

    a. address   c. house

    b. business   d. phone number

18. Lucy is making spaghetti for _____.

    a. food   c. dinner

    b. eat   d. hungry

19. "Are Jack and Jill at the park?"

"_____"

    a. Yes, they are.   c. Yes, he is.

    b. No, they aren't.   d. No, she isn't.

20. "Is Maynard sleeping?"

"_____"

    a. Yes, he is.   c. Yes, I am.

    b. No, he isn't.   d. No, they aren't.

TEST

_____ the window!

Don't _____ on the grass.

21. a. Open   c. Don't open
    b. Close   d. Don't close

22. a. sit   c. walk
    b. stand   d. run

23. That computer isn't old.
    It's _____.
    a. new   c. cheap
    b. young   d. good

24. Is Mr. Grand rich or _____?
    a. short   c. good
    b. happy   d. poor

25. My friends _____ the beach.
    a. is going   c. are going to
    b. are going   d. are going for

26. Grover _____ lunch.
    a. is taking   c. is drinking
    b. is eating   d. are having

27. Maria and I are busy.
    Don't talk to _____ now.
    a. us   c. her
    b. them   d. me

28. The man is hungry.
    Give _____ some food.
    a. he   c. his
    b. her   d. him

Are you enjoying _____ dinner?

_____ name is John.

29. a. my   c. his
    b. your   d. her

30. a. My   c. Her
    b. Your   d. His

Answer Key

1. b	11. d	21. b
2. d	12. b	22. c
3. a	13. a	23. a
4. c	14. c	24. d
5. c	15. b	25. c
6. b	16. d	26. b
7. d	17. a	27. a
8. a	18. c	28. d
9. b	19. b	29. b
10. c	20. a	30. d

CONTENTS

Chapter

5

CARTOON STORY

▶ 🎧 *Jamie and Vanessa are having a conversation after school. Listen. Listen and practice.*

CARTOON STORY

Page Summary

Grammar *To have*
Function Talking about family members

Culture Note

In the cartoon story, Jamie and Vanessa are looking at Vanessa's family photos. Jamie compliments Vanessa on her nice house and its features, including the fireplace. Pride in one's home is fairly universal, and Vanessa clearly enjoys showing the photos. Vanessa says *Wow!* to show her surprise when she hears how large Jamie's family is. Other common ways to show surprise are *You're kidding! Really!* and *Oh, my (goodness)!* In addition, people usually make some comment about the family members when they are shown a picture; for example, *She's so pretty!* or *He looks like your father.*

Warm-up

Tell the class one thing you have on your desk or in your bag, starting the sentence with *I have a. . . .* Then ask several students, one at a time, to tell the class one thing they have. Ask, *What do you have in your (bag/backpack), (Mike)?*

Pronunciation Tip

In rapid speech, the *t* sound at the end of *What* is linked to the next sound, and is often pronounced like a *d*: *WhaddyaHAVE?* or *Whadda nice HOUSE.*

🎧 *Jamie and Vanessa are having a conversation after school. Listen. Listen and practice.*

1. Direct students' attention to the illustrations. Ask students to describe what Jamie and Vanessa are wearing, and where they're sitting (on a bench, in the park).

2. Set the scene: Jamie and Vanessa are looking at Vanessa's family photos.
3. Play the recording (CD2, track 39) as students listen.
4. Play the recording (CD2, track 40) for students to practice the conversation.
5. Pair students. Have students practice the conversation.
6. Call on pairs to present the conversation to the class.

Expansion Activity 1

Have students each make a simple diagram of the house or apartment where they live. Have students form pairs, and then take turns describing the rooms and where each room is located, for example, *This is the kitchen. It's next to the living room.* Provide the names of the rooms, as needed.

Expansion Activity 2

On small slips of paper, write the words for six to eight items that students are very familiar with (a calculator, a telephone, a car). Put the slips of paper in a pile. Call one student at a time to the front of the room and have him or her choose a slip. Ask the student, *What do you have in your hand?* The student pantomimes using the object. For example, write on a slip, *a calculator.* The student pantomimes using a calculator. The class guesses what the object is, and says *You have a calculator.*

GRAMMAR • To Have

Page Summary

Grammar *To have*
Function Talking about family and possessions

Culture Note

To keep the conversation going in this kind of situation, the second speaker would typically then ask about the size of the other person's family or what the other person has: *How about you?*

Grammar Note

Do you have . . . ? is a *yes/no* question and the answer can be *yes* or *no*. The response includes *do* or *don't*; *have* is understood without being said.

! *Pronunciation Tip*
The voice rises on the *yes/no* question. The voice falls on both answers.

▶ PAIR WORK

1. Present the boxes at the top of the page. Make sure students understand that the short answers include only *do* or *don't*, and that *have* is understood without being said.
2. Model the example in the book with a student partner. Encourage students to personalize their answers.
3. Pair students. Have them take turns asking and answering the questions.
4. Call on different pairs to present each conversation for the class.

Expansion Activity 1

Ask students to each make a list of at least five more things they have, either at home or with them. Have students form pairs. Tell them to take turns asking their partners if they have the same things. For example, the first item on Student 1's list is *a laptop*. Student 1 asks Student 2, *Do you have a laptop?* Student 2 responds, and then asks about an item on his or her list.

Expansion Activity 2

Have students make a simple sketch of their families. (If students have photos with them, they could use these.) Have students form pairs and take turns describing the people in the pictures or sketches. Encourage students to use the *Wow! Really? You're kidding!* and vocabulary from page 82.

GRAMMAR • To Have

Yes/No Question	Short Answers	
Do you have a big family?	Yes, I do.	No, I don't.

▶ **PAIR WORK** • *Ask and answer questions.*

1. a big family
A: **Do you have a big family?**
B: **Yes, I do.** OR **No, I don't.**

1. a big family

2. a garden

3. a garage

4. a fireplace

5. a lamp

6. a bookcase

7. a computer

8. a wallet

9. a driver's license

GRAMMAR • To Have

Affirmative		
He She	has	a computer.

Word Bank			
bicycle	clothes dryer	violin	wallet
motorcycle	washing machine	guitar	handbag

 Look and listen.

WRITING • *Write a sentence for each picture.*

1. <u>She has a washing machine.</u>   2. <u>He has a clothes dryer.</u>

3. _____   4. _____   5. _____

6. _____   7. _____   8. _____

▶ **PRACTICE** • *Read the sentences out loud.*

GRAMMAR • To Have

Page Summary

Grammar *To have*
Function Describing personal possessions

Warm-up

To familiarize students with the third-person singular, walk around the room and comment on what several students have. Say, *(Student 1) has a dictionary. (Student 2) has two books,* and so on. Then stop at one student's desk and ask the class: *What does (Student 5) have?* Cue students to respond, using *has.* Then ask several students, one at a time, to tell the class what other students have.

Grammar Notes

- *She, he,* and *it* are followed by *has*; and *I, you, we,* and *they* are followed by *have.*
- Point out the difference between the question and answer in the third person: *What does he have? He has a computer.*

Pronunciation Tip

Has cannot be contracted here. This would make it impossible to distinguish *is* and *has.* To make this clear to the students, write on the board: *She has a washing machine* and *She's a washing machine.* Circle the *'s* and write *is,* then ask students, *Is she a washing machine?* (No, she's a woman.) Explain we can't use the contraction when *have* is the main verb in the sentence.

Look and listen.

Write on the board: *(Student's name) _____ a dictionary.* Elicit *has* and write it in the blank, and then cross out the student's name and replace it with *he* or *she.* Make sure that students understand that *she, he,* and *it* are followed by *has*; and *I, you, we,* and *they* are followed by *have.* Write on the board: *He/she has a computer. I have a computer.*

WRITING

1. Have students work alone to write a sentence for each picture using the words in the box on the right at the top of the page. Remind students that *a* is used before the nouns because they all start with consonant sounds.
2. Play the recording (CD2, track 41) and have students check their answers.

3. Go over the answers with the class by calling on individual students to read each sentence.

Answer Key

1. She has a washing machine.
2. He has a clothes dryer.
3. She has a handbag.
4. He has a wallet.
5. She has a bicycle.
6. He has a motorcycle.
7. He has a guitar.
8. She has a violin.

Pronunciation Tip

The main stress is on the stressed syllable of the noun (or compound noun) because that is the most important information: *She has a WASHing machine. He has a guiTAR.*

PRACTICE

1. Have students form pairs and practice reading the sentences out loud.
2. Call on individual students to read each sentence to the class.

Expansion Activity 1

Write on the board: *What does he have?* Remind students that they need to use *have* in the question, even with the third-person singular. Go around the room and put familiar objects (a pen, a pencil, a book, money) on the desks of some students. Have students form pairs and take turns asking each other questions about the students with the familiar objects on their desks. For example, tell Student 1 to ask Student 2, *What does (Student 3) have?* Student 2 responds, then asks a question of Student 1.

Expansion Activity 2

Use the illustrations to talk about what other things people in the pictures have, for example, in picture 1, *She has detergent.* 2. *He has blue jeans.* 3. *She has a blouse.* 4. *He has a watch.* 6. *He has boots.* Help students with vocabulary. Write any new words on the board for students to copy in their notebooks.

GRAMMAR • To Have

Page Summary

Grammar *To have*; third person singular, negative
Function Describing personal possessions

Warm-up

To familiarize students with the grammar, walk around the room and comment on things students have and don't have. Say, *(Hiro) has a notebook. He doesn't have a calculator. (Yolanda) has a pen. She doesn't have a pencil.* (Emphasize *doesn't*). Ask students to look at a student sitting next to them and to notice one thing the person has and one thing the person doesn't have. Then call on several students, one at a time, to tell the class what they have noticed.

Grammar Notes

- *She, he,* and *it,* and singular nouns are followed by *does not (doesn't)* + the base form of the main verb, in this case *have.*
- *Does* is called a helping verb here.
- There is no *-s* used on the main verb for the third-person singular. The final *s* is part of *does.* For example, it is not correct to say, *He doesn't has a car.*
- The contracted form, *doesn't,* is used with both pronouns *(He doesn't have a bike)* and proper nouns *(Ted doesn't have a bike). Doesn't* is more common than *does not* in spoken English and in all but formal writing.

! *Pronunciation Tip*

The words *have a* are often reduced in conversation; and the main stress is placed on the final noun: *She doesn't hava COAT.*

▶ ⌂ *Look and listen.*

1. Go over the box on the left at the top of the page. Remind students that *she* and *he* are followed by *does not* + the main verb and that there is no *-s* on the main verb for the third person singular. Ask students who in the class has or doesn't have a car, and then write on the board: *(Juan) has a car. (Yoko) doesn't have a car.* If necessary, repeat this with other words *(a dog, a daughter, a job)* and ask students to write the sentences on the board.
2. Have students look at the illustrations. Go over the words in the right box at the top of the page.
3. Play the recording (CD2, track 42) as students listen.

▶ WRITING

1. Have students work alone to write a negative sentence for each picture using the words in the box. Remind students to use *a* before a consonant sound and *an* before a vowel sound *(an umbrella).*
2. Play the recording (CD2, track 42) again and have students check their answers.
3. Go over the answers by calling on individual students to read each sentence.

Answer Key

1. She doesn't have a driver's license.
2. He doesn't have a girlfriend.
3. He doesn't have a lamp.
4. She doesn't have a coat.
5. He doesn't have a car.
6. She doesn't have an umbrella.
7. He doesn't have a watch.
8. She doesn't have a bookcase.

▶ PRACTICE

1. Pair students. Have students take turns reading the sentences out loud.
2. To go over the exercise as a class, call on one student to read the first sentence out loud. Tell that student to say the name of another student to read the next sentence, and so on.

Expansion Activity 1

Have students describe each illustration. Start with the whole class. Ask, *In picture 1, what is she doing?* Elicit, *She's driving. She's talking to the police officer.* Ask, *Where is she?* Elicit, *She's in her car.* Continue with questions about the second picture. Ask, *Is he happy or sad? Are they happy or sad? What is he wearing? What is he doing? What are they doing?* Then either continue with the whole class, or have students discuss the other pictures in pairs.

GRAMMAR • To Have

Negative		
He	doesn't	have a job.
She	(does not)	

Word Bank			
car	watch	umbrella	bookcase
lamp	coat	girlfriend	driver's license

▶  Look and listen. ▶ **WRITING** • *Write a negative sentence for each picture.*

1. <u>She doesn't have a driver's license.</u>   2. <u>He doesn't have a girlfriend.</u>

3._____   4._____   5._____

6._____   7._____   8._____

_____   _____   _____

▶ **PRACTICE** • *Read the sentences out loud.*

GRAMMAR • To Have

Yes/No Question			
Does	he she	have	a dictionary?

Short Answers					
Yes,	he she	does.	No,	he she	doesn't.

▶ **PAIR WORK** • *Ask and answer questions.*

1. A: **Does Dallas have a wallet?**
   B: **Yes, he does.**

2. A: **Does Daisy have a wallet?**
   B: **No, she doesn't. She has a handbag.**

3. Does Ken have a computer?

4. Does Jill have an orange?

5. Does Maria have a violin?

6. Does Carlos have a violin?

7. Does Becky have a dog?

8. Does Grover have a motorcycle?

9. Does Lucy have a motorcycle?

GRAMMAR • To Have

Page Summary

Grammar *To have*: short answers
Function Talking about possessions

Warm-up

Walk around the room and ask about what students have. Ask, *Does (Rob) have a backpack?* Model the response, *Yes, he does* or *No, he doesn't.* Repeat this with two more students, substituting other possessions. Then tell the students to ask a question about a classmate. Remind them not to speak directly to the person they're asking about, so that the activity stays in the third person. Call on several students, one at a time, to ask their questions. Have the whole class respond.

Grammar Notes

- *Does* is the helping verb here, and *Does . . . have* is used in a question with the third person singular *he/she*.
- In North American English, *does* and *doesn't*, without *have*, are used in the short answers with the third person singular.

▶ PAIR WORK

1. Go over the boxes at the top of the page. Review that *Does . . . have* is used in a question with the third person singular *he/she*. Write on the board:

   He <u>has</u> a dictionary.
   Q: *Does he <u>have</u> a dictionary?*
   A: *Yes, he _____. No, he _____.*

   Have students fill in the blanks.

2. Model the example in the book with a student partner.
3. Have students form pairs. Tell them to ask and answer the questions.
4. Call on different pairs to present each conversation to the class.

Expansion Activity 1

On the board, write *computer, car, dog, motorcycle, wallet, cat, bicycle.* Have students form pairs. Tell students to think of one person they know well (mother, wife, husband, friend) and to tell their partners who that person is. Students then take turns asking their partners if the partner's mother, wife, or other family member has the things listed on the board.

   A: *I'm thinking about my mother.*
   B: *Does your mother have a computer?*
   A: *No, she doesn't.*
   B: *I'm thinking about my brother.*
   A: *Does your brother have a car?*

Students can answer with true or made-up information, and can expand the exercise to include objects not listed on the page. Circulate to help with vocabulary and check pronunciation. Remind students to use short answers in their responses.

Expansion Activity 2

Work together with the class to make up a short story (about four to five sentences) about Becky and her cat. Ask questions, and write the students' responses on the board. For example, ask, *What is the cat's name? Is the cat young or old? Is it big or small? What color is it? Does Becky like cats or dogs?* When you are finished writing the entire story on the board, have the class read it aloud chorally. Then begin erasing some of the words and replacing them with blanks. Have the students read the story, filling in the blanks by remembering the words that were there. Erase more and more words until students are telling the whole story with only one or two word cues.

Page Summary

Grammar *To have*; third person plural
Function Talking about what people have and don't have

Warm-up

Have eight students form four pairs. Give each pair two different classroom objects, such as a book, a pen, a pencil, and a notebook. Indicate a pair and say what they have. Also say one thing they don't have. For example, say, *They have a book. They have a pencil. They don't have a dictionary.* Indicate a second pair. Call on a student to describe what the pair has or doesn't have. Call on other students to talk about the other two pairs.

Culture Note

Mr. and Mrs. Kilbride are a couple living in a rural area. Nowadays, satellite TV makes it possible for most rural areas, even remote ones, to have television. It appears, though, that Mr. and Mrs. Kilbride don't have some modern conveniences, such as a clothes dryer or TV. For the writing, students need to base their responses on what they hear and what they see in the illustration. In some cases, they cannot tell from the illustration alone what Mr. and Mrs. Kilbride have or don't have. For example, there might be a garden behind the house, but if students can't see something, they should assume the Kilbrides don't have it.

▶ 🎧 *Listen to Mr. and Mrs. Kilbride.*

1. Set the scene: Mr. and Mrs. Kilbride are sitting in front of their house. They are talking about what they have and what they don't have. Ask students, *Do they live in the city or in the country? Are they rich or poor?* to give the background.
2. Play the recording (CD2, track 43) as students listen and look at the illustration.

Option: For classes needing additional support, play the recording (CD2, track 43) again.

▶ WRITING

1. Go over the examples in the boxes at the top of the page. Point out that *have* is used with both the affirmative and the negative *(have/don't have)*.
2. Have students work alone to write the other sentences about Mr. and Mrs. Kilbride. Remind them to use *an* before a noun beginning with a vowel sound.

3. Go over the answers by calling on individual students to read each sentence.

Answer Key

1. They have a radio.
2. They don't have a television.
3. They have a car.
4. They don't have a motorcycle.
5. They don't have a garage.
6. They have an apple tree.
7. They don't have a garden.
8. They have a porch.
9. They have a dog.
10. They don't have a cat.
11. They don't have a clothes dryer.
12. They have a fireplace.

Expansion Activity 1

Review colors and items of clothing. Have students form pairs and describe three items of clothing that Mr. Kilbride has and three items that Mrs. Kilbride has. (They can include what is on the clothes line). Then call on pairs to tell the class their sentences.

Expansion Activity 2

Tell students to imagine that Mr. and Mrs. Kilbride got lucky and won the lottery (won a lot of money). Now they are rich. They buy some new things, and they get rid of some old things. In pairs, have students decide 10 things they have or don't have now and write a sentence for each, for example, *They have an airplane. They don't have an old car. They have a new car. They don't have a small house. They have a big house.* Then have pairs form small groups and compare ideas about what Mr. and Mrs. Kilbride now have. Tell them to choose from their lists and decide on 12 things they have. Call on pairs to tell the class what their group decided.

GRAMMAR • To Have

Affirmative	Negative
They have a radio.	They don't have a television.

🎧 *Listen to Mr. and Mrs. Kilbride.*

We don't have a television.

So we sit on the porch and listen to the radio.

▶ **WRITING** • *Write affirmative and negative sentences about Mr. and Mrs. Kilbride. After you finish, read the sentences out loud.*

1. (radio) __They have a radio.__

2. (television) __They don't have a television.__

3. (car) _____

4. (motorcycle) _____

5. (garage) _____

6. (apple tree) _____

7. (garden) _____

8. (porch) _____

9. (dog) _____

10. (cat) _____

11. (clothes dryer) _____

12. (fireplace) _____

GRAMMAR • To Have

Yes/No Question	Short Answers	
Do they have a computer?	Yes, they do.	No, they don't.

▶ **PAIR WORK** • *Ask and answer questions.*

1. a washing machine
A: **Do they have a
washing machine?**
B: **Yes, they do.**

2. a clothes dryer
A: **Do they have a
clothes dryer?**
B: **No, they don't.**

3. a television

4. a bookcase

5. a radio

6. money

7. jobs

8. a garden

9. a car

GRAMMAR • To Have

Page Summary

Grammar *To have*; third person plural
Function Talking about possessions

Grammar Note

Item 6 *(money)* is an uncountable noun, and item 7 *(jobs)* is a plural count noun, so neither takes an article *(Do they have money?/Do they have jobs?)* Often the question is phrased *Do they have any money?* which students will be learning in Chapter 6.

! Pronunciation Tip

The voice rises at the end of the question, and the stress falls on the last stressed syllable of the final noun or compound noun: *a BOOKcase, a WASHing machine.*

PAIR WORK

1. Go over the boxes at the top of the page. Point out that to form the *yes/no* question, they just need to add *Do*. Write on the board: *They have a computer. Do they have a computer?*
2. Model the example in the book with a student partner. Make sure students understand the pattern is the same for all the items: *Do they have* + noun.
3. Pair students. Have them take turns asking each other the questions.
4. Call on different pairs to present each conversation for the class.

Expansion Activity

Divide the class in half and have students form pairs. Half of the pairs look at picture 3. Tell them: *The people in picture 3 are very rich.* The other pairs look at picture 5. Tell them: *The people in picture 5 are very poor.* Then have the pairs make up five sentences about things the family in "their" picture has or doesn't have; for example, *(Picture 3): They have a television. They have a DVD player and a big new car. (Picture 5): They have an old radio. They don't have a car. They don't have jobs.* Then have pairs form groups of four, with each group made up of a "poor" pair and a "rich" pair. Tell one pair to ask the other pair about "their" family, using the items from their own sentences, for example, *Do they have a car? Do they have a DVD player?* The other pair answers according to what they wrote in their own sentences. Have pairs take turns asking questions.

Answer Key

1. A: Do they have a washing machine?
   B: Yes, they do.
2. A: Do they have a clothes dryer?
   B: No, they don't.
3. A: Do they have a television?
   B: Yes, they do.
4. A: Do they have a bookcase?
   B: No, they don't.
5. A: Do they have a radio?
   B: Yes, they do.
6. A: Do they have money?
   B: No, they don't.
7. A: Do they have jobs?
   B: No, they don't.
8. A: Do they have a garden?
   B: Yes, they do.
9. A: Do they a car?
   B: No, they don't.

CAR TALK

Page Summary

Grammar Possessive adjectives
Function Talking about cars

Warm-up

Ask the students a few questions about cars, for example, *What kind of cars do you like? What color? Do you like big cars or small cars?* Then say to the class, *Do you have a car? Raise your hand.* (Demonstrate raising your hand.) Then ask those students who have cars to say something about them: *Tell us about your car.* Elicit, for example, *My car is black. My car is fast.* Restate what each student says, substituting a possessive pronoun, for example, *Her car is black.* Have the class repeat each sentence. Note: If no students own cars, present the possessive adjectives using imaginary names, for example, *Toshi has a car. His car is white.* Write the sentences on the board and have students read out loud.

Culture Note

The United States is a country of cars. Most families have at least one car, often more, except in some large metropolitan areas such as New York City. Maintaining a car is essential, since so many people drive to work. For example, in picture 2, we can assume that Mr. Denby usually drives to work, and that taking the bus is unusual for him. The expression *to be in bad shape* is used for both people and objects. A car that is *in bad shape* has something seriously wrong with it. In picture 1, the problem is the engine, which is usually very serious.

Grammar Note

My, your, his, her, our, and *their* are possessive adjectives which come before nouns.

▶ ⌒ *Listen. Listen and practice.*

1. To review *has/have* and to help students remember the subject pronouns and learn possessive adjectives, write the following sentence pairs, with blanks, on the board. Elicit the possessive adjectives from the class, fill in the blanks, read the sentences out loud together, and have the students copy them.

   I have a car / My car is black.
   He has a car / _____ car is blue.

   She has a car / _____ car is red.
   We have a car / _____ car is black.
   They have a car / _____ car is black.

2. Read each sentence from the box at the bottom of the page out loud, pausing for students to repeat. Explain that the subject pronoun is the first one in the sentence. The possessive adjective is in **bold**. Say the first sentence *(I like my car.)* and then say *I* and *my*. Have students repeat. Say the second sentence *(You like your car)* and then say *you* and *your*. Continue with the other sentences.

3. Go over the key vocabulary:

   I'm afraid . . . (meaning *I think*)
   What's wrong with it?
   in bad shape
   they're asking . . . (a price)
   to take good care of . . .
   That's for sure! (strong agreement)
   How do you like . . . (to ask someone's opinion)

4. Play the recording (CD2, track 44) as students look at the illustrations and listen.
5. Play the recording (CD2, track 45) as students practice the conversations.
6. Have students form pairs to practice the conversations.
7. Call on pairs to present to the class.

Expansion Activity

Have students form pairs. Assign a different picture to each pair, and tell them to use the picture to make up several more lines of the conversation, using some of the key vocabulary. For example, in number 4, the couple talks about buying the car. He likes the color, but she doesn't. The sellers are asking too much money. They talk about a different price. After students practice their conversations, call on pairs to present to the class.

CAR TALK

▶ 🎧 *Listen. Listen and practice.*

POSSESSIVE ADJECTIVES

I like **my** car.	He likes **his** car.	We like **our** car.
You like **your** car.	She likes **her** car.	They like **their** car.

GRAMMAR • Possessive Adjectives

▶ 🎧 *Listen. Listen and repeat.*   ▶ **PAIR WORK** • *Practice the conversations.*

▶ **WRITING** • *Complete the conversations using these words:*

this	that	these	those		my	your	his	her	our	their

Whose sandwich **is this**?

It's **your sandwich**.

①

Whose chickens **are those**?

They're **our chickens**.

②

_____ sunglasses _____?

They're _____.

③

_____ bicycle _____?

It's _____.

④

_____ ball _____?

It's _____.

⑤

_____ pictures _____?

They're _____.

⑥

GRAMMAR • Possessive Adjectives

Page Summary

Grammar Possessive adjectives
Function Describing personal possessions

The Teacher's Notes for this activity continue on page 91.

Warm-up

Point to a female student's book. Say, *Whose book is this? It's her book.* Point to a male student's book. Say, *Whose book is this? It's his book.* Do this a few more times with other students. Ask the question, and have the class respond using *his* or *her*. Repeat with plural objects *(Whose books are these?)* and then with singular and plural objects on the other side of the room *(Whose book is that? Whose books are those?).*

Grammar Notes

- The focus here is on possessive adjectives. The students need to give a full-sentence response in order to practice this grammar point, even though in normal conversation, a speaker would probably just answer *It's yours* or *It's ours.* These possessive pronouns will be presented in another chapter.
- *Whose* is used to ask about possession. It's often used with a noun. It can be used without a noun if the meaning is clear in the situation, for example, *Whose is this?* (as the speaker points to an object).
- Remind students that some objects are plural in English even if they may not appear to be *(sunglasses, jeans)* and therefore need *are*.

∩ Listen. Listen and repeat.

1. Write on the board, *Whose book is this? It's her book. It's his book.* Read the sentences aloud for students to repeat. Then ask about a few plural classroom objects in order to elicit *our* and *their*, for example:

   Q: *Whose books are these?*
   A: *They're our books.*

2. Review the demonstrative adjectives *this, that, these, those,* using classroom objects.
3. Have students look at the illustrations.
4. Play the recording (CD2, track 40) as students listen to the conversations.
5. Play the recording (CD2, track 41) for students to repeat.

▶ PAIR WORK

1. Do items 1 and 2 with student partners.
2. Have students form pairs to practice the conversations, switching parts.
3. Call on pairs to present each conversation to the class.

▶ WRITING

1. Have students work alone to complete the conversations using the words in the boxes at the top of the page.
2. Play the recording (CD2, track 40) again and have the students check their work.
3. Go over the answers with the class by calling on different pairs to read each conversation. Encourage students to use gestures to indicate objects near or far away as they speak, in order to reinforce understanding of the demonstrative adjectives.

GRAMMAR • Possessive Adjectives

Answer Key

1. Whose sandwich is this? It's your sandwich.
2. Whose chickens are those? They're our chickens.
3. Whose sunglasses are these? They're my sunglasses.
4. Whose bicycle is that? It's his bicycle.
5. Whose ball is this? It's their ball.
6. Whose pictures are these? They're her pictures.
7. Whose flowers are those? They're my flowers.
8. Whose cat is that? It's our cat.
9. Whose envelopes are these? They're your envelopes.
10. Whose cell phone is this? It's her cell phone.
11. Whose dog is that? It's their dog.
12. Whose books are those? They're his books.

Expansion Activity

Hold up a few of the students' possessions, one at a time, and ask the class questions. Call on individual students to respond orally using a possessive adjective. For example, ask: *Whose watch is this? (It's his watch.) Whose backpack/jacket/handbag/hat is this? Whose shoes/keys/books are these? Whose coat/jacket/notebook is that? Whose pens/pencils/papers are those?*

PAIR WORK • *Read the conversations aloud.*

GRAMMAR • Possessive Nouns

▶ 🎧 *Listen. Listen and practice.*

Do you like Milton's green tie?

No, I don't like green very much.

①

Do you like the girls' blue uniforms?

Yes, I think blue is a beautiful color.

②

▶ **PAIR WORK** • *Look at the pictures and talk about the people's clothing.*

1. Ken's brown jacket
A: **Do you like Ken's brown jacket?**
B: **Yes, I think brown is a great color.** OR **No, I don't like brown very much.**

1. Ken's brown jacket

2. Maria's green dress

3. the boys' orange T-shirts

4. Susan's blue pants

5. Joe's purple shirt

6. the ladies' pink gloves

7. the men's black hats

8. Lucy's yellow blouse

9. Mr. Denby's gray sweater

GRAMMAR • Possessive Nouns

Page Summary

Grammar Possessive nouns
Function Talking about personal possessions

Warm-up

Indicate a possession of one student and ask about it, for example, *Whose jacket is this?* (If you get the response *It's her jacket,* say, *What's her name?*) Write the response on the board: *It's (Sara's) jacket.* Underline *'s.* Indicate a possession of a different student, and repeat the question. Model the response. Then ask about possessions of other students. Call on individual students to respond.

Grammar Notes

- To a singular noun, add an apostrophe (') + *s* to show possession *(the boy's jacket).*
- To a regular plural noun, add an apostrophe (') after the final *s* to show possession *(the boys' jackets).*
- To the name of one person, add an apostrophe (') + *s; (Ken's book).* This also applies if the name ends in *s (Carlos's book).*
- To irregular plural nouns *(men, women, children)* add an apostrophe (') + *s (men's, women's, children's).*
- *Green* can be either an adjective *(a green tie)* or a noun *(I don't like green).*

◯ Listen. Listen and practice.

1. Write on the board, *The boy's jacket.* Draw a simple stick figure of one boy. Also write, *the boys' jackets,* and draw two boys. Underline the endings on *boy's* and *boys'.* Point out how the position of the apostrophe changes. Next write, *This is Ken's book. These are the men's books.* Point out that *men* is plural, but it is irregular and therefore the possessive is formed with apostrophe (') + *s.*
2. Have students look at the illustrations.
3. Play the recording (CD2, track 48) as students listen. Write on the board *girls'* and *uniforms.* Point out that both words are plural, but one is possessive and the other is not.
4. Play the recording (CD2, track 49) as students practice the conversations.

▶ PAIR WORK

1. Model the first conversation with a student partner. Then have two students model the second conversation.
2. Have students form pairs. Tell them to look at the pictures and talk about the people's clothing.
3. Call on different pairs to present each conversation to the class.

Answer Key

1. A: Do you like Ken's brown jacket?
2. A: Do you like Maria's green dress?
3. A: Do you like the boys' orange T-shirts?
4. A: Do you like Susan's blue pants?
5. A: Do you like Joe's purple shirt?
6. A: Do you like the ladies' pink gloves?
7. A: Do you like the men's black hats?
8. A: Do you like Lucy's yellow blouse?
9. A: Do you like Mr. Denby's gray sweater?

Expansion Activity 1

Books are closed. Do a dictation. Read each question from the answer key above. Say each question twice, pausing for students to write. Call on different students to write the questions on the board. Have students check their spelling and the positions of the apostrophes.

Expansion Activity 2

Have students form pairs. Tell them to take turns asking other questions about clothing or objects, using the illustrations. Do the first illustration together. Ask a student: *Do you like Ken's motorcycle? Do you like Ken's shoes?* Note: Tell students to include the colors in their questions where possible. After students practice, call on a few pairs to present to the class.

FAMILY RELATIONSHIPS

Page Summary

Grammar Possessive nouns
Function Talking about family relationships

Warm-up

Have students open their books and cover all of page 93 except for the pictures of the Adams family. Say each number *(number 1)* and then the family relationship word, and have students repeat the word. Next, ask students to think of a well-known family in their country and say who the people are: *The father is . . . , The mother is . . . ,* and so on.

Culture Notes

- Divorce and remarriage have made it necessary to have many words to describe family relationships. If a father remarries, his new wife is his children's stepmother. Likewise, if a mother remarries, her new husband is her children's stepfather. If the new couple has children, the children from the first marriage and from the second marriage are half-brothers or half-sisters.
- Unlike some languages, English doesn't have words that specify birth order or exact family relationships. For example, there is not a particular word that means first-born son, or second-born daughter, or wife of second-born son. This can be puzzling for students whose first language does have expressions for these relationships.

Listen and repeat.

1. Play the recording (CD2, track 50) as students listen and repeat. Ask them to point at each person in the drawing as they say the appropriate word.
2. If students need more practice, play the recording (CD2, track 50) again.

WRITING

1. Have students work alone to complete the sentences.
2. Go over the answers by calling on different students to read each sentence.
3. Have students read the sentences out loud chorally or in pairs.

Answer Key

1. Ryan is Tom's son.
2. Tom is Ryan's father.
3. Becky is Linda's daughter.
4. Linda is Becky's mother.
5. Tom is Linda's husband.
6. Linda is Tom's wife.
7. Ryan is Becky's brother.
8. Becky is Ryan's sister.

Listen. Listen and practice.

1. Play the recording (CD2, track 51) as students listen.
2. Play the recording (CD2, track 52) again for students to practice.

Option: Play the audio (CD2, track 51) again with no pauses while students recite chorally along with it, trying to keep up with the actors and mimic their pronunciation, intonation, and speed.

PAIR WORK

1. Tell students to have similar conversations about their own families. Tell them to talk about any brothers or sisters they have, and their names. Note: You may need to teach a little additional vocabulary for this: *I don't have any brothers or sisters. I'm an only child.* (In this situation the other speaker can continue: *What about your parents? What are their names?*)
2. Have students form pairs and practice.
3. Call on several pairs to present their conversations to the class.

Option: Have pairs present their conversations to small groups rather than to the whole class in order to give more students speaking practice.

Expansion Activity

- Have students do a role play based on the conversation in **Listen and Practice**. One of them is Maria, and the other is a member of a famous family.
- After students practice, call on a pair to present their conversation to the class.

FAMILY RELATIONSHIPS

▶ 🎧 *Listen and repeat.*

THE ADAMS FAMILY

① father
② mother
③ son
④ daughter
⑤ husband
⑥ wife
⑦ brother
⑧ sister

▶ **WRITING** • *Complete the sentences. Then read the sentences out loud.*

1. Ryan is Tom's __son__.
2. Tom is Ryan's _____.
3. Becky is Linda's _____.
4. Linda is Becky's _____.

5. Tom is Linda's _____.
6. Linda is Tom's _____.
7. Ryan is Becky's _____.
8. Becky is Ryan's _____.

▶ 🎧 *Listen. Listen and practice.*

MARIA: Tell me about your family, Carlos. Do you have any brothers or sisters?

CARLOS: I have a brother and a sister.

MARIA: Oh, really? What are their names?

CARLOS: My brother's name is Luis, and my sister's name is Ana.

MARIA: So you have five people in your family.

CARLOS: That's right. How many people do you have in your family?

MARIA: Eight. I have two brothers and three sisters.

CARLOS: Wow! You have a big family.

▶ **PAIR WORK** • *Have similar conversations about your families. How many brothers and sisters do you have? What are their names?*

DESCRIBING PEOPLE • Appearance

▶ 🎧 *Listen. Listen and repeat.*

Stanley is tall. ⑥

Bill is average height. ⑤

Richard is short. ④

Jan has blond hair. ①

Sue has brown hair. ②

Rita has black hair. ③

Mrs. Lee is in her thirties. ⑧

Mr. Lee is in his forties. ⑨

Emma Lee ⑦ is thirteen.

▶ **WRITING** • *Describe the people at the picnic.*

1. <u>He's tall, he has blond hair, and he's about thirty-five.</u>

2. _____

3. _____

4. _____

5. _____

6. _____

7. _____

▶ **PRACTICE** • *Describe someone in your family.*

DESCRIBING PEOPLE • Appearance

Page Summary

Grammar Adjectives
Function Talking about peoples' appearance

Warm-up

Describe a few celebrities students are familiar with, for example, *Michael Jordan is tall. He has brown hair.* Then call on individual students to describe a few celebrities to the class. You can do a brief review of the professions that the class learned in Chapter 1: *He's an actor. She's a tennis player.* Write one of these sentences on the board and underline the article *a* or *an*. Then write *He's tall* and make an *X* before *tall* to show that there is no article with the adjective.

Grammar Note

- There are two sentence patterns here. One is: subject + [form of] *be* + adjective: *He is tall. She's short. He's in his forties.*
- The other pattern is subject + *has* + attribute: *He has blond hair. She has black hair.*
- With subject + *be* a contraction can be used: *He's tall*, but not with subject + *has*.
- *In her thirties* means anywhere between thirty and forty. Sometimes, the range is more specified: *She's in her early thirties, her mid-thirties, her late thirties.*

Culture Note

Average height varies from country to country. Someone is *short, average height, tall* only in relationship to others, as in the group shown here at a picnic.

▶ 🎧 *Listen. Listen and repeat.*

1. Write on the board: *He's tall. He has brown hair.* To be sure that students understand the difference, have them look at the illustrations. Say, *Stanley.* Have students make sentences about him: *He's tall. He has red hair.*
2. Play the recording (CD2, track 53) as students listen.
3. Play the recording (CD2, track 54) again for students to repeat.
4. Have students read the sentences out loud in pairs.

▶ **WRITING**

1. Have students work alone to write sentences describing the people at the picnic.

2. Go over the answers with the class by calling on individual students to read each sentence.

Answer Key
Answers will vary.

▶ **PRACTICE**

1. Tell students to practice the conversation, but to talk about their own families.
2. Have students form pairs and practice.
3. Call on several pairs to present their conversations to the class.

Option: Have pairs present their conversations to small groups rather than to the whole class in order to give more students speaking practice.

Expansion Activity 1

Make two sets of cards (five cards per set). One set has a name on each card. The other set has a feature on each card: *blond hair, about thirty-five, tall.* To play, draw one card from each set and read the information on both cards out loud, for example, *Sue, black hair.* Students listen and then write down the full sentence: *Sue has black hair.* Continue until the students have made 10 sentences. You can repeat any names or features in new combinations. Call on students to read the sentences out loud. Note: This can also be done as an oral activity if you just read the cues and have the students say the sentences instead of writing them.

Expansion Activity 2

Have students choose a category of people many of them are familiar with such as a sports team, movie stars, or music groups. Have one student at a time describe someone and the rest of the class guess who it is. This can also be done in small groups.

DESCRIBING PEOPLE • *Personality*

Page Summary

Grammar Adjectives
Function Talking about peoples' personalities

Warm-up

Review adjectives from Chapter 2, pages 22 and 23. List on the board: *happy, nervous, sad, strong, weak.* Write a name: *Ana.* Ask individual students to make sentences: *Ana is happy.* Continue with other names and other adjectives.

Grammar Note

Students often confuse adjectives ending in *-ed* and *-ing*, for example, *boring* and *bored.* One way to clarify this is to offer the example of a bad class: *The teacher is boring. The students are bored.* Ask, *Who is bored?* (the students). *Who is boring?* (the teacher).

▶ 🎧 *Look and listen. Listen and repeat.*

1. Play the recording (CD2, track 55) as students listen.
2. Play the recording (CD2, track 56) again for students to repeat.
3. Have students read the sentences out loud in pairs.

▶ WRITING

1. Have students work alone to describe three people who are important to them. Tell them to choose the best adjective from the words in the boxes to describe each of them.
2. Circulate and help students write their sentences.
3. Have students form small groups and take turns reading their sentences out loud.
4. Call on individual students to read their sentences.
5. To review possessives, have students report what they learned from other students. Model an example: *I talked to Tomas. His brother is funny. His sister is shy. I also talked to Sonya. Her father is hardworking.*

▶ PAIR WORK

1. Explain that *What's X like?* is a common way to ask for a description of a person or a thing.
2. Tell students they can talk about a real or an imagined best friend.
3. Have students form pairs and take turns describing their best friends.
4. Have students change partners and repeat.

Expansion Activity 1

Ask students to each write three or four sentences about a best friend, either real or imaginary. Tell students to look at earlier units for ideas on what to include. Model a few sentences on the board to help them get started: *My best friend is funny. She is shy. She doesn't like movies. She has a big black dog.* Have students form pairs and take turns reading their sentences. Call on a few students to read to the class.

Expansion Activity 2

Books are closed. Dictate the adjectives in the box. Say each word twice, pausing for students to write. Then have students open their books and check their spelling.

DESCRIBING PEOPLE • Personality

▶ 🎧 *Look and listen. Listen and repeat.*

Joe is funny.

Mr. Tuck is boring.

Ms. Dean is neat.

Donna is sloppy.

Lucy is talkative.

Annabelle is shy.

Al is hardworking.

Fred is lazy.

▶ **WRITING** • *Describe five people who are important to you. Use the best adjective to describe each person.*

Example: <u>My brother is sloppy.</u>

1. _____

2. _____

3. _____

4. _____

5. _____

IMPORTANT PEOPLE			
mother	sister	girlfriend	aunt
father	brother	boyfriend	uncle

ADJECTIVES			
funny	boring	talkative	shy
neat	sloppy	hardworking	lazy

▶ **PAIR WORK** • *Use two or three adjectives to describe your best friend.*

A: **What's your best friend like?**
B: **She's talkative, very funny and a little lazy.**

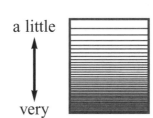

a little

very

CARTOON STORY

▶ 🎧 *Jason is looking for a pay phone. Listen. Listen and practice.*

▶ **STORY QUESTIONS** • *Look at the pictures for the answers.*

1. Where is Jason? What's he looking for?
2. What is Jason's problem?
3. Does the old man have change for a dollar?
4. Why is Jason calling the operator?
5. What is Pat's phone number?
6. Look at the lady with the red hair. Why is she angry with Jason?
7. What does Jason say to the lady?

CARTOON STORY

Page Summary

Grammar *To have*
Function Making phone calls

The Teacher's Notes for this Cartoon Story continue on page 97.

Warm-up

Model making a polite request. Write on the board:

> A: *Excuse me, do you have . . . ?*
> B: *Let's see . . . Yes, I do. Here you are.*

Call on a student. Ask, *Excuse me, do you have a pencil?* Cue the student to respond with the sentences on the board. Tell that student to make a polite request of another student. Continue for several rounds.

Culture Note

In the cartoon story, Jason is looking for a pay phone. With the increase in cellular phone use all over the world, pay phones are becoming harder to find. Once Jason finds the phone, his next hurdle is paying for the call. Since he doesn't have a calling card, he has to find change. To get a phone number, the caller typically follows a series of computerized voice prompts, such as *What city?* and *What listing?* until finally the phone number is given twice.

🎧*Jason is looking for a pay phone. Listen.*
  Listen and practice.

1. Direct student's attention to the illustrations. Ask them to describe the people: *What is Jason wearing? What color is his jacket? Is the woman in picture 7 happy?* Continue with people on page 97.
2. Set the scene: Jason wants to call Pat Lacy. First, he needs to get her phone number, and then she isn't home.
3. Play the recording (CD2, track 57) as students listen.
4. Play the recording (CD2, track 58) for students to practice the conversation.
5. Have students form pairs to practice the conversation.

▶ STORY QUESTIONS

1. Tell students to look at the pictures for the answers.
2. Have students form pairs. Tell them to take turns asking and answering the questions about the pictures.
3. Go over the answers by asking the questions of individual students.

Option: Go over the questions one page at a time. Then replay the audio for the whole story.

Answer Key

1. He's at the market. He's looking for a pay phone.
2. He doesn't have any change.
3. Yes, he does.
4. He doesn't have Pat Lacy's phone number.
5. Pat's phone number is 473-2906.
6. He has the wrong number.
7. Is this 473-2906? OR I'm sorry.
8. May I use the phone?
9. He's looking at his watch.
10. I'm finished.
11. No, she isn't. She's at work.
12. No, he isn't. He's sleeping.
13. Yes, she is.
14. Pat's wearing a shirt and pants.
15. She's watching her favorite TV show.
16. Jason feels sad.

CARTOON STORY

Expansion Activity 1

Have students form groups of four to practice the conversation. Tell them to use props and gestures to mime telephoning, and to move around as they practice. Call on a group to present to the class.

Expansion Activity 2

At the end of the story, Jason says "This isn't my day." Review with the students the reasons why he says this. (He can't find a phone, he doesn't have change or Pat's phone number, Pat isn't home, and finally, she doesn't want to talk to him.) Ask students to think about what makes a "bad day." Have them form pairs and tell each other about what a bad day is like; for example, *I wake up late. I get to school late.* Encourage students to ask each other questions. Call on a few students to tell the class about their partner's bad day.

CARTOON STORY

▶ **STORY QUESTIONS (continued)** • *Look at the pictures for the answers.*

8. What does the girl in the green sweater ask Jason?
9. What is Jason doing while she's talking on the phone?
10. What does the girl say after using the phone?
11. Is Pat home the first time Jason calls? Where is she?
12. Is Jason looking at his watch? What's he doing?
13. Is Pat home now?
14. What is Pat wearing?
15. What is Pat doing while she's talking with Jason?
16. How does Jason feel? Is he sad or angry?

VOCABULARY

NOUNS

Family Members

mother
father
wife
husband
brother
sister
son
daughter

Other

chicken
clothes dryer
driver's license
envelope
fireplace
garage
guitar
hair

handbag
lamp
oil
violin
wallet
washing machine

VERB

sell

ADJECTIVES

boring
cute
funny
hardworking
lazy
lucky
neat
sloppy
talkative
top

POSSESSIVE ADJECTIVES

our
their

DETERMINER

any

CONJUNCTION

so

EXPRESSIONS

Describing people

He's tall.
   …short.
   …average-height.
She has blond hair.
She's in her thirties.
She's about thirty-five.

Talking about cars

How do you like our new car?
   I like it very much.
She takes good care of her car.
   That's for sure.
Your car is in bad shape.
   What's wrong with it?

Asking for a phone number

What city?
   Maywood. I'd like the number of Pat Lacy.
How do you spell the last name?
   L-A-C-Y.
The number is 473-2906.
   Thank you.

Getting the wrong number

Hello. Is Pat there?
   No, you have the wrong number.
Is this 473-2906?
   No, it isn't.
I'm sorry.

Asking to speak with someone

Hello. Can I speak to Pat, please?
   Pat isn't here right now. She's at work.
Hello. Is Pat there now?
   Yes, she is. Just a minute, please.

Talking on the phone

Hi, Pat. This is Jason Brown.
   Oh, hi, Jason.
What are you doing?
   I'm watching my favorite TV show.
   Can you call me later?

Other

May I use the phone?
Oh, no…I don't have any change.
This isn't my day.

I'm finished.
Oh, really?
That's right.

It's over there.
Wow!
What a nice house!

Let's see…
Here you are.
Thanks.

VOCABULARY

The games below provide additional opportunities to use the vocabulary, grammar, and expressions presented in the unit. Before students play any of the games, have them review the lists of words and circle any words they don't know. Then put students into small groups and have them review the circled words together. Circulate so you can help in case no one in a group knows a particular word.

Game 1: Describing People
Have students form pairs. Tell them to take turns describing their classmates and guessing who it is. Model an example:

> A: *He's tall. He has brown hair. He's wearing a blue shirt.*
> B: *Is it Tony?*
> A: *Yes, it is. / No it isn't.*

Game 2: Telephone Game
Review the conversation under *Talking on the phone.* Then have students form groups of six to eight. Tell one student to start. That student begins the conversation in the book, substituting his or her name and the name of another student in the group. They continue the conversation, substituting a different activity in response to *What are you doing?* When they finish, the student who received the call makes a new call to another group member. Students continue until everyone makes and receives a call. The challenge is that each student needs to come up with a new activity without slowing down the conversation.

Game 3: Family Tree
Have students draw a family tree of their own families. Ask them to write the names and the family relationships. Tell them to refer back to page 93, the Adams Family, as needed. Circulate and help them. Then have students form pairs and sit back to back. One partner describes his or her family and the other draws the family tree and labels it. When they are finished, they compare the trees. As a follow-up, ask students to tell the class something about their partners, for example, *Alex has a brother. His name is Mario.*

PRONUNCIATION

Page Summary

Focus /ae/ and /e/

▶**A** 🎧 *Listen and repeat.*

1. Have students look at the words as you play the recording (CD2, track 59) and they listen and repeat. If they have trouble with the /æ/ sound, you can show them that it's easier to make the sound if you smile as you say it.
2. Have students form pairs to practice reading the words out loud.

▶**B** 🎧 *Listen and repeat.*

1. Have students look at the words as you play the recording (CD2, track 60) and they repeat.

▶**C** 🎧 *Listen to each pair of words. Listen again and repeat.*

1. Have students look at each pair of words and listen as you play the recording (CD2, track 61).
2. Play the recording (CD2, track 62) again and have the students listen and repeat each word pair.
3. Say one of the words in each pair and have students point to the correct picture.

▶**D** 🎧 *Look at the words in Part C. Listen and circle the words you hear.*

1. Have students circle the words they hear as you play the recording (CD2, track 63).
2. Have students form pairs and compare their answers.
3. Play the recording (CD2, track 63) again as a final check.

4. Go over the answers with the class by saying the number of an item; for example, *number 1,* and have the class say the letter of the correct word (*a* or *b*).

Answer Key	
1. a. pan	4. a. tan
2. b. men	5. b. guess
3. b. Jen	6. a. bad

▶**E** 🎧 *Listen and practice.*

1. Have students listen and read the sentences silently as you play the recording (CD2, track 63).
2. Play the recording (CD2, track 64) again and have the students practice reading the sentences out loud.
3. Have students form pairs to practice reading the sentences out loud.

Expansion Activity

Dictate the words for Part C in random order. Then write the answers on the board for students to check their work.

PRONUNCIATION

▶ **A** 🎧 *Listen and repeat.*

/æ/

1. fat   4. that   7. sad
2. black   5. bad   8. happy
3. cat   6. apple   9. pants

▶ **B** 🎧 *Listen and repeat.*

/e/

1. ten   4. sell   7. heavy
2. yes   5. red   8. yellow
3. men   6. dress   9. sweater

▶ **C** 🎧 *Listen to each pair of words. Listen again and repeat.*

1. a. pan   b. pen   2. a. man   b. men

3. a. Jan   b. Jen   4. a. tan   b. ten

5. a. gas   b. guess   6. a. bad   b. bed

▶ **D** 🎧 *Look at the words in Part C. Listen and* (circle) *the words you hear.*

▶ **E** 🎧 *Listen and practice.*

1. Jen has a red hat.
2. The happy chef is at his desk.
3. My best friend is an acrobat.
4. The men are standing next to the bank.
5. Texas is having bad weather.
6. Is Dan ready for the next dance?

GRAMMAR SUMMARY

TO HAVE Affirmative		
He She	has	a car.
I You We They	have	

Negative		
He She	doesn't (does not)	have a car.
I You We They	don't (do not)	

Interrogative		
Does	he she	have a car?
Do	I you we they	

Short Answers						
Yes,	he she	does.	No,	he she	doesn't.
	I you we they	do.		I you we they	don't.

POSSESSIVE ADJECTIVES		
It's	my your his her our their	house.

Questions with WHOSE	
Whose	radio is that? books are those?

POSSESSIVE NOUNS
It's John's radio. They're the girls' books.

CONTENTS

▶ **TOPICS**

Apartments

Furniture and rooms

Food

Eating habits

▶ **GRAMMAR**

There is / there are

Some / any

Countables / uncountables

like, want, need

▶ **FUNCTIONS**

Asking about and
describing apartments

Buying furniture

Expressing preferences
in food

Ordering fast food

Shopping for food

Asking a favor

▶ **PRONUNCIATION**

/ɑ/ vs. /ʌ/

Chapter

6

CARTOON STORY

CARTOON STORY

Page Summary

Grammar *There is / there are*
Function Describing an apartment

The Teacher's Notes for this activity continue on page T103.

Culture Note

In the cartoon story, Carlos and Maria are at his apartment. It is the first time she has been there and she makes remarks about what a nice place it is. Some students might confuse *apartment* and *apartment building*. *Apartments* are the individual units within an *apartment building*. Typically, someone rents an apartment. If they own the unit, it is a condominium, or "condo."

Warm-up

Review introductions. Ask two students to come to the front of the class. Greet one of them. Then ask, *Who's your friend?* Cue the student, *This is (Teresa.)* Continue with *Nice to meet you,* and so on as modeled in the cartoon story.

! Pronunciation Tip

Who's your is pronounced *Whoozyur.*

Grammar Notes

- *Who's* is a contraction for *Who is.* Students might confuse this with the possessive *whose (Whose book is this?)* that they learned in Chapter 5 on pages 90–91. One test is to say the sentence without the contraction. If *Who is* makes sense, the contraction *Who's* is being used. Because *who's* and *whose* sound the same in spoken English, this is only a test for students to use if they are confused about the meaning of something they hear.
- In the last line, *We'd better go, We'd* is a contraction for *we had better*, which will be taught later.

⌢ Listen. Listen and practice.

1. Direct student's attention to the illustrations. Set the scene: These are Carlos and Maria. Ask them to describe the situation: *Where are they? What are they wearing? Are they happy?* Encourage students to describe what they see using their own words.
2. Play the recording (CD3, track 1) as students listen.
3. Play the recording (CD3, track 2) for students to practice the conversation.
4. Have students form pairs to practice the conversation.

▶ STORY QUESTIONS

Ask the questions of individual students.
Option: Have students form pairs. Tell them to take turns asking and answering the questions. Then go over the answers with the class.

Answer Key

1. Yes, he does.
2. Yes, there is. No, it isn't (working).
3. Mrs. Jones is tired today. She needs a vacation.
4. The view from Carlos' apartment is fantastic.
5. Yes, she is very hungry. There are some ham and cheese sandwiches.
6. Yes, there is. The coffee cups are on the shelf behind Maria.
7. There's a bird in the window. It's singing.

Expansion Activity 1

To review some of the vocabulary from earlier chapters, have the students each write three sentences about where they live. Write on the board, *Well, this is my apartment/house.* Have students form pairs. Tell them to describe where they live. Tell them to start with the sentence on the board, and to end the conversation with the exchange in picture 15 *(This is a nice place you have./Thanks. I'm glad you like it.)*

Expansion Activity 2

Write on the board the exchange:

> *Are you hungry?*
> *Very.*
> *I hope you like . . .*
> *Yes, I do.*

Compile a list on the board of foods the students know. Have students form pairs and practice this exchange substituting different foods. Encourage them to use the list on the board or other foods they know. Call on pairs to present to the class.

▶ **STORY QUESTIONS**

1. Does Carlos live on the top floor of his apartment building?
2. Is there an elevator in the building? Is it working?
3. How is Mrs. Jones today? What does she need?
4. How is the view from Carlos' apartment?
5. Is Maria hungry? What's in the refrigerator?
6. Is there some coffee on the stove? Where are the coffee cups?
7. What does Maria see in the window? What's it doing?

GRAMMAR • There's a + singular noun

▶ 🎧 *Listen and repeat.*

There's a bird in the window.   There's a lamp on the table.
_____ computer on the desk.   _____ newspaper on the bed.
_____ mirror on the wall.   _____ dog under the bed.

Yes/No Question	Short Answers	
Is there a telephone in the bedroom?	Yes, there is.	No, there isn't.

▶ **PRACTICE** • *Answer the teacher; then ask each other these questions.*

A: **Is there a mirror on the wall?**   A: **Is there a picture on the wall?**
B: **Yes, there is.**   B: **No, there isn't.**

1. Is there a lamp on the table?   5. Is there a dog under the bed?
2. Is there a clock on the table?   6. Is there a telephone on the desk?
3. Is there a magazine on the bed?   7. Is there a computer on the desk?
4. Is there a newspaper on the bed?   8. Is there a dictionary on the desk?

▶ **PAIR WORK** • *Ask if these items are in your partner's bedroom.*

Example: clock
Student A: **Is there a clock in your bedroom?**
Student B: **Yes, there is.** OR **No, there isn't.**

1. clock   4. piano   7. lamp
2. radio   5. television   8. desk
3. telephone   6. computer   9. mirror

Page Summary

Grammar *There's a* + singular noun
Function Asking about and describing the location of objects in a bedroom

Grammar Notes

- The word order is inverted in the question: *There is a book. Is there a book?*
- *Is there a book?* is a *yes/no* question and the answer is *Yes, there is* or *No, there isn't.*
- Like the other negative short answers earlier in the book, the alternative *No, there's not* is also possible.
- Contractions are often used in statements *(There's a book)*, but can't be used in affirmative short answers.

! *Pronunciation Tip*

There's a is pronounced *Thereza. Is there a* sounds like one word: *Iztherea.*

▶ 🎧 *Listen and repeat.*

1. To familiarize students with the grammar point and to review prepositions of location, make a few observations about things in the classroom, for example, *There's a (dictionary) in the bookcase. There's a (pencil) on the desk. There's a (notebook) under the (book).* Next write on the board: *There is a pencil on the desk.* Cross out the *i* in *is* and replace it with an apostrophe. Under *There is*, write *there's* to show the contraction. Ask, *What do you see in the room?* Tell students to respond, using *There's a.* Ask several students, one at a time, to tell the class what they see. Have the class repeat each sentence.
2. Have students look at the illustration. Say different objects one at a time *(dog, computer, desk)* and have students point to them.
3. Play the recording (CD3, track 3) as students listen and repeat.
4. Have students form pairs and read the sentences out loud.

▶ PRACTICE

1. Go over the examples in the grammar boxes. Write on the board: *There is a telephone.* Draw a circle around *is*, and draw an arrow pointing to the beginning of the sentence to show the inverted word order in the question. Write: *Is there a telephone?* and then write the short answer responses on the board. Point out that a contraction can be used in the negative *(No, there isn't)*, but not in the affirmative *(Yes, there is).*

2. Ask the questions of the class. Have them respond chorally.
3. Have students form pairs and ask each other the questions.

Answer Key

1. B: Yes, there is.	5. B: Yes, there is.
2. B: No, there isn't.	6. B: No, there isn't.
3. B: No, there isn't.	7. B: Yes, there is.
4. B: Yes, there is.	8. B: No, there isn't.

! *Pronunciation Tip*

Primary stress is on the item because that is the focus of the question: *Is there a CLOCK in your bedroom?*

▶ PAIR WORK

1. Have students form pairs and take turns asking about the items. Encourage students to answer with true information.
2. Call on pairs to present the conversations to the class.

Expansion Activity

Write on the board another room in a home; for example *living room.* Ask, *What do people have in the living room?* and put any new vocabulary *(sofa, coffee table, stereo)* on the board. Have students form pairs. Tell them to do Pair Work again, this time asking about items in the living room. Tell them to use any items on the page, plus any other items they may know. Circulate and help with vocabulary. Call on a few students to summarize for the class what their partner has in the living room.

GRAMMAR • There are + plural noun

Page Summary

Grammar *There are* + plural noun
Function Asking about and describing location of objects in a kitchen

---

Warm-up

To familiarize students with the grammar, walk around and ask about what is in the room, using *Are there any . . . (books, students, dogs) in this room?* Model the response, *Yes, there are* or *No, there aren't.* Call on a pair to ask and answer. Then have the whole class form pairs and ask each other the question, substituting different plural objects.

Grammar Notes

- *Are there any . . . ?* is a *yes/no* question about whether something exists in a particular place; for example, *Are there any cups on the shelf?* is a question only about cups on the shelf.
- The word order is inverted in the question: *There are pots. Are there any pots?*
- *Are there any cups on the shelf?* is a *yes/no* question and the answer is *Yes, there are* or *No, there aren't.* Note: *Any* can be added to a negative short answer, *No, there aren't any,* but not to the affirmative answer. (This is beyond the scope of this chapter, but some students might ask about *any.*)
- If students ask about *any* at this point, just say that it is used in a question or a negative answer with plural or uncountable nouns, while *some* is used in the positive statement. This grammar will be more fully covered later in the book.

❗ *Pronunciation Tip*
In spoken English, the contracted form *there're* is common.

▶ 🎧 *Listen and repeat.*

1. Have students look at the illustration and notice what objects are in the kitchen and where they are located. To review this vocabulary, say different objects one at a time *(pots, bottles, cups)* and have students point to them. You can do this faster and faster, repeating the words for objects that students take longer to locate.
2. Play the recording (CD3, track 4) as students listen and repeat.
3. Call on individual students to read the sentences out loud.

▶ PRACTICE

1. Say, *There's a clock in this room. What else is there in the room?* As soon as a student comes up with a plural object *(desks, tables, students)*, write the word on the board, underlining the *s*. Draw two blanks in front of the word; elicit *there are*. Draw an arrow from the word *are* to the front of the sentence to show how the word order changes in the question.
2. Ask the questions of the class. Have them respond chorally and individually.
3. Have students form pairs with new partners and ask each other the questions.

Answer Key

1. Yes, there are.	5. No, there aren't.
2. No, there aren't.	6. Yes, there are.
3. Yes, there are.	7. No, there aren't.
4. Yes, there are.	8. No, there aren't

❗ *Pronunciation Tip*
The strongest stress is on the item being asked about: *Are there any POTS in your kitchen?*

▶ PAIR WORK

1. Have students form pairs and take turns asking about the items. Encourage students to answer with true information.
2. Call on pairs to present the conversations to the class.

Expansion Activity

Have students form pairs to talk about their own kitchens. Have one partner ask questions, using *Are there any,* and the other partner describe his or her kitchen. Tell the listening partner to take notes, for example, *four chairs.* When both partners have had a turn, have students form new pairs and tell their new partner about the old partner's kitchen. Note: Encourage students to make up information if they cannot remember exact quantities, for example, *five pots.* For extra challenge, have students draw what their partner tells them.

GRAMMAR • There are + plural noun

▶ 🎧 *Listen and repeat.*

There are some apples in the bowl.
_____ dishes in the sink.
_____ spoons on the counter.

There are some bottles on the table.
_____ cups on the shelf.
_____ pots on the wall.

Yes/No Question	Short Answers	
Are there any chairs in the kitchen?	Yes, there are.	No, there aren't.

▶ **PRACTICE** • *Answer the teacher; then ask each other these questions.*

A: **Are there any dishes in the sink?**
B: **Yes, there are.**

1. Are there any pots on the wall?
2. Are there any oranges in the bowl?
3. Are there any apples in the bowl?
4. Are there any cups on the shelf?

A: **Are there any pots in the sink?**
B: **No, there aren't.**

5. Are there any glasses on the shelf?
6. Are there any spoons on the counter?
7. Are there any knives on the counter?
8. Are there any dishes on the table?

▶ **PAIR WORK** • *Ask if these items are in your partner's kitchen.*

Example: pots
Student A: **Are there any pots in your kitchen?**
Student B: **Yes, there are. OR No, there aren't.**

1. flowers
2. apples
3. oranges

4. books
5. chairs
6. pots

7. cups
8. bottles
9. magazines

LIFE SKILL • Buying Furniture

▶ 🎧 *Listen. Listen and practice.*

1 May I help you? — FURNITURE — Yes, I need a coffee table.

2 The coffee tables are over there.

3 Do you see one you like? — Yes. I like this one. — $295

4 How much is it? — Two hundred ninety-five dollars. — I'll take it.

1. lamp / $75

2. table / $330

3. chair / $139

4. desk / $265

5. armchair / $550

6. sofa / $898

7. bed / $980

8. dresser / $469

▶ **PAIR WORK** • *Have similar conversations.*

A: May I help you?

B: Yes. I need a _____.

A: The _____ are over there. Do you see one you like?

B: Yes. I like this one. How much is it?

A: _____.

B: Good. I'll take it.
   OR   Oh, that's too expensive.

Page Summary

Grammar Singular and plural nouns
Function Buying furniture

Warm-up

Books are closed. Ask students to name different pieces of furniture. Make a list on the board. Then say, *Think of a piece of furniture you need in your home.* Model an example, *I need a small lamp.* Call on students, one at a time, to say something they need.

Culture Note

I'll take it is a commonly use expression for *I've made up my mind. I'm going to buy that one.*

! Pronunciation Tip

The main stress is on the verb: *I'll TAKE it.*

Grammar Notes

- *I need a coffee table* is singular. *The coffee tables are over there* is plural.
- *Do you see one you like?* = *Do you see a particular table you like?*
- *I like this one,* = *I like this table.*
- *How much is it?* = *How much is the one I like?*
- *I'll take it* = *I'll take the one (that) I like.*

▶ ◯ Listen. Listen and practice.

1. Play the recording (CD3, track 5) as students listen.
2. Play the recording (CD3, track 6) as students listen and practice the conversation.

▶ PAIR WORK

1. Do a quick scanning activity before students begin pair work. Ask students how much different items on the page cost, for example, say, *How much is the lamp?* A student responds, *It's seventy-five dollars.* Choose the items at random to keep students listening actively.
2. Model an example with a student partner, using *lamp.*
3. Have students form pairs. Tell them to have similar conversations.
4. Call on different pairs to present some of the conversations to the class.

Expansion Activity

Have students form pairs. Write on the board: *This one is only. . . .* Tell students to make up similar conversations, but if the partner says, *Oh, that's too expensive,* then the other partner presents a different item at a lower price. They continue offering items at lower prices until the partner says, *I'll take it.* They can use the items in the book, or other items they know. After students practice, call on a few pairs to present to the class.

Page Summary

Grammar *There is/there are*
Function Asking about and describing apartments

Warm-up

Have students look at the illustrations and describe what they see in each of the rooms. Have them identify objects (*There is a lamp in the bedroom*), say where objects are located (*The lamp is on the table*), and say how many objects they see (*There are three pots*). Do this as a whole-class activity or in pairs. You may want to put some of the vocabulary on the board (*pillow, toilet, curtains, piano bench*).

Grammar Notes

- For this activity, students need to understand that *some* is used in affirmative sentences: *There are some pens on the table.*
- *Any* is used in negative sentences: *There aren't any pens on the table.*
- Both *some* and *any* can be used in questions, but *any* should be emphasized in this lesson because it is more common: *Are there any books on the table?*
- *A* or *an* are used when there is only one object, or when the speaker expects that there will be only one object: *Is there a fireplace in your house?*

▶ WRITING

1. Write on the board: *There's a book on the table* and *There are some books on the table.* Underline the differences in the two sentences (*'s a* for the singular form and *are some* + final *s* for the plural.) Read the examples out loud and have students repeat.
2. Have students work alone to write their sentences about the location of the objects. Remind students to use the contraction *There's.*
3. Have students form pairs to compare answers.
4. Go over the answers by calling on individual students to read each sentence.

Answer Key

1. There are some pictures in the living room.
2. There's a dresser in the bedroom.
3. There's a stove in the kitchen.
4. There are some books in the living room.
5. There's a mirror in the bathroom.
6. There are some pots in the kitchen.
7. There are some flowers in the bedroom.
8. There's a piano in the living room.

▶ PAIR WORK

1. Write on the board: *There are some books on the table.*

   Under this sentence, write _____ _____ _____ *books on the table?* Remind students of what they learned on page 105, that *any* is added to the question for plural count nouns, to elicit *Are there any. . . .*

2. Have students form pairs. Tell them to ask and answer the questions.
3. Call on different pairs to present each conversation for the class.

Expansion Activity 1

Have each student take a piece of paper and divide it into four sections. Tell them to label the sections: Bedroom, Bathroom, Kitchen, Living Room as in the illustration. (Students can modify these labels to match their own homes). Have students form pairs and take turns asking about items in rooms in their partner's home. The partner listens to the answers and adds the item(s) to the appropriate rooms on the piece of paper. Students can either draw the items or write phrases (*two lamps*). Circulate and help with vocabulary. When pairs are finished, call on a few students to present to the class a few sentences about their partner's home.

Expansion Activity 2

Have students use the illustration in the book for more practice. Tell them to make up questions of their own. This time, if the partner says *No, there isn't,* the partner must add something that *is* in the room, for example, *No, there isn't. There's a (chair.)*

   A: *Is there a dishwasher in the kitchen?*
   B: *No, there isn't. There's a sink.*

▶ **WRITING** • *Give the location of these objects.*

1. (pictures) <u>There are some pictures in the living room.</u>
2. (dresser) <u>There's a dresser in the bedroom.</u>
3. (stove)_____
4. (books) _____
5. (mirror)_____
6. (pots) _____
7. (flowers) _____
8. (piano) _____

▶ **PAIR WORK** • *Ask and answer questions.*

chairs / kitchen
A: **Are there any chairs in the kitchen?**
B: **Yes, there are.**

piano / bedroom
A: **Is there a piano in the bedroom?**
B: **No, there isn't.**

1. piano / living room
2. flowers / living room
3. flowers / bedroom
4. mirror / bathroom
5. mirror / bedroom
6. pots / kitchen
7. window / bathroom
8. pictures / living room
9. pictures / bedroom

GRAMMAR • Countables and Uncountables

▶ 🎧 **BASIC FOOD GROUPS** • *Look and listen. Listen and repeat.*

1 Fats, oils, and sweets

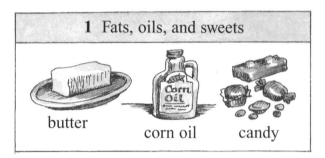

butter   corn oil   candy

2 Dairy

milk   yogurt   cheese

3 Grains

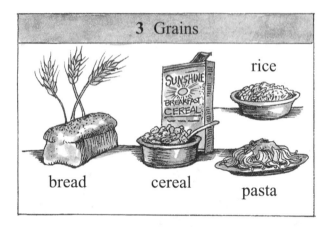

rice

bread   cereal   pasta

4 Meat and other protein

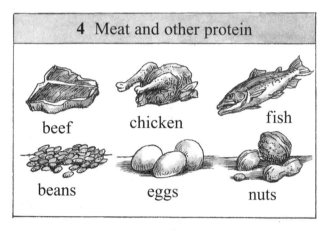

beef   chicken   fish

beans   eggs   nuts

5 Fruit

apples   oranges   bananas

peaches   pears   grapes

6 Vegetables

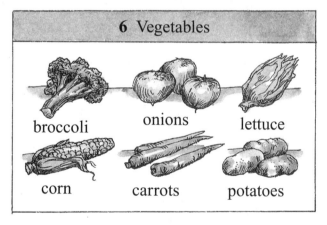

broccoli   onions   lettuce

corn   carrots   potatoes

Countable	Eat orang**es**. Orang**es** are good for you.
Uncountable	Drink orange juice. Orange juice is delicious.

▶ **WRITING** • *List six countable foods and six uncountable foods.*

Countable	**Uncountable**
Example: ___eggs___	Example: ___chicken___

Countable		Uncountable	
1._____	4._____	1._____	4._____
2._____	5._____	2._____	5._____
3._____	6._____	3._____	6._____

GRAMMAR • Countables and Uncountables

Page Summary

Grammar Countables and uncountables
Function Categorizing countables and uncountables

Warm-up

Ask students to turn back to page 105. Review what is in the kitchen as a way to present countables and uncountables. Say, *There are some apples in the bowl. Can you count them? (Yes.) There is some soda on the table. Can you count it? (No.)* (If students say *yes* about the soda, tell them that you can count the bottles of soda, but not the actual soda in the bottle.) Write two column heads on the board: *Countable* and *Uncountable*. Have the whole class work together to contribute to the lists. Common countables in the picture include: *cups, apples, flowers*. Common uncountables in the picture: *olive oil, soda, wine*. You can then expand the lists to other items, either those on the page or such everyday things as coffee, chocolate, hamburgers. Be sure to include a few examples such as (uncountable) *soda*, (countable) *cans of soda*, (uncountable) coffee, (countable) cups of coffee.

Grammar Notes

- Countable nouns can be counted. The singular is *a(n)* + noun or *one* + noun: *an apple, one apple*. The plural is noun + *s: apples*.
- Uncountable nouns do not use *a* or *one* in the singular, and there is no plural form: *milk / some milk*.

▶ BASIC FOOD GROUPS

🎧 *Look and listen. Listen and repeat.*

1. Play the recording (CD3, track 7) as students look and listen.
2. Play the recording (CD3, track 8) as students listen and repeat.

▶ WRITING

1. Have students work alone to list six countable and six uncountable foods.
2. Go over the answers with the class by making a two-column chart on the board. Label the columns *Countables* and *Uncountables*. Call students to present their lists. Write the items in the appropriate

column. Note: Individual lists will vary, but final answers on the board should be those in the answer key.

Answer Key

Answers will vary, but include the following:

Countables	Uncountables
apples	butter
oranges	corn oil
bananas	candy
peaches	milk
pears	yogurt
grapes	bread
onions	rice
carrots	pasta
potatoes	beef
	chicken
	fish
	broccoli
	lettuce
	corn

Expansion Activity

Divide the class into teams. Have the teams to line up at the board. Tell them you will say an item (use both countable and uncountable). The first team member must listen for the cue, and write an appropriate sentence. For example, say *apples*. A correct response is any sentence with *apples*: *There are three apples / There is an apple*. When the team member finishes writing, he or she goes to the end of the line. Continue until all students have a chance to write a sentence. Have the class read over the sentences and see which are correct. Teams get a point for each correct sentence.

GRAMMAR • Partitives

Page Summary

Grammar Partitives with nouns

Warm-up

Write on the board: *Yolanda is going to the supermarket.* Write on the board a list of things she needs: *water, cereal, rice, pasta, corn oil.* Say, *She needs* and read the list. Then say, *She needs some water. She needs two bottles of water.* Have students repeat. Then say, *cereal.* Cue students to respond: *She needs some cereal.* Then write on the board and say *boxes of.* Cue an individual student to respond: *She needs two boxes of cereal.* Have the whole class repeat. Continue with the other items, substituting the appropriate partitive *(bag of rice, box of pasta, bottle of corn oil).* Be sure that the students understand that it is OK to say *one box of rice, a box of rice,* or *two boxes of rice,* so that they know that partitives can be either plural or singular.

NOTE

You may want to point out to students that *bunch* is used for any fruit or vegetable that either grows with many parts on a stem or is sold tied up in a group: *a bunch of grapes, bananas,* or *carrots.*

Grammar Note

Partitives are used to refer to a specific quantity of an uncountable or countable noun *(a can of soup, a bag of potatoes)* or to a limited number of a countable noun *(a bunch of grapes).*

▶ 🎧*Listen and repeat.*

1. Have students look at the illustrations.
2. Play the recording (CD3, track 9) as students listen and repeat.

▶ **WRITING**

1. Have students work alone to fill in the blanks with the appropriate partitive.
2. Go over the answers with the class by calling on different students to read the phrases aloud.

Answer Key

1. a bottle of water
2. a bunch of grapes
3. a can of soup
4. a box of cereal
5. a jar of olives
6. a bag of cookies
7. a bottle of ketchup
8. a box of chocolates
9. a bunch of bananas
10. a jar of mustard
11. a can of beans
12. a bag of potatoes

Expansion Activity 1

Present other partitives: *a carton of (milk), a loaf of bread.* Have students form pairs. Tell them to play a game: *I went to the store. I bought. . . .* Tell them to take turns saying what they bought at the store. You can create variety in the game by giving them some shopping "guidelines," for example, *two bottles* (of something), + *three boxes* (of something), + *one bag* (of something). Write the guidelines on the board for students to refer to as they talk. Circulate to check for pronunciation, particularly the final *s* sound on *grapes, potatoes,* etc.

Expansion Activity 2

Play a listening game. Books are closed. Say a partitive *(a bottle of),* and call on one student to respond with an item on the page *(a bottle of ketchup).* Have the whole class repeat the response. Or say the item *(potatoes)* and call on one student to respond with the whole phrase: *a bag of potatoes.* Have the whole class repeat the response. For added challenge, expand to items not on this page.

GRAMMAR • Partitives

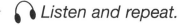 *Listen and repeat.*

| can | jar | bottle | bag | box |

WRITING • *Fill in the blanks with **bottle, jar, can, bag, box,** or **bunch**.*

1. a __bottle__ of water

2. a __bunch__ of grapes

3. a _____ of soup

4. a _____ of cereal

5. a _____ of olives

6. a _____ of cookies

7. a _____ of ketchup

8. a _____ of chocolates

9. a _____ of bananas

10. a _____ of mustard

11. a _____ of beans

12. a _____ of potatoes

There's a	bowl of soup on the table.
There are some	sandwiches on the table.
There's some	mustard next to the sandwiches.

▶ **NOTE** • We say **there's some mustard**, not ~~there are some mustard~~.
Mustard is uncountable.

▶ **WRITING** • *Complete the sentences using* **There's a, There are some,** *or* **There's some**.

1. <u>There's a</u> plate of spaghetti on the table.

2. <u>There's some</u> tomato sauce on the spaghetti.

3. _____ glasses on the table.

4. _____ bottle of water next to the glasses.

5. _____ fruit on the table.

6. _____ dishes on the table.

7. _____ cookbook on the counter.

8. _____ lettuce on the counter.

9. _____ tomatoes next to the lettuce.

10. _____ coffee on the stove.

▶ **PRACTICE** • *Read the sentences out loud.*

Page Summary

Grammar Countables/uncountables: affirmative
Function Describing food in a kitchen

Warm-up

Write *a/an* and *some* on the board. Talk about some objects in the room; for example, say, *There's a pencil on the desk. There are some books on the bookcase. There are some papers on the table. There is some water in the bottle.* Ask students, *What do you see?* Call on individual students. Cue students to elicit examples of both countables and uncountables. Write their responses on the board, and underline *a* or *some.* Have the whole class repeat.

Grammar Notes

- *There are some* is used with countables with the quantity is unspecified: *There are some books./There are (two) books.*
- *There's some* is used with uncountables when a partitive is not used: *There's some sauce* but *There are two cans of sauce.*
- *There's a* is used with both countables (*There's a banana*) and uncountables + a partitive (*There's a bottle of ketchup*).

▶ NOTE

1. Go over why *some mustard* is used (quantity is unspecified).
2. Present examples of when to use *There are some* (+ countable plural noun), *There's some* (+ uncountable noun), and *There's a* (+ countable singular noun).
3. Elicit examples of each from students.

▶ WRITING

1. Have students work alone to complete the sentences using *there's a, there are some,* or *there's some.*
2. Go over the answers with the class by calling on different students to read each sentence out loud.

Answer Key

1. There's a plate of spaghetti on the table.
2. There's some tomato sauce on the spaghetti.
3. There are some glasses on the table.
4. There's a bottle of water next to the glasses.
5. There's some fruit on the table.
6. There are some dishes on the table.
7. There's a cookbook on the counter.
8. There's some lettuce on the counter.
9. There are some tomatoes next to the lettuce.
10. There's some coffee on the stove.

▶ PRACTICE

Have students form pairs to read the sentences out loud.

Option: Read the sentences chorally with the class.

Expansion Activity

Have students turn back to page 105 and describe the illustration using the structures on page 110, for example, *There's a bowl of apples. There are some bottles on the table.* This can be done in pairs or as a whole-class activity. To do as a class, call on individual students to say their sentences.

Page Summary

Grammar Countables/uncountables: negative
Function Talking about food

Warm-up

Place some books, notebooks, pencils, and a variety of other classroom objects on a table. Point to the books and say, *There are some books.* Move the books off the table, and then say, *There aren't any books left.* Repeat this with several more objects, except pause for students to make the sentences with *There aren't any* instead. Then ask several students, one at a time, to come to the table and take your part.

Next, to help students understand that *there aren't any left/there aren't any more* are used in situations in which there's a finite quantity of something that gets used up, write the following examples on the board:

1. This morning I made some coffee. We drank it all. There isn't any left. There isn't any more coffee.
2. Teresa bought two apples. She ate two apples. There aren't any more apples. There aren't any apples left.

Then write part of a situation: *Jason bought three cookies. He ate them.* Elicit from students the following sentences: *There aren't any more cookies. There aren't any cookies left.*

To help students understand that "left" means "remaining," you do a few simple word problems. For example, say, *Melinda bought two apples. She ate one apple. How many apples are left?* Elicit the answer: *one.*

Grammar Notes

• *There isn't any* is used with uncountables and *There aren't any* is used with countables.
• *There isn't any soup* only means none exists (we don't know if there was any before), whereas *There isn't any soup left* or *There isn't any more soup* tells us that there was soup in the past but not now. (In items 3 and 7, the meaning is that none exist. For the other items, the implication is that the objects and people existed in the past, but don't now.)
• We can say either *There aren't any sandwiches left* or *There aren't any more sandwiches.* The meaning is the same.
• In this exercise, *chocolate* is uncountable, because it refers to chocolate ice cream. *Chocolates* are individual pieces of chocolate candy.

▶ WRITING

1. Write on the board:

    1. There isn't any soup.
    2. There isn't any soup left.
    3. There isn't any more soup.

Explain the difference in these sentences. (There is no difference between sentences 2 and 3; both imply that that there once was soup, but that has changed.) Then point to picture 3 and ask: *How is this different?* (There's no emphasis on change. We're only talking about the situation now.)

1. Go over the boxes at the top of the page. Write on the board examples for both countables and uncountables, using the negative.
2. Have students work alone to complete the sentences with *there isn't any* or *there aren't any.*
3. Go over the answers by calling on different students to read each sentence.

Answer Key

1. There aren't any bananas left.
2. There isn't any more milk.
3. There aren't any gas stations around here.
4. There aren't any roses left.
5. There isn't any water left.
6. There aren't any more cookies.
7. There aren't any jobs for clowns.
8. There isn't any more chocolate.
9. There aren't any good men left.

▶ 🎧 *Listen to the conversations.*

Play the recording (CD3, track 10) as students listen to check their work.

Expansion Activity

Books are closed. Do a dictation. Choose six sentence answers from the page that start *There isn't any* or *There aren't any* (use the answer key above). Say each sentence twice, pausing for students to write. Then have students open their books and check their work.

There isn't any	soup left.	There aren't any	more sandwiches.

▶ **WRITING** • *Complete with* **There isn't any** *or* **There aren't any**.

I'm sorry. <u>There aren't any</u> bananas left.

1. Susan and the grocer

Sorry, Jinx. <u>There isn't any</u> more milk.

2. Max and Jinx

_____ gas stations around here.

3. The mailman and Daisy

I'm sorry. _____ _____ roses left.

4. Miss Brady and Dallas

_____ water left.

5. Jane and Milton

_____ more cookies.

6. Jimmy and his mom

I'm sorry. _____ _____ jobs for clowns.

7. Bobo and Ms. Grimes

I'm sorry. _____ _____ more chocolate.

8. Lucy and Ben

_____ good men left.

9. Candy and Rosie

▶ 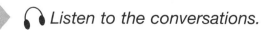 *Listen to the conversations.*

CARTOON STORY

STORY QUESTIONS

1. Where are Becky and her mother?
2. What does Becky want for dinner?
3. What do they need to make spaghetti?
4. Where is the tomato sauce?
5. Do they need any onions?
6. What about garlic?

DISCUSSION QUESTIONS

1. Where do you shop for food?
2. What foods do you buy there?
3. Do they have everything you need?
4. What fruits are in season now?
5. What's your favorite fruit?
6. How much is a bunch of bananas?

CARTOON STORY

Page Summary

Grammar Countables/uncountables
Function Shopping for food

Warm-up

Books are closed. Say, *Becky and her mother are at the grocery store. Becky wants spaghetti for dinner.* Find out who has eaten spaghetti, who likes it, and so on. Then ask, *What do they need to make spaghetti?* Elicit ideas and write them on the board. Help with vocabulary as needed.

Culture Note

In the cartoon story, Becky's mother calls her *sweetie.* This is a term of endearment similar to *honey.* Remind students of the term of endearment that Dallas used at the beginning of Chapter 3 when he was talking to Daisy: *My little angel.*

Pronunciation Tip

Point out that the *s* in *aisle* is silent, and that the *ai* is pronounced like *I.*

🎧 *Becky and her mother are shopping at the neighborhood market. Listen. Listen and practice.*

1. Direct students' attention to the illustrations. Ask them to describe Becky and her mother, where they are, and any details they notice.
2. Set the scene: Becky and her mother are shopping at the neighborhood market. They are buying what they need to make spaghetti for dinner.
3. Play the recording (CD3, track 11) as students listen.
4. Explain that *Absolutely!* is a strong *yes.* Point out Becky's body language in picture 6 (she shrugs her shoulders to indicate "I don't know" in response to her mother's question).
5. Play the recording (CD3, track 12) for students to practice the conversation.
6. Have students form pairs to practice the conversation.

STORY QUESTIONS

1. Tell students to take turns asking and answering the questions about the story.
2. Go over the answers by asking the questions of individual students.

Answer Key

1. They're at the neighborhood market.
2. She wants spaghetti for dinner.
3. They need some tomato sauce.
4. It's in aisle 6.
5. Yes, they need some onions. (Yes, they do.)
6. Yes, they need some garlic.

DISCUSSION QUESTIONS

Note: This can be done in pairs, small groups, or as a class.

1. Make sure students understand that they should answer with true information. Before they begin, check that they understand the phrase "in season" (question 4).
2. Have students discuss the questions.
3. If students work in pairs or small groups, call on individual students to report their answers to the class.

Answer Key

Answers will vary.

Expansion Activity 1

Have students form pairs. Tell them to decide on something they want to eat for dinner (or for a snack if they don't cook). Tell them to role-play going to the store to buy what they need, at least three things. When students are finished practicing, call on pairs to role-play for the class.

Expansion Activity 2

Have students form small groups. Tell them to take turns describing their favorite holiday food. Encourage group members to ask questions. Call on a few students to present their favorite foods to the class.

Page Summary

Grammar *Do you like*
Function Expressing preferences in food

Warm-up

On the board, list five or six common foods the students are familiar with, such as ice cream. Point to a food, and ask a student: *Do you like (ice cream)?* Continue with several more students, substituting different foods. Then have students ask each other the questions. Call on Student 1 to start. Student 1 asks Student 2 a question. Student 2 answers, and then asks a different question of Student 3. Students continue.

Grammar Notes

- The affirmative answers *Yes, of course* and *Yes, very much* can be used with both countables and uncountables. Likewise, the negative responses *No, not very much* and *No, not at all* can be used with both countables and uncountables.
- *It's okay* is used with uncountables, and *They're okay* with countables. These expressions are less enthusiastic than *Yes, of course* or *Yes, very much*.

Culture Note

Point out that the gesture "thumbs up" is a *yes* response, and that "thumbs down" is a *no* response.

▶ 🎧*Listen. Listen and practice.*

1. Play the recording (CD3, track 13) as students listen.
2. Play the recording (CD3, track 14) again for students to practice.

▶ **PAIR WORK**

1. Model the examples with student partners. Point out that *It's okay* is used with uncountables, and *They're*

okay with countables. Be sure to use examples of *No, not very much* and *No, not at all* with both countable and uncountable nouns, so that students understand it is grammatically acceptable to use either response. Model each, pausing for students to repeat.

2. Have students form pairs and talk about the foods on the page.
3. Call on several pairs to present their conversations to the class.

Expansion Activity 1

Compile a list on the board of other foods. Have students form pairs with new partners and have them practice similar conversations about these foods.

Expansion Activity 2

Work with the students to make a list on the board of six to eight foods one might find at a party. Have students form groups of about six. Tell them to imagine they are at a party. The foods listed on the board are on a table. Tell them to have similar conversations to those at the top of the page. Encourage them to switch partners in the group and ask different questions.

▶ 🎧 *Listen. Listen and practice.*

Do you like grapes?

Do you like strawberries?

Yes, very much.

How's the coffee?

They're okay.

It's delicious.

Do you like chocolate cake?

Yes, of course. Everyone likes chocolate cake.

Do you like cheese?

No, not very much.

▶ **PAIR WORK** • *Talk about these foods.*

No, not at all.

1. chicken
A: **Do you like chicken?**
B: **Yes, of course.**
   OR **It's okay.**
   OR **No, not very much.**

2. French fries
A: **Do you like French fries?**
B: **Yes, very much.**
   OR **They're okay.**
   OR **No, not at all.**

1. chicken

2. French fries

3. pizza

4. mushrooms

5. coffee

6. peanuts

7. cheese

8. hot dogs

LIFE SKILL • Reading Advertisements

Save $$ this week! JUNIOR'S MARKET $$ sale! $$

1. T-Bone STEAK $5.⁹⁰ lb.
2. AVOCADOS 99¢ each
3. Florida ORANGE JUICE 32 ounce carton $1.⁶⁹
4. Sponge MOPS $6.²⁵ each
5. TOMATOES 88¢ lb.
6. Sparkle Detergent $7.⁸⁵
7. Bandera BANANAS 39¢ lb.
8. Scrubb Toothbrushes ·selected types· $1.⁷⁹ each
9. In our bakery BREAD $2.⁹⁹

▶ **WRITING** • *Answer the questions about the items on sale this week at Junior's Market.*

1. How much is the T-bone steak? It's five dollars and ninety cents a pound.
2. How much are the avocados? They're ninety-nine cents each.
3. How much is the orange juice? It's a dollar sixty-nine.
4. How much are the sponge mops? _____
5. How much are the tomatoes? _____
6. How much is the detergent? _____
7. How much are the bananas? _____
8. How much are the toothbrushes? _____
9. How much is the bread? _____

▶ **PAIR WORK** • *Ask and answer questions about the items that are on sale this week.*

LIFE SKILL • Reading Advertisements

Page Summary

Grammar *How much is/are*
Function Shopping for food

Warm-up

Have students cover the bottom half of the page and discuss what items are on sale, using the phrases *There is, There are some, There aren't any*, and so on. Also ask them *yes/no* questions to elicit these phrases, for example, *Are there any apples on sale? Is there any cereal on sale?*

Grammar Notes

- *How much is* is used with singular items. *How much are* is used with plural items.
- Some foods have both a countable and an uncountable form. We can say either *How much <u>is</u> the T-bone <u>steak</u>?* or *How much <u>are</u> the T-bone <u>steaks</u>?*

Culture Notes

1. *For sale* means something is being sold. *On sale* means it is being sold at a special (lower) price.
2. For students who are only familiar with the metric system, 1 pound = 0.454 kilograms, 32 ounces = 1 quart = 0.946 liter. Meat is typically sold by the pound. Orange juice is sold in different units, such as pints (16 ounces), quarts (32 ounces), or half-gallons (64 ounces). This is also true for milk.
3. *"a (pound)"* and *"per (pound)"* are used interchangeably.

▶ WRITING

1. Explain the difference between *on sale* and *for sale*, and the measurement conversions (see Culture Notes). Make sure students understand that *each* means *one*.
2. Go over the example answer in the book. Point out the different ways the prices are given.
3. Have students work alone to answer the questions about items on sale this week.
4. Go over the answers with the class by asking the questions of individual students.

Answer Key

1. It's five dollars and ninety cents a pound.
2. They're ninety-nine cents each.
3. It's a dollar sixty-nine.
4. They're six dollars and twenty-five cents each.
5. They're eighty-eight cents a pound.
6. It's seven dollars and eighty-five cents.
7. They're thirty-nine cents a pound.
8. They're one dollar and seventy-nine cents each.
9. It's two dollars and ninety-nine cents.

▶ PAIR WORK

1. Tell students to ask and answer questions about the items on sale, switching parts.
2. Call on different pairs to present each question/answer exchange to the class.

Expansion Activity

Have students form pairs. Tell each pair to take a piece of paper, divide it into nine sections, and to make an advertisement similar to the one at the top of the page. Have them use other foods and items that are in this unit or earlier units. Tell them to make up their own prices. Encourage students who are comfortable drawing to make illustrations, but for those who aren't, it is enough to write the word for the item and the price. When pairs are finished, have two pairs form groups of four. Have a student from one pair say an item that is on sale on their paper, and a student from the other pair ask the price, for example:

A: *Apples.*
B: *How much are the apples?*
A: *They're $1.49 a pound.*

Have students in the pairs take turns and switch parts.

LIFE SKILL • Shopping for Food

Page Summary

Function Asking for a favor

Warm-up

Review commands as a way to introduce the expression *Can you do me a favor?* Say to a student, *Close the door, please.* Then say *(more polite), Can you do me a favor? Close the door please.* Continue with different students, substituting a variety of commands in the classroom. Then have a few students ask for a favor.

Culture Note

The expression *Can you do me a favor?* is a very common expression that is used when someone wants to soften a request. Often the conversation will start with *Can you do me a favor?* The response is often *Sure, (what do you need)?* If the other person wants to know what the favor is first, however, it might be just *What do you need?* Since Lucy and Grove know each other well, she expects him to say *Sure* here.

! *Pronunciation Tip*

The expression *Can you do me a favor?* is usually said in a gentle tone of voice since the speaker is making a request.

▶ ⌒ *Listen. Listen and practice.*

1. Play the recording (CD3, track 15) as students listen.
2. Play the recording (CD3, track 16) again for students to practice.
3. Have students form pairs to practice the conversation, switching parts.

▶ WRITING

1. Have students work alone to make a list of five things they need at the store. Tell them to write down things they really need, or make up five things. Also tell them to specify quantities (2 cans of soup) if this is important to them.
2. Circulate and help students write their lists.
3. Have students form pairs and practice their conversations.
4. Call on pairs to present their conversations to the class.

Expansion Activity 1

Have students form pairs and have similar conversations to the one on the page. Tell them to use the advertisement from Junior's Market on page 114, and to select at least three items to ask their partner to buy for them. Tell them to include at least two other items that are not on sale. Have them switch parts and repeat. Call on pairs to present for the class.

Expansion Activity 2

Have students form pairs to do a role play. One of them is a shopper. The other is an employee at the supermarket. Shoppers use their shopping lists from Writing. The shopper doesn't know where anything is, and must ask the supermarket employee where each item is located. The employee makes up the location, for example:

A: *I need some chicken soup.*
B: *It's in Aisle 5.*
A: *Thank you.*

LIFE SKILL • Shopping for Food

▶ 🎧 *Listen. Listen and practice.*

LUCY: Can you do me a favor?

GROVER: Sure.

LUCY: I need some things at the store.

GROVER: What do you need?

LUCY: Some apples, chicken soup and a quart of milk.

GROVER: Let's see…apples, chicken soup and a quart of milk.

LUCY: That's right.

GROVER: Anything else?

LUCY: Yes! Some laundry detergent. Get Sparkle. It's on sale.

GROVER: Okay.

LUCY: Thanks, Grover.

GROVER: No problem.

▶ **WRITING** • *Make a list of five things you need at the store. After you finish, pair up and have a conversation like the one above.*

LIFE SKILL • Ordering Fast Food

▶ 🎧 *Listen and repeat.*

MENU

1. hamburger

2. chicken sandwich

3. salad

4. French fries

DRINKS

5. soda

6. orange juice

7. coffee

8. milk

DESSERTS

9. ice cream

10. apple pie

11. chocolate cake

12. cookies

▶ 🎧 *Listen. Listen and practice.*

A: Can I help you?

B: Yes. I'd like a hamburger.

A: Do you want everything on it? Lettuce, onions and tomato?

B: Yes. I'd also like a coffee and some apple pie.

A: Okay. Anything else?

B: No, that's all.

▶ **PAIR WORK** • *Have similar conversations. Order anything from the menu above.*

LIFE SKILL • Ordering Fast Food

Page Summary

Function Ordering fast food

Warm-up

Books are closed. Write on the board: *Fast Food*. Ask students what fast food places they go to, and what their favorite fast foods are: *What is your favorite fast food?* Call on different students, or have students ask one another the questions.

Culture Notes

• If someone orders fast food inside the restaurant, the final question is typically something like, *Is that for here or to go?* If students will be in this situation, they should know to anticipate this question.
• The phrase *everything on it* can have different meanings depending on the type of fast food; for example, a hamburger with *everything on it* may have lettuce, onions, pickles, and tomato. A hot dog might have mustard, pickle relish, and onions. *Everything on it* is also referred to as *the works*. When in doubt, it's a good idea to check what *everything on it* includes.

Grammar Notes

• The phrase *a coffee* is a short form for the partitive *a cup of coffee* that is used in restaurant situations. In the same way, other items are treated as countable in a restaurant setting: I'd like *two orange juices* (instead of two glasses of orange juice), *three milks* (instead of three cartons of milk), *two fries* (instead of two orders of fries).
• In other contexts, such as visiting someone, the phrase *I'd like some (coffee)* is commonly used.
• In the conversation, the customer orders *some pie*. He could also say *apple pie*, which is a short form for *a piece of apple pie*. If he says *an apple pie*, he's asking for the entire pie rather than one piece.

▶ ⌒ *Listen and repeat.*

Play the recording (CD3, track 17) as students listen and repeat the menu items.

▶ ⌒ *Listen. Listen and practice.*

Play the recording (CD3, track 18) as students listen. Play the recording (CD3, track 19) as students listen and practice.

▶ **PAIR WORK**

1. Have students form pairs to have similar conversations. Have them to order anything from the menu in the book. Circulate and make sure they switch parts. Have them each order several times.
2. Call on pairs to present to the class.

Expansion Activity 1

Go over the partitives for the items on the menu: *a bag of French fries, a can of soda, a glass of orange juice, a cup of coffee, a carton of milk, a dish of ice cream, a slice of apple pie / chocolate cake* (or *a piece of apple pie / chocolate cake*). Have students practice saying what they want to order, using the partitives.

Expansion Activity 2

Work with the class to create a fast food menu on the board that includes items not on the menu in the book, for example, *pizza, tacos, apple juice, tea, chocolate ice cream,* or *strawberry ice cream*. Encourage students to add food items they like to order at fast food restaurants. Have students form pairs with new partners and have similar conversations to the one in the book, using the menu on the board.

TOPIC • Eating Habits

Page Summary

Function Talking about eating habits

Warm-up

Talk about different foods to get students thinking about the topic of eating habits, and to introduce some vocabulary they will encounter in the reading. Start: *I like fruit. I like bananas, I like apples. I don't like pears. What fruit do you like?* Indicate individual students to answer. Then say, *Every morning I drink (a cup of) coffee. What do you drink?* Call on different students to answer. Then write on the board, *I have a sweet tooth. I like candy, cookies, and ice cream. Who else has a sweet tooth? Raise your hand.* Write on the board, *nutritious.* Say, *I know candy isn't nutritious. It isn't good for me, but I like to eat candy. Fruit is nutritious.* Continue, *My favorite food is. . . . I love to eat it. What is your favorite food?* Call on individual students to answer.

Culture Note

Dallas is having a barbecue in his backyard. Barbecuing is very popular in the United States, especially in the summer.

▶ 🎧 *Listen and read.*

1. Have students cover the text for the top pictures, and look only at the illustrations. Ask them to describe what's happening. Ask questions: *Where are they? What are they eating?* Cue students to use the partitives: *a piece of cake, a can of soda, a glass of water.* After students finish with the top illustrations, have them uncover the bottom illustrations, keeping the text covered, and follow the procedure above.
2. Have students read along as you play the recording (CD3, track 20) or read the text out loud.
3. Check students' understanding by asking questions: *Where does Jimmy eat every day? What does he like to eat? Why doesn't Mrs. Wellington want dessert? Where is Dallas? What is he cooking? Why is he putting on hot sauce? Does Jane like meat? What does Jane like to eat?*
4. Ask students if they have any questions.

▶ QUESTIONS

1. Write on the board, *In your opinion.* Explain that this means they should answer the question with their own ideas. There isn't one correct answer. Encourage students to give reasons. To model this, start by saying, *In my opinion (Jane) is having the best lunch because* + (give your reason). Then ask a student the first question. Ask the student *why* he or she thought that person was having the best lunch.
2. Have students form pairs. Tell them to take turns asking and answering the questions.
3. Have pairs form groups of four and compare their ideas.
4. Call on individual students to answer the questions for the class.

Answer Key

Answers will vary.

Expansion Activity 1

Ask students to discuss their favorite restaurants. Write the following prompts on the board: *Name, Location, Type of Food, Size, Why it's my favorite:* Do an example together with the class (using a restaurant near the school, if possible). Write the responses on the board. It isn't necessary to use complete sentences. Then have students form pairs and discuss their favorite restaurants. After students finish, call on one or two students to tell the class about their favorite restaurant.

Expansion Activity 2

Have students conduct a class survey to find out what they eat for lunch. Divide the students into groups of about six. Ask them to find out what each person in the group has for lunch, and to have one person in each group take notes. Then call on one representative from each group to report to the class what group members eat. Compile the information on the board. Ask students to look at the results and make observations: *We like to eat (pizza). We don't like to eat (sandwiches). We like (bananas). We don't like (apples).*

TOPIC • Eating Habits

▶ 🎧 *Listen and read.*

Every day Jimmy eats lunch at the school cafeteria. Today he's having a cheeseburger with French fries, an apple, a cherry soda, and a piece of chocolate cake. Jimmy has a big appetite.

Mrs. Wellington likes to eat in fancy restaurants. Today she's having grilled salmon, string beans, and a baked potato for lunch. She doesn't want anything for dessert because she doesn't like sweets.

Dallas is having a barbecue in his backyard. He's cooking chicken and steaks on the grill. Dallas loves spicy food, so he puts hot sauce on everything.

Jane is a vegetarian, so she doesn't eat any meat. She thinks the most nutritious foods are fruits and vegetables. Right now, Jane is making a salad for lunch.

▶ **QUESTIONS**

1. In your opinion, who's having the best lunch today?
2. Is it more fun to eat at home, in a restaurant, or outdoors?
3. What kind of foods do you like?
4. Do you like spicy foods?
5. What foods are best for your health?
6. What foods are not good for you?
7. Do you like desserts? Do you have a "sweet tooth"?
8. What's your favorite dessert?

VOCABULARY

NOUNS

Fruit
grape(s)
strawberries

Vegetables
broccoli
corn
green bean(s)
lettuce
potato(es)
tomato(es)

Dairy foods
butter
cheese
milk
yogurt

Grains
bread
cereal
pasta
rice

Meat/Protein
beef
eggs
fish
nuts

Fast foods
French fries
hamburger
pizza

Beverages
milk
orange juice
soda

Desserts
apple pie
chocolate cake
cookies
ice cream

Other food items
baked potato
garlic
mushrooms
salad
salmon
steak
tomato sauce

Rooms
bathroom
bedroom
kitchen

Furniture
armchair
bed
dresser

Other
aisle
appetite
bag
barbecue
bottle
box
building
can
counter

detergent
elevator
every day
floor
fork
grill
jar
knife
mirror
pot

refrigerator
shelf
sink
sponge mop
spoon
stove
toothbrush
vacation
vegetarian

PRONOUNS
everyone
everything

VERBS
cook
get
hope
know
live
need
want

ADJECTIVES
delicious
fancy
nutritious
spicy

ADVERBS
also
then

EXPRESSIONS

Shopping
May I help you?
   Yes. How much is…?
Twenty-five dollars.
   I'll take it.

Ordering fast food
May I help you?
   Yes, I'd like…
Anything else?
   No, that's all.

Talking about likes and dislikes
Do you like…?
   Yes, of course.
   Yes, very much.
   No, not very much.
   No, not at all.

Asking for a favor
Can you do me a favor?
   Sure.

Asking for and giving an opinion
How do you like the view?
   It's fantastic!

Talking about quantity
There isn't any milk left.
There aren't any more cookies.

Do you want sugar in your coffee?
   Yes, a little.

Describing a condition
The elevator isn't working.

Other
I hope…
I'm glad…
What about…?
Absolutely.
Very good.
No problem.

VOCABULARY

The games below provide additional opportunities to use the vocabulary, grammar, and expressions presented in the unit. Before students play any of the games, have them review the lists of words and circle any words they don't know. Then put students into small groups and have them review the circled words together. Circulate so you can help in case no one in the group knows a particular word.

Game 1: Food Dictation

Draw a large square on the board, divide it into four sections, and label the sections: *Fruit and Vegetables, Dairy Foods, Meat/Protein, Grains*. Have students each take a piece of paper and copy what you drew. Choose items from the vocabulary list for each of these categories, for a total of 12 items. Say each word twice, pausing for students to write. Call on volunteers to write their answers on the board in the correct categories. Have the class read each word out loud.

Game 2: Shopping Trip

Tell students to imagine they have moved to a new home. They need new furniture. Have students form pairs. One partner is the shopper, and the other is the salesperson. Each shopper buys at least one item for three of the rooms. Have students take turns. If your class did the Expansion Activity on page 106, you can remind them of the expressions *This one is only* and *Oh, that's too expensive.* Encourage the "shopper" to end the exchange with the expression *I'll take it!*

Game 3: Timed Vocabulary

Have students turn back to page 117 and work in teams to identify as many food items as they can within three minutes. Each team makes a list, and the team with the most (correctly spelled!) items at the end of 3 minutes wins the game.

PRONUNCIATION

A 🎧 *Listen and repeat.*

Play the recording (CD3, track 21) as the students listen and repeat the words.

B 🎧 *Listen and repeat.*

1. Play the recording (CD3, track 22) as the students listen and repeat the words.
2. Have students form pairs to practice reading the words from Parts A and B out loud.

C 🎧 *Listen to each pair of words. Listen again and repeat.*

1. Have students look at each pair of words and listen as you play the recording (CD3, track 23).
2. Play the recording (CD3, track 24) again and have the students listen and repeat each word pair.

D 🎧 *Look at the words in Part C. Listen and circle the words you hear.*

1. Have students look at the words in Part C. Tell them to listen and circle the words they hear as you play the recording (CD3, track 25).
2. Have students form pairs and compare their answers.
3. Play the recording (CD3, track 25) again as a final check.
4. Go over the answers with the class by saying the number of an item; for example, *number 1*, and have the class say the letter of the correct word (*a* or *b*).

Answer Key

1. b. cup	4. a. lock
2. b. hut	5. a. dock
3. a. cot	6. b. hug

E 🎧 *Listen and practice.*

1. Play the recording (CD3, track 26) and have students listen and repeat each sentence.
2. Have students form pairs to practice reading the sentences out loud.

Expansion Activity 1

Dictate the 12 words from the page, mixing up the order. Say each word twice, pausing for students to write. Then write the answers on the board for students to check their work.

Expansion Activity 2

Listening. Put on the board *a: luck, b: lock*. Have students write the numbers 1–12 on a piece of paper. Read the words in Part C in random order. Students do not write whole words, but only *a* or *b* after each number to indicate the sound that they have heard. This exercise can be repeated several times. You can use a code to remember the order in which you have read the words; for example, the first time, go through the list backwards: start with 6 and read *hug, hog, duck, dock, luck, lock*, etc. (Students will write *b, a, b, a, b, a, . . .*) The next time through you can read the words in an order that will produce a, a, b, b, a, a, b, b, and so on.

PRONUNCIATION

▶ **A** 🎧 *Listen and repeat.*

/ɑ/

1. top	4. sloppy	7. want
2. box	5. hot	8. father
3. shop	6. pot	9. doctor

▶ **B** 🎧 *Listen and repeat.*

/ʌ/

1. under	4. some	7. lucky
2. lunch	5. funny	8. young
3. truck	6. money	9. mother

▶ **C** 🎧 *Listen to each pair of words. Listen again and repeat.*

 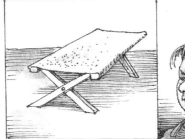

1. a. cop   b. cup

2. a. hot   b. hut

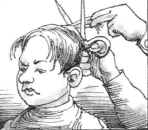 

3. a. cot   b. cut

4. a. lock   b. luck

5. a. dock   b. duck

6. a. hog   b. hug

▶ **D** 🎧 *Look at the words in Part C. Listen and* (circle) *the words you hear.*

▶ **E** 🎧 *Listen and practice.*

1. The young cop is at the bus stop.
2. Your ugly socks are under the box.
3. Does Bob want a cup of coffee?
4. My brother loves hot popcorn.
5. Mother and father are watching us.
6. A long hot summer is not funny.

GRAMMAR SUMMARY

THERE IS/THERE ARE Affirmative

There's (There is)	a dish	
There are	some cups	on the table.
There's (There is)	some cake	

Negative

There isn't (There is not)	a dish	
There aren't (There are not)	any cups	on the table.
There isn't (There is not)	any cake	

Interrogative

Is there	a dish	
Are there	any cups	on the table?
Is there	any cake	

Short Answers

	there is.			there isn't.
Yes,	there are.	No,		there aren't.
	there is.			there isn't.

TO LIKE Affirmative

He She	likes	
I You We They	like	chocolate.

Negative

He She	doesn't (does not)	
I You We They	don't (do not)	like chocolate.

Interrogative

Does	he she	
Do	I you we they	like chocolate?

Short Answers

	he she	does.		he she	doesn't.
Yes,	I you we they	do.	No,	I you we they	don't.

CONTENTS

Chapter

7

CARTOON STORY

Jason is going to a dating service called Grand Expectations. He has an appointment with the president, Lotta Bagonia. Listen. Listen and practice.

CARTOON STORY

Page Summary

Grammar Review
Function Describing daily habits and routines

The Teacher's Notes for the Cartoon Story continue on page 123.

The Teacher's Notes for the Cartoon Story continue on page 123.

Culture Notes

- In the cartoon story, Jason is going to a dating service to help him find a girlfriend. This type of dating service requires people to pay a membership fee. If he joins, the service will arrange dates with girls he is interested in.
- The question *What do you do for a living?* is one way to ask someone about their job.
- The phrase *I bet* is used when the speaker thinks something is likely to be true. In the cartoon story, Lotta thinks Jason must meet a lot of interesting people (thus her comment, *I bet you meet a lot of interesting people*). His response *All kinds* has two possible interpretations; one is a simple affirmative of *there are many kinds*. The other interpretation is that he is being sarcastic and is implying that he meets a wide range of people, from ordinary to strange.

Warm-up

Discuss free-time activities. Start by telling students a few things you do in your free time. For example, say, *In my free time I (read books)*. Write on the board the prompt, *What do you do in your free time?* Call on individual students to say what they like to do. Then call on a few students to ask other students what they like to do in their free time.

! Pronunciation Tip

The phrase *what do you do* is linked together in conversation: *whuddyaDO.*

Grammar Notes

- In the sentence *Women love men who are good dancers*, the adjective clause *who are good dancers* describes *men*. It answers the question *What kind of men? (good dancers)*, and identifies which men women love. It starts with the relative pronoun *who*.

- Because students haven't studied relative clauses yet, in this lesson you can just mention that the clause functions in a similar way to adjectives they already know. One way to present this is to write on the board the following phrases: *tall men, strong men, men who are good dancers*. Point to each phrase and ask the question: *What kind of men? (tall men / men who are tall).*

▶ 🎧 *Jason is going to a dating service called Grand Expectations. He has an appointment with the president, Lotta Bagonia. Listen and practice.*

1. Direct students' attention to the illustrations. Set the scene: *This is Jason and this is Lotta. Jason has an appointment with Lotta at a dating service called Grand Expectations. Lotta is the president.* Ask them to describe the situation. *Where are they? What are they wearing? What are they doing?* Encourage students to describe what they see using their own words.
2. Play the recording (CD3, track 27) as students listen.
3. Write on the board the following phrases: *friendly women, intelligent women*. Point to each phrase and ask the question: *What kind of women?* Elicit from the class: *Women who are friendly. Women who are intelligent.* Then write on the board: *good dancers*. Ask, *What kind of women does Jason like?* Elicit from the class, *Women who are good dancers.*
4. Play the recording (CD3, track 28) for students to practice the conversation.
5. Have students form pairs to practice the conversation.

▶ QUESTIONS

1. Have students form pairs. Tell them to take turns asking and answering the questions.
2. Then go over the answers with the class by asking the questions of individual students.

CARTOON STORY

Answer Key

1. He's looking for a girlfriend.
2. She's the president of Grand Expectations.
3. Yes, he does. Wow! They look nice.
4. He's a bank teller.
5. He plays the piano and he takes dance lessons.
6. He likes classical music.
7. He takes dancing lessons at the Rainbow Studio.
8. He likes women who are friendly and intelligent.
9. He doesn't become a member of Grand Expectations because it's too expensive.

Expansion Activity 1

Have students each write down three interests they have. Then give them 5 minutes to walk around the room, talk to as many classmates as they can, and see if they can find anyone else who has the same interests. Tell them to ask the questions: (1) *What do you do in your free time?* (2) *What other interests do you have?* After 5 minutes, have students return to their seats. Call on students to tell the class what they learned. Model an example: *I like to play tennis. Teresa likes to play tennis.* (Have students review Chapter 6, page 117, for the third person singular as needed.)

Expansion Activity 2

Write the following exchange on the board:

A: *I need a chair for my living room. How much is that one?*
B: *($1,000)*
A: *($1,000)!*
B: *Where are you going?*
A: *I don't need a chair for my living room that much!*

Review furniture and objects used in the kitchen. With students, compile a list on the board. Have students form pairs and practice the exchange above, substituting different items. Encourage them to use the list on the board or other objects they know. Remind students of the importance of intonation to express disbelief: *one thousand DOLLars!* and *I don't need a chair THAT much!* Call on pairs to present to the class.

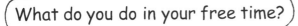

▶ **QUESTIONS**

1. Why is Jason going to a dating service?
2. Who is Lotta Bagonia?
3. Does Jason like the pictures of the new members? What does he say?
4. What does Jason do for a living?
5. What does he do in his free time?
6. What kind of music does Jason like?
7. Where does Jason take dancing lessons?
8. What kind of women does Jason like?
9. Does Jason become a member of Grand Expectations? Why or why not?

GRAMMAR • Simple Present Tense

▶ 🎧 *Listen as Luis talks about his daily routine. Listen and repeat.*

GRAMMAR • Simple Present Tense

Page Summary

Grammar Simple present tense
Function Describing daily habits and routines

Warm-up

To familiarize students with the grammar point, talk about a few of your own daily habits, for example, say: *I take the bus to school.* Then ask several students: *How do you get to school?* Then say, *I have dinner at (7 o'clock).* Then ask several students: *What time do you have dinner?* Continue with a couple more activities: *I go to bed* or *I go home.*

Grammar Notes

- The simple present is used here to talk about something that is done regularly. For example, *I get up at 6 o'clock* means every day.
- In item 9, the sentence is *I come home at 4 o'clock.* Students often confuse *come* and *go.* *I come home at 4 o'clock* means *I arrive home.* *I go home at 4 o'clock* means *I leave (school) at 4 o'clock.* It isn't necessary to present this now, but students who have studied English before may ask about it.

🎧 *Listen as Luis talks about his daily routine. Listen and repeat.*

1. Have students look at the illustrations.
2. Set the scene: Luis is talking about his daily routine.
3. Play the recording (CD3, track 29) as students listen.
4. Play the recording (CD3, track 30) as students listen and repeat.
5. Have students form pairs and read the sentences out loud.

Expansion Activity 1

Have students form pairs. Tell them to use the illustrations to talk about their own routines. For example, one partner points to picture 1 and says: *I get up at 7 o'clock.* The other partner says the same sentence with his or her own information. Pairs continue. Note: Tell students to only talk about what they do. If they don't do something Luis does (for example, eat breakfast), tell them to skip it. This will avoid introducing the negative. In addition, encourage them to change any details to keep an affirmative sentence, for example, *I take the train to school* instead of *bus.*

Expansion Activity 2

Have students form small groups. Tell them to take turns pantomiming one of the activities on the page. One student pantomimes, and the rest of the group guesses the activity. The speakers will need to substitute *you* for *I.* Write an example on the board: *You get up.* Note: If a student pantomimes eating, 4, 8, and 11 are all appropriate responses.

GRAMMAR • Simple Present Tense

Page Summary

Grammar Simple present tense
Function Describing daily habits and routines

Warm-up

To familiarize students with the grammar, ask individual students questions about their daily routines, for example, *When do you get home? When do you leave home? Where do you study? Where do you eat lunch?* Then say, *In the evening, I like to (watch TV).* Ask a couple of students, *What do you like to do in the evening?*

❗ *Pronunciation Tip*

The stress in the question changes according to what the speaker wants to emphasize. For example, if the speaker says *WHERE do you have lunch?* the focus is on the location. If the speakers says *Where do you have LUNCH?* the focus is on the meal.

▶ 🎧 *Listen. Listen and practice.*

1. Have students look at the illustration and describe what they see. They can identify objects *(the sun, a car).* They can also say what the people are doing. *(She's sitting. He's driving.)*
2. Play the recording (CD3, track 31) as students listen.
3. Play the recording (CD3, track 32) as students listen and practice.
4. Have students form pairs and practice the conversations.

▶ WRITING

1. Have students work alone to answer the questions about their daily routines, using complete sentences.
2. On the board, model how to answer the first question. Some students might not eat breakfast or lunch. Since *don't* will be introduced on page 126, you can put the negative form on the board as well: *I don't eat breakfast. I don't eat lunch.*
3. Go around the classroom and check as students write their answers.

▶ PAIR WORK

1. Have students form pairs and take turns asking five questions about their daily routines. Encourage students to answer with true information.
2. Call on pairs to present the exchanges to the class.

Expansion Activity

Ask students to work alone to make up a character and write information about what the character does each day. Have them write six short sentences, modeled after the ones on pages 124 and 125. To make it easier for them to come up with the information, suggest that they pick an occupation, and use that as a basis for their sentences; for example, *I am a doctor. I get up very early. I eat lunch at the hospital*, and so on. (Review occupations as needed.) After students finish writing, have them form pairs. Tell them to take turns asking about their daily routines. Students answer using the information they made up for their character.

GRAMMAR • Simple Present Tense

▶ 🎧 *Listen. Listen and practice.*

When do you get up in the morning?

I get up at six-thirty.

How do you get to work?

I drive to work.

1

2

Where do you have lunch?

I have lunch at Al's Cafe.

AL'S CAFE

What do you do in the evening?

I listen to music.

3

4

▶ **WRITING** • *Answer the following questions about your daily routine.*

1. When do you get up in the morning? <u>I get up at...</u>

2. What do you have for breakfast?_____

3. When do you leave the house? _____

4. How do you get to school/work?_____

5. Where do you have lunch?_____

6. When do you come home? _____

7. What do you do in the evening? _____

8. When do you go to bed? _____

▶ **PAIR WORK** • *Ask your partner five questions about his or her daily routine.*

GRAMMAR • Simple Present Tense

▶ 🎧 *Look and listen. Listen again and repeat.*

1. I get up early in the morning. I don't sleep late.

2. I drive to work. I don't take the bus.

3. I walk to work. I don't have a car.

4. I work fast. I don't waste time.

5. I exercise every day. I don't sit in front of a TV.

6. I only eat foods that are good for me. I don't like junk food.

Page Summary

Grammar Simple present tense; affirmative and negative
Function Describing daily habits and routines
The Teacher's Notes for this activity continue on page T127.

Warm-up

Talk about your daily habits. Say what you do and what you don't do, for example, *I drink coffee in the morning. I don't drink tea. I eat cereal for breakfast. I don't eat eggs.* Then ask several students: *What do you eat for breakfast?* Have them tell you one thing they eat and one thing they don't eat. Continue with other activities you do thoughout the day. After you model what you do and what you don't do, call on students to make their own sentences. Put one affirmative and one negative sentence on the board for students to refer back to as they do the exercise in the book.

Culture Notes

• The expression *sit in front of the TV* means to watch a lot of TV. The expression *work around the house* means to do chores.
• Discount stores are popular. Many people don't like to pay full price. If there is a local discount store that your students are familiar with, use it as an example.

Grammar Notes

• *Do* is a helping verb here. The negative is formed with the helping verb: *I don't have a car.* You can clarify this by using the example of *do homework* (from page 124): *I do homework, I don't do homework,* putting both sentences on the board and underlining the main verb *do* and the helping verb *don't* with different colors of chalk.

• In this activity, *don't* is used to present contrasting ideas of what I do and what I don't do, for example, *I get up early. I don't sleep late.* Each pair of sentences follows this pattern.

⌒⍛ Look and listen. Listen again and repeat.

1. Have students look at the illustrations.
2. Play the recording (CD3, track 33) as students look and listen.
3. Play the recording (CD3, track 34) as students listen and repeat.

▶ PRACTICE

1. Have students form pairs to practice reading the statements on pages 126 and 127.
2. Call on individual students to read the sentences to the class.

▶ PAIR WORK

1. Have students look at the grammar boxes. Write on the board: *I get up early* and *Do you get up early?* Point out the word order in the question. Also point out that in the short answer, only the helping verb is used: *Yes, I do./No, I don't.*
2. Model the example with a student partner.
3. Have students form pairs. Tell them to ask and answer the questions. Encourage them to use true information about themselves.
4. Call on different pairs to present some of the conversations to the class.

Expansion Activity 1

Write on the board the following list of expressions: *go to bed late, drink coffee, go dancing, play tennis, go to the park, like movies, go to concerts, work on the weekend.* Have students form pairs with new partners. Tell them to continue Pair Work, using the activities on the board instead. In addition, tell students to continue asking questions when they have finished the list, substituting their own ideas. After students finish practicing, call on a few pairs to present to the class.

Expansion Activity 2

Write on the board: *work around the house.* Elicit from students examples of work people might do around the house on a weekend *(do laundry, wash dishes, clean the house, cut the grass).* Compile a list on the board. Help with vocabulary as needed. Then have students form pairs and ask and answer about these activities. When students have finished, take a quick class poll. Ask: *Who does laundry? Raise your hand.* Model raising your hand.

"I shop at discount stores. I don't spend a lot of money on clothes."

"I study after school. I don't hang out with my friends."

"I play the piano in my free time. I don't play cards with my friends."

"I relax on the weekend. I don't work around the house."

▶ **PRACTICE** • *Read out loud the statements of each character on pages 126-127.*

Yes/No Question	Short Answers	
Do you get up early?	Yes, I do.	No, I don't.

▶ **PAIR WORK** • *Ask and answer questions.*

     play the piano

A: **Do you play the piano?**

B: **Yes, I do.** OR **No, I don't.**

1. get up early
2. walk to school/work
3. sleep late on Saturday
4. exercise every day
5. eat junk food
6. like French fries
7. study a lot
8. relax on the weekend
9. watch a lot of TV

GRAMMAR • Simple Present Tense

Where	does	he she	live? work?		He She	lives works	in Hollywood.		Irregular: go - goes

▶ 🎧 *Listen. Listen and repeat.*

▶ **PAIR WORK** • *Practice the conversations.*

▶ **WRITING** • *Fill in the answers. Then read the conversations aloud.*

Who does Grover talk to every day?

He talks to his wife.

①

What street does Jane live on?

②

When does Carlos get up in the morning?

③

How does Suzi get to school?

④

GRAMMAR • Simple Present Tense

Page Summary

Grammar Simple present tense third person singular; *Wh-* questions
Function Asking about and describing daily habits and routines
The Teacher's Notes for this activity continue on page T129.

The Teacher's Notes for this activity continue on page T129.

Warm-up

Talk about daily habits. Ask a female student: *When do you get up?* Write her response on the board: *I get up at (6 o'clock).* Underline the subject *(I)* and the verb *(get up).* Next, write on the board: *When does she get up?* and *She gets up at 6 o'clock.* Underline *does (she) get up* and *She gets up.* Model the question and the answer, pausing for the class to repeat. Repeat this procedure with a male student, substituting the question *When do you eat dinner?* and *he* in the examples you write on the board. Continue with two more students. Then have students do a chain question-and-answer activity. Student 1 asks a question of Student 2 and Student 2 answers. Then you indicate a student (Student 3) to report what Student 2 said. Student 3 asks the next question of someone he or she chooses. For each exchange, you indicate Student 3. Before students begin, call on students to model the following example. (For the example, tell Student 1 which question to ask). After students model the example, make sure they understand that Student 3 makes up the question to ask.

S1: *Where do you eat lunch, (S2)?*
S2: *I eat lunch at school.*
S3: *She eats lunch at school.*
S3: *When do you come home, (S4)?*

Grammar Notes

• In British English people live *in* a street. In American English people live *on* a street.
• In American English a person lives *on* a street, but *in* a place (a building, a city, a town, a state). *He lives in New York in an apartment building on Madison Avenue.*
• Some of the words on pages 128 and 129 frequently are used together. If students learn the words as set combinations, they will develop more fluency, for example, *talk to, get up at, live on.*

Listen. Listen and repeat.

1. Have students look at the illustrations.
2. Play the recording (CD3, track 35) as students look and listen.
3. Play the recording (CD3, track 36) for students to repeat.

PAIR WORK

1. Have students form pairs to practice the conversations. Remind them to switch parts.
2. Call on different pairs to present each conversation for the class.

WRITING

1. Remind students how to form *Wh-* questions. Write on the board: *He wants a hamburger.* Circle the *s* at the end of *wants*, draw an arrow to the beginning of the sentence, write *Does*, erase the *s* at the end of *wants*, and cross out *hamburger* to show how the *Wh-* question is formed.
2. Have students work alone to answer the questions.
3. Have students form pairs to compare answers.
4. Play the recording (CD3, track 35) or read the conversations out loud again.
5. Go over the answers by calling on pairs to say each conversation. Make sure students are aware of the spelling for *go/goes.*

Answer Key

1. He talks to his wife.
2. She lives on Hill Street.
3. He gets up at 7 o'clock.
4. She walks to school.
5. He wants a hamburger.
6. She buys groceries at Junior's market.
7. He likes country music.
8. He has dinner at 6 o'clock.
9. She goes to bed at 10 o'clock.

▶ **PAIR WORK**

1. Have students form pairs and ask each other the same questions.
2. Model the example with a student partner. Remind students about the difference in the grammar (*Who do you talk to* versus *Who does he talk to*). Encourage students to make up information if necessary, for example, someone they talk to every day.
3. Call on pairs to present to the class.

Expansion Activity

Work together with the whole class. Have students answer the questions on pages 128 and 129, except this time, the questions are about Jason, for example, *Who does Jason talk to every day? What street does Jason live on?* and so on. Tell students to make up information. Ask each question (in question 4, substitute *dance school* for *school*), and call on a student to answer. Write the answer on the board. When you are finished, have the students read the sentences out loud. Then have students form pairs and take turns asking questions about Jason, using the answers on the board. Note: The main purpose here is to give the students an opportunity to use their imaginations while they practice the grammar. If one student can't come up with an idea (for example, where Jason lives), encourage other students to help out.

What does Jimmy want for lunch?

⑤

Where does Lucy buy groceries?

Junior's Market

⑥

What kind of music does Dallas like?

Country Music at Montana's

⑦

When does Milton have dinner?

⑧

When does Maria go to bed?

⑨

▶ **PAIR WORK** • *Ask each other the same questions.*

A: **Who do you talk to every day?**

B: **I talk to my sister.**

GRAMMAR • Simple Present Tense

Affirmative		
He She	walks	to school every day.

Negative		
He She	doesn't (does not)	take the bus.

Irregular verbs:
do - does
watch - watches
relax - relaxes

▶ **WRITING** • *Write affirmative and negative sentences about the people in the pictures. After you finish, read the sentences out loud.*

(1) Ellen Grayson (work) __works__ as a receptionist at an employment agency. (2) She (like) __doesn't like__ her job because it's boring. (3) She (do) _____ the same thing every day. (4) Ellen's problem is that she (have) _____ any fun. (5) She really (need) _____ a vacation.

It's Saturday afternoon. (1) Ernie is happy because he (work) _____ on Saturdays. (2) He (stay) _____ home and (watch) _____ TV all day. (3) Ernie's wife is upset with him because he (help) _____ her with the housework. (4) She (think) _____ Ernie is lazy.

(1) Jane Doe (live) _____ in a small house on Hill Street. (2) Her house (have) _____ a big yard, but it (have) _____ a nice porch. (3) Every day Jane (relax) _____ on the porch with her cats. (4) Jane (love) _____ cats, but she (like) _____ dogs very much.

▶ **DISCUSSION** • *Do these people remind you of anyone you know — a friend, a neighbor, or a member of your family? What do they have in common?*

Example: **"Ellen reminds me of my neighbor. He also works in an office, and he doesn't like his job."**

GRAMMAR • Simple Present Tense

Page Summary

Grammar Simple present tense third person singular; affirmative and negative
Function Talking about daily habits and routines

Warm-up

Ask students to turn back to page 128. Say: *Jane lives on Hill Street. She doesn't live on Main Street.* Next say: *Carlos gets up at 7 o'clock. He doesn't get up at 6 o'clock.* Pause for students to repeat. Then say: *Suzi walks to school. She doesn't . . .* and then call on a student to finish the sentence, for example, *She doesn't take the bus.* Then write on the board: *He wants / He doesn't want.* Call on a student and say: *Jimmy.* Elicit the sentence: *He wants a hamburger. He doesn't want (pizza).* Next, write: *He has / he doesn't have.* Call on a student and say: *Milton.* Elicit from that student: *He has dinner at 6 o'clock.* Call on another student and say: *He doesn't have. . . .* Elicit from that student: *He doesn't have dinner at (7 o'clock).*

Grammar Notes

• The contracted form *(doesn't)* is more common than the full form *(does not)*, especially in spoken English.
• If students ask about the spelling differences *(-s* versus *-es* for third person singular), you may want to mention the rules: With most regular verbs add *-s*, but with those ending in *-sh*, *-ch*, *-ss*, and *-x*, add *-es*: *pushes, watches, passes, relaxes.*

Pronunciation Tip
The *t* sound at the end of *doesn't* is often reduced and barely heard: *He doesnhav fun.*

▶ WRITING

1. Go over the examples in the boxes at the top of the page. Read the sentences and have students repeat. Point out the verbs that take *-es*, not *-s*.
2. Have students work alone to write affirmative and negative sentences about the people in the pictures. Encourage them to use contractions.
3. Have students form pairs and read the sentences out loud.
4. Go over the answers by calling on students to read for the class.

Answer Key

1. works	1. doesn't	1. lives
2. doesn't like	work	2. doesn't have, has
3. does	2. stays, watches	3. relaxes
4. doesn't have	3. doesn't help	4. loves, doesn't like
5. needs	4. thinks	

▶ DISCUSSION

1. Present the discussion questions.
2. To make sure students understand the phrase *have in common*, give an example. Write on the board: *Jane loves cats. My sister loves cats.* Say, *They love cats. They have this in common.*
3. Have students look at the example at the bottom of the page. Then ask, *What do Ellen and the neighbor have in common? (They work in an office and they don't like their jobs.)*
4. Have students form pairs or small groups to have their discussion.
5. After students are finished, call on a few students to report on their discussion.

Expansion Activity
Books are closed. Do a dictation. Dictate the description of Jane Doe. Say each sentence twice, pausing for students to write. Then read the whole paragraph through slowly, pausing for students to write and make corrections. Have students form pairs to compare what they wrote. Call on one student at a time to read out loud a sentence in the paragraph. As a final check, have students open their books and check their work.

Page Summary

Grammar Simple present tense third person singular; *yes/no* questions
Function Talking about daily habits and routines

Warm-up

Do a quick review of *to have*, third person singular, *yes / no* questions (Chapter 5). Ask Student A: *Does (Student B) have a green backpack?* Student A answers: *Yes, he (she) does* or *No, he (she) doesn't.* Say (to Student A): *Ask (Student B) about (Student C).* Continue around the room, encouraging students to ask and answer as quickly as possible.

▶ PAIR WORK

1. If necessary, review the process for forming *yes/no* questions. Write on the board: *Carlos plays the guitar.* Draw a circle around the *s* in *plays*, draw an arrow to the beginning of the sentence, draw a blank, and say *How do we make the yes/no question?* Write *does* in the blank, and erase the *s* at the end of *plays.*

2. Have students work in pairs to ask and answer the questions about the pictures. Remind them that if they give a negative answer, they need to add another sentence to correct the information on the page.

3. Go over the answers with the class by calling on pairs to read the conversations out loud.

Option: Have students cover the text and repeat the activity, looking only at the pictures.

Answer Key

1. B: No, she doesn't.
   She hates her job.
2. B: Yes, he does.
3. B: Yes, she does.
4. B: No, he doesn't.
   He takes the bus.
5. B: No, he doesn't.
   He watches television.
6. B: Yes, she does.
7. B: No, she doesn't.
   She drives a big car.
8. B: Yes, he does.
9. B: No, he doesn't.
   He wants a piano.

Expansion Activity

Have the class turn back to the cartoon story on page 122. Review the story by asking *yes/no* questions that will elicit short answers. If the answer is negative, tell students to make the correction. *Does Jason want a girlfriend? (Yes, he does.) Does Jason like the pictures of the girls? (Yes, he does.) Does Jason work at a hospital? (No, he doesn't. He works at a bank.) Does he meet boring people? (No, he doesn't. He meets interesting people.) Does Jason play the guitar? (No, he doesn't. He plays the piano.) Does Lotta think she can find a girl for Jason? (Yes, she does.) Does Jason like to dance? (Yes, he does.) Does Jason leave? (Yes, he does.)*

GRAMMAR • Simple Present Tense

Yes/No Question		
Does	he she	work on Saturday?

Short Answers					
Yes,	he she	does.	No,	he she	doesn't.

▶ **PAIR WORK** • *Ask and answer questions.*

1. A: **Does Ellen like her job?**
   B: **No, she doesn't. She hates her job.**

2. A: **Does Mr. Wick need a secretary?**
   B: **Yes, he does.**

3. Does Amy study at the library after school?

4. Does Milton drive to work?

5. Does Ernie work on Saturdays?

6. Does Jane shop at discount stores?

7. Does Lulu drive a small car?

8. Does Carlos play the guitar?

9. Does Ken want a guitar?

GRAMMAR • Simple Present Tense

Where	do	they	live? work?

They	live work	in Hollywood.

▶ 🎧 *Listen. Listen and repeat.*

▶ **PAIR WORK** • *Practice the conversations.*

▶ **WRITING** • *Fill in the answers.*
Then read the conversations aloud.

Where do Lisa and her friends hang out?

They hang out at the mall.

①

Where do the boys play baseball?

②

Where do Jack and Jill study after school?

③

Where do Lucy and Grover shop?

④

GRAMMAR • Simple Present Tense

Page Summary

Grammar Simple present tense and third person plural; *Where*
Function Talking about popular entertainment
The Teacher's Notes for this activity continue on page T133.

Warm-up

Talk about what the students do for entertainment. Call on individual students and ask: *What do you do in your free time?* Write their activities on the board, for example, *go to the movies.* Elicit answers from six students. Then ask the first student where he or she does the activity, for example, *Where do you go to the movies?* After the student responds, ask the second student where he or she does the activity. Then call on different students to ask Students 3–6 about where they do their activities. Next, ask students questions about a local sports team in order to elicit the pronoun *they*, for example, *Where do they play their games?*

Culture Note

In picture 1, Lisa and her friends *hang out* at the mall. *Hang out* is an informal phrasal verb. It means to spend a lot of time at a particular place, or with certain people. Sometimes it means that the people are just relaxing and being together and not doing anything in particular (*Let's hang out at the mall on Saturday*). Other times, there may be an activity (*Let's hang out and watch a movie on Saturday night*). The question *Who do you hang out with?* means *Who are you friends with?*

Pronunciation Tip

The strongest stress in the response is on the location because the question is about *where* something is, for example, *They play baseball at the PARK.*

Listen. Listen and repeat.

1. Have students look at the illustrations and describe what they see. They can identify objects (*books, groceries*). They can also say what the people are doing. (*They're standing at the mall. He's reading a book at the library.*)

2. Play the recording (CD3, track 37) as students look and listen.
3. Play the recording (CD3, track 38) for students to repeat.

▶ PAIR WORK

1. Have students form pairs to practice the conversations.
2. Tell them to switch parts and repeat.

▶ WRITING

1. Have students work alone to answer the questions.
2. Go over the answers by calling on different pairs to read each conversation out loud.

Answer Key

1. They hang out at the mall.
2. They play baseball at the park.
3. They study at the library.
4. They shop at Junior's Market.
5. They work at the post office.
6. They eat lunch at the cafeteria.
7. They exercise at Bruno's gym.
8. They go dancing at the palace.
9. They have picnics at the beach.

▶ GROUP WORK

1. Have students form small groups.
2. Present the example. Make sure students understand they are to ask each other the questions and to answer using true information.
3. Tell students to take turns asking the questions. One student can ask the same question of all group members, or one student can choose another student to ask each of the questions.
4. When groups are finished, call on individual students to report to the class something they learned about the other group members, for example, *Tomas hangs out downtown. He studies at home.*

Expansion Activity 1

Ask students to work alone and to use their own answers from Group Work to write sentences about what they do. When they are finished, have students form pairs and read each other's sentences. Encourage students to make suggestions and corrections if something isn't clear.

Expansion Activity 2

Ask the class to look at picture 9 again: *Where do people have picnics in the summer?* Have a class discussion about picnics where you live. *Do people picnic? What kind of food do people like to take? Where do they go? What are the favorite places to go? Who has been to these places? What did they do there besides eat?*

Where do these people work?

5

Where do Becky and Jimmy eat lunch?

6

Where do Ken and Suzi exercise?

7

Where do Carlos and Maria go dancing?

8

Where do people have picnics in the summer?

9

▶ **GROUP WORK** • *Ask each other where you hang out, eat lunch, study, exercise, shop.*
A: **Where do you hang out?** B: **I hang out at the Amazon Cafe. I go there with my friends.**

GRAMMAR • Simple Present Tense

Affirmative	Negative
They listen to classical music.	They don't like rock music.

▶ **WRITING** • *Write affirmative and negative sentences about Mr. and Mrs. Grand. After you finish, read the sentences out loud.*

1. (live in a big house) <u>They live in a big house.</u>

2. (worry about money) <u>They don't worry about money.</u>

3. (have a lot of employees) _____

4. (work in the garden) _____

5. (have a big car) _____

6. (take the bus) _____

7. (love fine food) _____

8. (like fast food) _____

9. (wear expensive clothes) _____

10. (shop at discount stores) _____

GRAMMAR • Simple Present Tense

Page Summary

Grammar Simple present tense, third person plural: affirmative and negative sentences
Function Talking about habits and routines

Warm-up

Books are closed. Write on the board: *They work at the post office. They don't work at the mall.* Read the sentences out loud and have the class repeat. Write another example: *They study at the library. They don't study at the post office.* Read the sentences out loud and have the class repeat. Then write: *They eat lunch at home.* Call on an individual student to make the negative sentence *They don't eat at the mall.* Write it on the board, and have the whole class say it. To reinforce that the form of the main verb doesn't change for third person plural, write an example with the third person singular *(He likes pizza/He doesn't like pizza)* and with the third person plural *(They like pizza/They don't like pizza).* Have students read the sentences out loud.

Grammar Notes

- The form of the third person plural affirmative is *They* + base form of main verb.
- The form of the third person plural negative is *They + do not (don't)* + base form of main verb.

Culture Notes

- In picture 3, the sentence is *They have a lot of employees.* In the illustration we see their driver (chauffeur), their gardeners, a musician who plays music while they dine, and their server (waiter). We can assume there is also a chef in the kitchen who prepares the food.
- In picture 7, *fine food* refers to gourmet food.
- In picture 10, the implication is that they don't shop at discount stores because they are rich and they don't need to. However, many people, rich or poor, buy some items at discount stores.

▶ WRITING

1. Have students work alone to write their sentences.
2. Go over the answers by calling on different students to read the sentences out loud.

Option: First have students compare answers in pairs. Then go over them as a class.

Answer Key

1. They live in a big house.
2. They don't worry about money.
3. They have a lot of employees.
4. They don't work in the garden.
5. They have a big car.
6. They don't take the bus.
7. They love fine food.
8. They don't like fast food.
9. They wear expensive clothes.
10. They don't shop at discount stores.

Expansion Activity

Have students form pairs. Ask them to imagine what Mr. and Mrs. Grand do for their daily routine. Ask: *What time do they get up? Eat breakfast? What do they do all day? What do they do for fun?* Tell pairs to work together to write a paragraph about Mr. and Mrs. Grand's activities. Tell them to use both affirmative and negative sentences. When students are finished, have two pairs form a group, and take turns reading their paragraphs out loud. Call on a few pairs to read for the class.

Page Summary

Grammar Simple present tense, third person plural: *yes/no* questions
Function Talking about daily habits and routines

Warm-up

Ask two students, one at a time: *Do you get up early?* Continue asking until you get the same answer from two students. Then, turn to a third student, gesture to the other two and ask: *Do they get up early?* Write on the board: *Yes, they do./No, they don't.* Elicit the response from the student, and then have the whole class repeat. Follow the same procedure with different students: *Do you like classical music? Do you go dancing on the weekend? Do you study every day?*

Grammar Notes

- The form of the question for third person plural is *do* + subject + base form of main verb.
- The negative answer to the *yes/no* question usually uses the contracted form *don't* rather than the longer *do not: No, they don't.*

Culture Notes

- In the conversation below picture 1, the name of the store is shortened to just *Junior's*. This is done in conversation when the speakers know the situation well (and, in this case, know that Junior's is the name of a market).
- In item 5, the question *Do Mr. and Mrs. Grand have money problems?* means do they have enough money to live comfortably and to take care of their needs. Often it is used in the negative to describe people who have plenty of money; for example, *They don't have any money problems = They are rich* or *They have no worries about money.*

▶ **PAIR WORK**

1. Go over the examples in the boxes at the top of the page. Point out that *do* is used in both the question and the answer.
2. Have students form pairs to ask and answer the questions.
3. Go over the answers with the class by calling on pairs to read the conversations out loud.

Answer Key

1. B: Yes, they do.
2. B: No, they don't. They work at the bank.
3. B: No, they don't. They live on Pine Street.
4. B: Yes, they do.
5. B: No, they don't. They are rich. (They have a lot of money.)
6. B: No, they don't. They take the bus.
7. B: Yes, they do.
8. B: Yes, they do.
9. B: No, they don't. They have an apple tree.

Expansion Activity 1

Have students each make up a list of five things that Lucy and Grover buy at Junior's Market, for example, *a box of cereal, a bag of potatoes, some orange juice,* and so on. (Review food and partitives, pages 108–110, as needed.) After students write their lists, have them form pairs. Tell them not to show their lists to their partners. Write on the board: *Do Lucy and Grover buy _____ at Junior's?* Tell students to take turns asking questions. To ask a question, they look at their lists, choose an item, and use it in the question. The partner listens to the question. If the partner has the same item on his or her list, the response is: *Yes, they do.* If it's not on the list, the response is: *No, they don't.*

Expansion Activity 2

Have students form pairs. Tell them to choose one of the illustrations and to write a short story (three to four sentences) about it. For example, if they choose picture 7, they can write about where the video arcade is, the names of the boys, how old they are, if they are good at playing video games, what time they go home from playing, and so on. After they finish writing, call on students to present to the class.

GRAMMAR • Simple Present Tense

Yes/No Question		
Do	they	get up early? walk to school?

Short Answers					
Yes,	they	do.	No,	they	don't.

▶ **PAIR WORK** • *Ask and answer questions.*

1. A: **Do Lucy and Grover shop at Junior's?**
   B: **Yes, they do.**

2. A: **Do Max and Louise work at the library?**
   B: **No, they don't. They work at the bank.**

3. Do Mr. and Mrs. Garcia live on Lime Street?

4. Do Joe and Eddie need money?

5. Do Mr. and Mrs. Grand have money problems?

6. Do the girls walk to school?

7. Do the boys play video games after school?

8. Do Daisy and Dallas enjoy country music?

9. Do Mr. and Mrs. Lee have an orange tree?

TOPIC • Music

▶ 🎧 **MUSICAL STYLES** • *Listen.*

classical   jazz

rock   country   rap

▶ 🎧 **LISTENING TO MUSIC** • *Check (✓) the musical styles you hear.*

1. ☐ classical   ☐ jazz   ☐ rock   ☐ country   ☐ rap
2. ☐ classical   ☐ jazz   ☐ rock   ☐ country   ☐ rap
3. ☐ classical   ☐ jazz   ☐ rock   ☐ country   ☐ rap
4. ☐ classical   ☐ jazz   ☐ rock   ☐ country   ☐ rap
5. ☐ classical   ☐ jazz   ☐ rock   ☐ country   ☐ rap

▶ **DISCUSSION** • *First answer the teacher; then form small groups and ask each other these questions.*

1. What kind of music do you like?
2. Is there any kind of music that you don't like?
3. What's your opinion of jazz?
4. What kind of music is popular in your country?
5. Who are your favorite singers and groups?
6. Do you like to sing? When? Where?
7. Do you play a musical instrument?
8. Where do you go to hear live music?

TOPIC • Music

Page Summary

Grammar *Yes/no* and *Wh-* questions
Function Talking about musical styles and preferences

Warm-up

Ask students to say the names of different music groups that are popular and the type of music that they play. Ask students who their favorite groups are and the reasons why.

Culture Note

Although rap music started out as urban music by African-American musicians, it is now popular all over the world. It has also influenced many other types of music.

▶ MUSICAL STYLES

🎧 *Listen.*

1. Direct students' attention to the illustrations. Ask them to describe the different musicians, and to identify any musical instruments they know.
2. Set the scene. Students will listen to excerpts of music representing the musical styles listed.
3. Play the recording (CD3, track 39) as students listen.

🎧 LISTENING TO MUSIC

1. Tell students to listen and to check the musical styles they hear.
2. Play the recording (CD3, track 40) as students listen and check the boxes.
3. Play the recording (CD3, track 40) again for students to review their answers.

Answer Key

1. jazz	4. rap
2. country	5. rock
3. classical	

▶ DISCUSSION

1. Ask the questions of individual students.
2. Have students form small groups and ask each other the questions.

Answer Key

Answers will vary.

Expansion Activity

Ask students to work in pairs, with one student taking notes, to write a radio advertisement for a concert of a popular music group in their country or in another country. Each pair can decide which group they want to use. Tell them to include the date, the time, the location, the price of tickets, and any other details they think are important. After students practice saying their advertisements, call on students to present their advertisements to the class.

TOPICS • Movies and Television

Page Summary

Grammar *Yes/no* and *Wh-* questions
Function Talking about popular entertainment

Warm-up
Say the names of several actors who are popular in your country. Ask the students if they like these actors, and what movies they have seen them in.

Culture Note
In addition to the types of TV shows listed in the book, reality TV shows and soap operas are very popular. Soap operas deal with a variety of family and social problems, such as illness, unemployment, and family fights. Viewers often become very loyal to a show and watch it regularly to follow the lives of the characters.

▶ MOVIES
🎧 *Listen and repeat.*

Play the recording (CD3, track 41) as students listen and repeat.

▶ DISCUSSION
1. Ask the questions of individual students. Encourage students to give reasons for their answers. For example, ask them to explain why someone is their favorite actor.
2. Have students form small groups and ask each other the questions.

Answer Key
Answers will vary.

▶ TV PROGRAMS
🎧 *Listen and repeat.*

Play the recording (CD3, track 42) as students listen and repeat.

▶ DISCUSSION
1. Ask the questions of individual students. Encourage students to give reasons for their answers. For example, ask them to explain why someone is their favorite actor.
2. Have students form small groups and ask each other the questions.

Answer Key
Answers will vary.

Expansion Activity 1
Have one student from each group give the class a summary of the group's TV viewing habits. Ask, *When do students in your group watch TV?* and so on. After all groups have reported, ask the class to summarize their TV watching habits, for example, *We like reality TV shows. We also like sports programs. We watch TV a lot on the weekend.*

Expansion Activity 2
Ask each student to think of a TV show they watch regularly. Tell them to write three or four sentences describing what happens on the show. When students are finished, have them form small groups and take turns reading their sentences out loud. Encourage students to ask each other questions.

TOPICS • Movies and Television

▶ 🎧 **MOVIES** • *Listen and repeat.*

comedies

dramas

adventure movies

science fiction movies

westerns

cartoons

▶ **DISCUSSION** • *Answer the teacher; then form small groups and ask each other these questions.*

- What kind of movies do you like?
- What's your favorite movie?
- Who's your favorite actor?

- Are there any good movies playing now?
- Who do you go to the movies with?
- Are there any movie theaters around here?

▶ 🎧 **TV PROGRAMS** • *Listen and repeat.*

comedies

dramas

news programs

sports programs

▶ **DISCUSSION** • *Answer the teacher; then form small groups and ask each other these questions.*

- When do you watch TV?
- How many hours a day do you watch TV?
- What kind of TV programs do you like?

- What's your favorite program?
- When is it on?
- Do you watch... (name of program)?

VOCABULARY

NOUNS

Music
classical
country
jazz
rap
rock

Movies
adventure
cartoon
comedy
drama
science fiction
western

Other
actor
appointment
cards
discount store
employee
group
member
movie theater
musical instrument
opinion
picnic
president
program
secretary
teeth
video game

VERBS
become
brush
do
exercise
find
hang out
hear
stay
worry

ADJECTIVES
lazy
popular

ADVERBS
early
fast
late
mostly

PREPOSITION
after
around

CONJUNCTION
because

EXPRESSIONS

Talking about routines

What time do you get up?
   I get up at…
When does he go to bed?
   He goes to bed at…

Talking about yourself

I get up early.
I don't sleep late.
I work fast.
I don't waste time.

Asking someone's opinion

What's your opinion?
   They look nice.

Asking about price

How much does it cost?
   Two thousand dollars.

Other

Oh, yeah.   Great!   I bet…
It's the same thing   Excellent!   I'm sure…

VOCABULARY

The games below provide additional opportunities to use the vocabulary, grammar, and expressions presented in the unit. Before students play any of the games, have them review the lists of words and circle any words they don't know. Then put students into small groups and have them review the circled words together. Circulate so you can help in case no one in the group knows a particular word.

Game 1: Tell the Story

Make a four-column chart on the board for students to copy. Tell each student to choose a character and to fill in the chart about the character. They can choose a real person or make up a character. After students complete their charts, have them form pairs. Tell them to take turns telling each other about their characters' daily routines. Remind them to use *Wh-* questions such as *What time does he/she (get up)? Where does he/she (eat dinner)?*

Who	What he / she does every day (5 things)	What time	Where

Game 2: Interview

Have students form pairs for a role play. Assign roles. One of them is an interviewer for a radio talk show, and the other is a famous actor. (This student chooses which famous movie actor to be.) The interviewer asks the actor questions about his or her daily routines. The actor describes his or her day. Encourage students to think about what an actor might do, and to make up information; for example, *I get up early. I get up at 7 o'clock. I exercise every morning. Then I eat breakfast. I don't eat a lot. I like to eat . . . ,* and so on. The interviewer can also ask about a movie the actor is making now, and what the actor is doing every day to make the movie.

Game 3: Dictation Challenge

Dictate the following words from key vocabulary: *do, employee, opinion, video game, hang out, lazy, popular, brush, exercise, picnic.* Say each word twice, pausing for students to write. Then challenge students to use five of these words to write five questions or sentences. Tell them they only need to use one of the dictated words in each sentence or question, and they can add any other words they need. Tell them to raise their hands when they are finished. Circulate and check their sentences. Students get one point for each correct sentence or question. When all of the students are finished, call on different students to present one of their sentences or questions.

PRONUNCIATION

Page Summary

A 🎧 *Listen and repeat. Notice the pronunciation of the -s endings.*

1. Have students look at the words. Tell them to listen and notice the pronunciation of the *-s* endings as you play the recording and they repeat the words (CD3, track 43).
2. Have students form pairs to practice reading the words out loud.

B 🎧 *Listen and write these verbs in the correct columns.*

1. Have students write the words in the correct columns as you play the recording (CD3, track 44).
2. Check answers by making three columns on the board and labeling them: */s/*, */z/*, and */iz/*. Have three students come to the board and write the verbs in the columns.
3. Say each word, pausing for students to repeat.

Answer Key		
/s/	/z/	/iz/
looks	cleans	washes
sleeps	gives	dances
makes	goes	closes
eats	opens	teaches

C 🎧 *What do these people do every day? Listen to the verb in each sentence.*

1. Have students look at the illustrations.
2. Play the recording (CD3, track 45) and have the students listen to the sentences.

D 🎧 *Complete the sentences in Part C. Then read each sentence out loud.*

1. Have students work alone to fill in the verbs.
2. Have students form pairs and read the sentences out loud.
3. Play the recording (CD3, track 45) again as a final check.
4. Go over the answers with the class by calling on individual students to read the sentences out loud.

Answer Key	
1. He *eats* an apple.	5. He *takes* the bus.
2. She *brushes* her teeth.	6. She *drives* her car.
3. He *reads* the newspaper.	7. He *drinks* coffee.
4. She *washes* the dishes.	8. He *watches* TV.
	9. She *plays* the piano.

Expansion Activity

Books are closed. Dictate the sentences from Part C. Say each sentence twice, pausing for students to write. Then have students open their books and look at Part C to check their work. Remind them to check their spelling of *brushes*, *washes*, and *watches*.

PRONUNCIATION

▶ **A** 🎧 *Listen and repeat. Notice the pronunciation of the **s** endings.*

/**s**/	/**z**/	/**iz**/
want**s**	live**s**	brush**es**
take**s**	play**s**	exercis**es**
keep**s**	stud**ies**	relax**es**

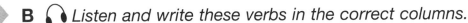

	cleans	

▶ **B** 🎧 *Listen and write these verbs in the correct columns.*

cleans	looks	dances	opens	makes	goes
washes	gives	sleeps	closes	teaches	eats

▶ **C** 🎧 *What do these people do every day? Listen to the verb in each sentence.*

1. He __eats__ an apple.   2. She _____ her teeth.   3. He _____ the newspaper.

4. She _____ the dishes.   5. He _____ the bus.   6. She _____ her car.

7. He _____ coffee.   8. He _____ TV.   9. She _____ the piano.

▶ **D** *Complete the sentences in Part C. Then read each sentence out loud.*

GRAMMAR SUMMARY

SIMPLE PRESENT Affirmative

He She	lives	in New York.
I You We They	live	

Negative

He She	doesn't (does not)	live in New York.
I You We They	don't (do not)	

Interrogative

Does	he she	live in New York?
Do	I you we they	

Short Answers

Yes,	he she	does.
	I you we they	do.

No,	he she	doesn't.
	I you we they	don't.

Questions with WHO, WHAT, WHEN, WHERE

Who	lives in that house?	Mrs. Brown.
What	does your brother do?	He's a mechanic.
When	do you have lunch?	At one o'clock.
Where	do the girls study?	At the library.

CONTENTS

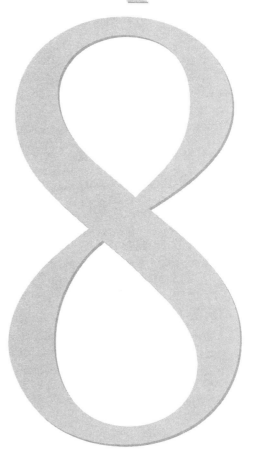

Chapter

8

CARTOON STORY

▶ 🎧 *It's Sunday afternoon and Jason is taking a walk in the park. Listen and practice.*

QUESTIONS

1. Who does Jason meet at the park?
2. Why does Lisa come to the park on weekends?
3. Is she enjoying the music today?
4. What does Lisa do?
5. Are her students lucky? Why?
6. Do you think Lisa likes Jason? Why?

CARTOON STORY

Page Summary

Grammar Review
Function Starting a conversation

Culture Notes

- In the cartoon story, Jason is taking a walk in the park and decides to start a conversation with Lisa, who is sitting on a bench. He makes "small talk" with her, chatting about the kinds of general topics that people use to get a conversation going with someone new. Ask students to consider the topics they like to talk about to start a conversation. Put a list on the board: *job, weather, sports*.

- Review that *What do you do?* is a way to ask someone what their job is. Remind students that in Chapter 7 they learned *What do you do for a living?*

- Review that the phrase *I bet*, also from Chapter 7, is used when the speaker thinks something is likely to be true. Here, Lisa realizes Jason is flirting with her a little and is interested in talking to her more. She uses the sentence with *I bet* to deflect the compliment, yet keep the conversation going.

▶ QUESTIONS

1. Tell students to take turns asking and answering the questions.
2. Then go over the answers with the class by asking the questions of individual students.

Option: Answer the questions as a class. Read each question, and then say a student's name. After the student says the answer, have the rest of the class repeat it.

Answer Key

1. He meets Lisa.	4. She's a teacher.
2. They have entertainment at the park on weekends.	5. Jason thinks they're lucky because she is so nice.
3. Yes, she is.	6. Answers will vary.

Warm-up

To review greetings and to get students to think about possible topics for small talk, have students form pairs, and tell them to pretend they don't know each other. One partner is sitting in a café. The other person walks in and wants to start a conversation. They greet each other, and then ask each other a few questions to get acquainted. After pairs practice their conversations, call on one or two pairs to role-play for the class.

Expansion Activity 1

Have students form pairs and role-play the conversation between Jason and Lisa. When they finish the lines in the book, have them create more lines to continue the conversation. *(Where do you teach? What other music do you like?)* After students finish, call on a few pairs to role-play for the class.

▶ ∩ *It's Sunday afternoon and Jason is taking a walk in the park. Listen and practice.*

1. Direct students' attention to the illustrations. Set the scene: *It's Sunday afternoon and Jason is taking a walk in the park. It's a beautiful day. He stops to talk to Lisa.* Ask students to describe the situation, for example, ask: *Where's Lisa? What is she doing? What are Jason and Lisa wearing? Does Lisa have long hair?* Encourage students to describe what they see using their own words.
2. Play the recording (CD3, track 46) as students listen.
3. Play the recording (CD3, track 47) again for students to practice the conversation.
4. Have students form pairs to practice the conversation.

Expansion Activity 2

Have students form pairs with new partners and role-play the conversation between Jason and Lisa. This time have them think of ways to change the situation. For example, Jason is lost and asks Lisa where the bus stop is, or Lisa comes to the park only on Sundays to exercise. She likes to run, or she has a different occupation: she's a doctor at the hospital near the park. She comes to the park to eat lunch. Encourage students to review earlier units, as needed, to create their role plays. Call on pairs to present to the class.

STARTING A CONVERSATION

Page Summary

Grammar Review
Function Starting a conversation

Warm-up

Greet several students, one at a time, using the questions on page 142 *(Beautiful day, isn't it? Is it okay if I sit here? My name's _____. What's your name? What do you do?).* Pause for them to respond. Then have a few students greet each other.

Culture Notes

• In conversation 3, one of the choices is: *You call this music?* This is a common construction used to show disapproval in a variety of situations. Here, Henry clearly doesn't like the music. In a restaurant, if the coffee is bad, someone might say: *You call this coffee?* Likewise, if the salad is terrible: *You call this salad?*

• In conversation 4, one of the choices is: *It's none of your business.* This is a blunt way for Henry to make it clear to Amanda that he doesn't want to continue with that topic. A less blunt way would be to say something like: *I'd rather not say.* This can be used in many situations to avoid answering a question.

! *Pronunciation Tip*

The voice falls on the tag question *Beautiful day, isn't it?* because Amanda is looking for confirmation of information she already believes, and she is fairly sure that Henry will agree. The voice rises on tag questions where the speaker actually needs to get information or isn't sure of the answer: *That's Tim's book, isn't it? (I really don't know whose book it is.)*

▶ WRITING

1. Have students look at the illustrations.
2. Set the scene: Amanda and Henry are meeting for the first time. Tell students to listen to Amanda's questions and Henry's possible answer below each picture. Then they write the answer they like best. Encourage students to give their own answers to each question instead.
3. Play the recording (CD3, track 48) as students listen.
4. Have students work alone to write their answers in the speech bubbles.
5. Have students form pairs and read the conversations out loud. Remind them to switch parts so that each of them has a chance to say Henry's responses.

▶ PAIR WORK

1. Have students form pairs. Tell them to have a conversation using some of Amanda's questions as well as any other questions they want to add.
2. Remind students that in a good conversation, each speaker asks and answers questions in order to keep the conversation going. To help make this clear, give students examples of follow-up questions they can ask. For example, when Henry says, *No, I think it's terrible,* a good follow-up question would be: *Oh, well, what kind of music do you like?* When Henry says, *I'm looking for a job,* a good follow-up question would be: *What kind of job?*
3. After students practice, call on a few pairs to present their conversations to the class.

Option: For more practice with question formation, reverse the conversations. One partner gives one of the answers *(No, this is my first time)* and the other must supply the correct question *(Do you come here often?).* For more challenge, have the second student cover the page.

Expansion Activity 1

Have students form pairs. Tell them to use the lines in the illustrations to start a similar conversation, but set a different scene first. The situation is: Amanda and Henry are at a sports club. They are both exercising in the weight room. Amanda asks Henry to get a glass of juice with her. Then they talk about what they do. He is a reporter for a newspaper. She is a teacher. They both like jazz.

Expansion Activity 2

Do a dictation. Choose six of Henry's responses to dictate. Say each response twice, pausing in between for students to write. When they are finished, have students read the sentences out loud chorally.

STARTING A CONVERSATION

▶ 🎧 **WRITING** • *Amanda Standfast and Henry Bell are meeting for the first time. Listen to Amanda's questions and Henry's possible answers below each picture. Write the answer you like best or give your own answer to each question. After you finish, practice the conversation with a partner.*

- I don't think so.
- No, it's too cold.
- No, I hate this weather.
- Other.

- I come here once or twice a week.
- Yes, I come here every day.
- No, this is my first time.
- Other.

- It's okay.
- No, I think it's terrible.
- You call this music?
- Other.

- I'm a salesman.
- I'm looking for a job.
- It's none of your business.
- Other.

▶ **PAIR WORK** • *Start a conversation with the person next to you. Use some of Amanda's questions, and ask some original questions. In a good conversation, each speaker asks and answers questions.*

GRAMMAR REVIEW • Simple Present Tense

🎧 *Listen. Listen and repeat.*

▶ **PAIR WORK** • *Practice the conversations.*

▶ **WRITING** • *Fill in the questions and answers. Then read the conversations aloud.*

1. Ben and Sara / a dishwasher?	have

Do Ben and Sara have a dishwasher?

No, they don't.

2. Jean / blond hair?	have

Does Jean have blond hair?

Yes, she does.

3. Lucy and Grover / a fireplace?	have

4. Jason / a big car?	have

5. Mr. and Mrs. Doe / rock music?	like

6. Suzi / roses?	like

7. Becky and Jimmy / ice cream?	like

8. Mr. Ruffcorn / birds?	like

GRAMMAR REVIEW

Page Summary

Grammar Review
Function Talking about what people have and like

The Teacher's Notes for this activity continue on page T145.

Warm-up

To review the grammar, ask individual students questions about their classmates, for example, *Do (Tanya) and (Jose) have black backpacks? Does (Sarah) have long hair? Does (Shigeo) have dark hair?* Then write on the board: *Tomas, brown hair, have.* Call on a student to make the question: *Does Tomas have brown hair?* Then write: *Mr. and Mrs. Ramos, classical music, like.* Call on a different student to make the question: *Do Mr. and Mrs. Ramos like classical music?*

Listen. Listen and repeat.

1. Have students look at the illustrations and describe what they see.
2. Play the recording (CD3, track 49) as students listen.
3. Play the recording (CD3, track 50) for students to repeat.

PAIR WORK

Have students form pairs to practice the conversations.

WRITING

1. Go over the examples in the book.
2. Tell students to work alone to write the question and answer for each picture.
3. Play the recording (CD3, track 49) again for students to check their answers.
4. Go over the answers by calling on pairs to read each question and answer.

Answer Key

1. Do Ben and Sarah have a dishwasher? / No, they don't.
2. Does Janet have blonde hair? / Yes, she does.
3. Do Lucy and Grover have a fireplace? / Yes, they do.
4. Does Jason have a big car? / Yes, he does.
5. Do Mr. and Mrs. Doe like rock music? / No, they don't.
6. Does Suzi like roses? / Yes, she does.
7. Do Becky and Jimmy like ice cream? / Yes, they do.
8. Does Mr. Ruffcorn like birds? / No, he doesn't.
9. Does Maria want a hamburger? / Yes, she does.
10. Do Bob and Alice want dessert? / No, they don't.
11. Do Amy and Billy want a dog? / Yes, they do.
12. Does Joe want a job? / No, he doesn't.
13. Does Jane need glasses? / Yes, she does.
14. Do Max and Judy need food? / No, they don't.
15. Do Joe and Eddie need money? / Yes, they do.
16. Does Larry need a comb? / No, he doesn't.

GRAMMAR REVIEW

▶ PAIR WORK

1. Have students form pairs with new partners. Tell them to ask each other questions using *have*, *like*, *want*, and *need*, plus any other vocabulary that they would like to include *(Does Tomas like big cars?)*. Encourage students to answer with real information, and remind them to ask their partners about other students in the class, so that the focus remains on the third person form of the verbs.
2. Model the examples in the book with a student partner, switching parts.
3. After students practice, call on pairs to present to the class.

Expansion Activity

To give students practice in using follow-up comments and questions to keep a conversation going, have them each choose four conversations and write a few more lines to continue each conversation. Do the first one as an example:

> *Do Ben and Sarah have a dishwasher?*
> *No they don't. They're washing the dishes.*
> *Are they happy?*
> *No, they aren't.*

As students write, circulate and help with vocabulary. When students are finished, have them form pairs and practice the conversations each of them wrote. Then, call on a few pairs to present to the class.

9. Maria / a hamburger?   want

10. Bob and Alice / dessert?   want

11. Amy and Billy / a dog?   want

PET SHOP

12. Joe / a job?   want

EMPLOYMENT

13. Jane / glasses?   need

RE PONC KAZE LQYIB DFRGKN   R..E...

14. Max and Judy / food?   need

15. Joe and Eddie / money?   need

16. Larry / a comb?   need

▶ **PAIR WORK** • *Ask each other questions using **have, like, want** and **need**.*

A: **Do you like science fiction movies?**
B: **Yes, I do.** OR **No, I don't.**

A: **Do you need a new pair of shoes?**
B: **Yes, I do.** OR **No, I don't.**

GRAMMAR REVIEW • Simple Present Tense

▶ 🎧 *Look at the pictures and listen to the conversations.*

▶ **WRITING** • *Begin the questions using* **What, Where, When, How, How often, What kind of**.

▶ **PAIR WORK** • *Practice the conversations.*

1
How often does Suzi exercise?

Three times a week.

2
_____ food do Bob and Alice like?

Mexican food.

3
_____ does Ken see his friends?

On the weekend.

4
_____ do Mr. and Mrs. Baker live?

On Rock Street.

GRAMMAR REVIEW • Simple Present

Page Summary

Grammar Simple present tense; *Wh-* questions
Function Talking about daily habits and routines

The Teacher's Notes for this activity continue on page T147.

The Teacher's Notes for this activity continue on page T147.

Warm-up

Talk about how often people do things. Write on the board: *Max goes to the park on Monday and Friday. He goes two times a week.* Then say, *Jason goes to the park on Monday, Wednesday, and Friday.* Ask, *How often does he go?* Elicit, *He goes three times a week.* Ask individual students questions about their activities, for example, *Do you do take the bus?* If they give an affirmative answer, ask, *How often do you do take it?* Then say, *Max goes to the park <u>in the afternoon</u>* (emphasizing the last part of the sentence) in order to elicit, *<u>When</u> does he go to the park?* After several rounds, have students ask the questions.

Culture Note

The expression *see (one's) friends* means to get together to hang out or to do an activity.

Grammar Notes

• All these questions are information questions used to ask about something specific.
• Because the *do/does* part of the question is included on the page, the focus here is on which question word is needed for each situation.

▶ ⌢ *Look at the pictures and listen to the conversations.*

1. Have students look at the illustrations.
2. Play the recording (CD3, track 51) as students look and listen.

▶ WRITING

1. Tell students to work alone to add the correct question word to each balloon.
2. Go over the example in the book. Point out that the answer does not need to be a complete sentence because the meaning is clear.
3. Play the recording (CD3, track 51) again for students to check their answers.
4. Go over the answers by calling on pairs to read each conversation.

Answer Key

1. How often does Suzi exercise?
2. What kind of food do Bob and Alice like?
3. When does Ken see his friends?
4. Where do Mr. and Mrs. Baker live?
5. What languages does Maria speak?
6. How often does Carlos brush his teeth?
7. When do your neighbors watch TV?
8. What kind of work does Pam do?
9. How do Becky and Jimmy go to school?

▶ PAIR WORK

1. Have students form pairs. Tell them to ask each other the same questions. Tell them they can answer with true or made up information.
2. Model the example with a student partner.
3. Call on pairs to present conversations to the class.

Expansion Activity 1

Work with the students to compile a list of about eight other daily activities. Then have students form pairs with new partners and have similar conversations, substituting the new activities.

GRAMMAR REVIEW • Simple Present

Expansion Activity 2

Question scramble. Write the following words on the board:

1. dance lessons / How / does Jason take / often /?
2. of food / and Grover / What kind / do / Lucy / like /?
3. the park / Lisa go / When / to / does /?
4. Jason / work / does / do / What kind of /?
5. do / hang out / Where / your friends /?
6. How / do you / do laundry / often /?

Have students work alone to put the words in order to create questions. When students are finished, have them form pairs and read their questions out loud. Then call on students to read the questions and answers for the class.

Answer Key

1. How often does Jason take dance lessons?
2. What kind of food do Lucy and Grover like?
3. When does Lisa go to the park?
4. What kind of work does Jason do?
5. Where do your friends hang out?
6. How often do you do laundry?

5. _____ languages does Maria speak?
   English and Spanish.
   Good morning. Buenos días.

6. _____ does Carlos brush his teeth?
   Twice a day.

7. _____ do your neighbors watch TV?
   After dinner.

8. _____ work does Pam do?
   She's a nurse.

9. _____ do Becky and Jimmy go to school?
   They take the bus.

▶ **PAIR WORK** • *Ask each other the same questions.*
A: **How often do you exercise?**   B: **I exercise every day.**

BEAUTIFUL HOMES

▶ **CLASS ACTIVITY** • *Look at the different homes in the pictures. Which home is the most beautiful? The most modern? The most expensive? Which house is your favorite?*

1. a house in the city

2. a house by the sea

3. a log cabin in the mountains

4. a farm house in the country

▶ **WORK ALONE** • *The home in the pictures below has many nice features. Which features are important to you? Which features are not very important? Number the six features in their order of importance. Number one is the most important and number six is the least important.*

___ a porch ___ fruit trees ___ a garden ___ a balcony ___ a patio ___ a swimming pool

BEAUTIFUL HOMES

Page Summary

Grammar Review
Function Describing the features of homes

Warm-up

Books are closed. Talk about students' ideas of beautiful homes. Ask the class: *What makes a home beautiful? Is it big or small? What features does it have?* Give some examples of features: *large rooms, a flower garden, trees, lots of light.* Call on different students. On the board, compile a list of features.

Culture Notes

- Where a house is located can make a huge difference in how expensive it is. In the class activity, students may factor this in when deciding which of the homes is the most expensive. All of them could, in fact, be quite expensive depending on where they are located. In the language of real estate, this fact is summed up with the words "Location, location, location!"
- The expression *in the city* refers to an urban setting, while *in the country* refers to a rural setting.
- A log cabin is a small house that is made out of wooden logs. During pioneer times and the westward expansion in the United States, many people built log cabins because wood was plentiful. Nowadays, most are built in the mountains or as second homes for leisure activities.

▶ CLASS ACTIVITY

1. Have students look at the illustrations. Discuss the features of each house with the class.
2. Present the discussion questions.
3. Have students answer the discussion questions as a class. Call on individual students for their answers. Encourage students to give reasons for their answers. For example, ask, *Why do you think number 2 is the most beautiful?*
4. Then take a class vote on which house is the most beautiful, the most modern, and so on. For example, ask, *Who thinks number 1 is the most expensive? Raise your hand.* Compile their answers on the board.

▶ WORK ALONE

1. Have students look at the illustrations. Point out that the left picture is the front yard, and the right picture is the back yard of the same house.
2. Say each feature *(a porch)*, and have students point at it in the illustration.

3. Tell students to work alone to rank the features listed from one to six; one is most important and six is least important.
4. Have students form small groups to compare answers.
5. Ask one student from each group to summarize for the class how their group ranked the features, for example, *Three of us think a garden is most important.*

Expansion Activity 1

As a preview to the introduction of *because* coming up later in this chapter, write a simple sentence on the board using *because*.

> *I sleep because I am tired.*

Label the subjects and verbs of the sentence as follows to show that *because* requires a two-part sentence:

> S V   because   S V
> I sleep because   I am tired.

Then have students work alone to write about the feature they considered the most important and the feature they considered the least important about the house at the bottom of the page. Tell them to write at least three sentences explaining why the one feature is most important and three sentences about why the other one is the least important, using *because* to connect their ideas. When students are finished, have them form pairs and take turns reading their sentences out loud.

Expansion Activity 2

Work together as a class. Discuss the house in the illustration. Ask students to elaborate on each of its features. Encourage them to use their imaginations and think up details. For example, ask, *What kind of fruit trees are they? What kind of flowers are in the garden? Who lives in this house? What do they like to do? What do they use the patio for? Do they have parties?* Call on different students for their ideas. To expand this further, write the students' answers on the board, and then have the students form pairs and use the answers to summarize what they have discussed as a class.

JANET'S DREAM HOUSE

Page Summary

Grammar Review
Function Describing the features of a dream house

Warm-up

Write *a dream house* on the board. Explain that a dream house is the perfect house, the house you want to have. Everyone, of course, has different ideas about what makes a dream house. Some people want a small house by the ocean. Other people want a big house with many features. Ask students to think for a minute about what their dream house is like. Don't elicit their ideas. Tell them they will write about their dream house later. The main purpose here is to get them to think about the topic. Explain that they are going to listen to someone talk about her dream house.

▶ ∩ Listen to Janet talk about her dream house.

1. Set the scene: Janet is describing her dream house.
2. Have students look at the illustration and identify the items in Janet's thought bubble.
3. Play the recording (CD3, track 52) as students listen, covering the text.
4. Play the recording (CD3, track 52) again as students listen and follow along in their books.

▶ QUESTIONS

1. Have students work alone to answer the questions.
2. Go over the answers by calling on different students.

Option: First have students form pairs and compare answers. Then go over them as a class.

Answer Key

1. It is in the country.
2. It has three bedrooms.
3. There's a fireplace, a piano, and a big, comfortable sofa.
4. Her favorite place on hot, sunny days is her swimming pool in the back yard.

▶ DISCUSSION

Ask students what features make a house special. List their ideas on the board.

▶ WORD POWER

1. Go over the lists of words on the page. Point out that the words in the pairs on the left have the same meaning, whereas the words in the pairs on the right are opposites.
2. Say the words from the right column in random order, and have students say the opposite word. For example, say, *small* and elicit, *large*.

Option: Expand this activity to include other adjectives that the students have learned: *old, beautiful, weak, married*. You say the adjective, they give the opposite.

▶ COMPOSITION

1. Present the activity. Tell students their paragraphs should have two parts: First, they describe their dream house, and then they say what they like best about it and why.
2. Have students form small groups. Tell them to take turns reading their compositions out loud.
3. Call on several students to read their compositions to the class.
4. After students present their compositions, ask individual students to compare their dream house with the dream house of one of the presenters, for example, *My dream house is very big. Julio's is small with large windows.*

Option: Ask students to compare Janet's ideas of a dream house with their own.

Expansion Activity

Have students form pairs. Ask them to use their paragraphs describing their dream house to role-play a conversation between a real estate agent and a customer. The student who is the agent tries to sell his or her dream house to the customer. He or she explains all the features. The customer asks questions, but doesn't agree to buy the house. Have students switch parts and repeat the role play. For more challenge, students can try to use some of the shopping vocabulary they have already learned: *How much does it cost? I need / I like / I don't need a _____ that much!*

JANET'S DREAM HOUSE

▶ 🎧 *Listen to Janet talk about her dream house.*

My dream house is an old-fashioned house in the country. It has large windows because I like a house that is sunny and cheerful. In the living room, there's a fireplace, a piano, and a big, comfortable sofa. My dream house is ideal for a family of four. It has three bedrooms, and there's a bathroom next to each bedroom. Best of all, there's a swimming pool in the backyard. That's my favorite place in the summertime when the weather gets hot.

▶ **QUESTIONS**

1. Where is Janet's dream house?
2. How many bedrooms does it have?
3. What's in the living room?
4. Why does Janet's dream house have large windows?
5. Where is Janet's favorite place on hot, summer days?

▶ **DISCUSSION** • *What are some features that make a house special?*

▶ **WORD POWER** • *Here are some typical words we use to talk about our homes.*

big = large	quiet ≠ noisy
ideal = perfect	large ≠ small
quiet = peaceful	cheap ≠ expensive
new = modern	modern ≠ old-fashioned
cheerful = sunny	front yard ≠ back yard
cozy = small, comfortable and warm	hot, summer days ≠ cold, winter nights

▶ **COMPOSITION** • *Write a paragraph describing your dream house. For ideas, look at the pictures on these pages. Look at the vocabulary in WORD POWER, and Janet's description of her dream house. What do you like best about your dream house?*

LIFE SKILL • Locating Places

▶ 🎧 *Look and listen. Then read out loud.*

There's a parking lot on Rock Street, **next to** the hotel.

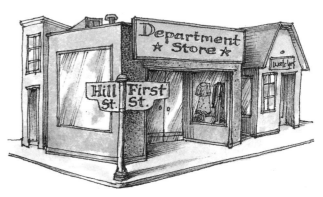

There's a bakery on Central Avenue, **between** the coffee shop and the bank.

There's a bookstore on Pine Street, **across from** the school.

There's a department store on First Street, **on the corner of** First and Hill.

▶ **PAIR WORK** • *Ask and answer questions. Use **between, next to, across from, and on the corner of** in your answers.*

1. barbershop?

A: **Excuse me. Is there a barbershop around here?**

B: **Yes. There's a barbershop on Main Street, between the flower shop and the hotel.**

2. gas station?

A: **Excuse me. Is there a gas station around here?**

B: **Yes. There's a gas station on Hill Street, on the corner of Hill and Lake.**

1. barbershop?

2. gas station?

LIFE SKILL • Locating Places

Page Summary

Grammar Prepositions of location: *next to, between, across from, on the corner of*
Function Locating places in the community

The Teacher's Notes for this activity continue on page T151.

Warm-up

To introduce the prepositions of location *next to, between, across from,* and *on the corner of,* describe the buildings near your school or in an area familiar to the students. Use each of the prepositions and names of community buildings, such as *post office, library, bookstore, bank,* and *restaurant.* After you give an example, write the preposition on the board. Next, ask students to describe the location of other buildings. Call on individual students. Have the whole class repeat each student's sentence.

Grammar Notes

- Review that American English uses <u>on</u> *(Main Street)* whereas British English uses <u>in</u> *Main Street.*
- Emphasize to the students that many of these words typically occur together and that it is helpful to learn them that way: *next <u>to</u>, across <u>from</u>,* and *on the corner <u>of</u>.*

⌒ Look and listen. Then read out loud.

1. Have students look at the illustration and identify the buildings.
2. Play the recording (CD3, track 53) as students listen.
3. Have students read the sentences out loud chorally.

Option: Have students form pairs and take turns reading the sentences.

▶ PAIR WORK

1. Have students form pairs to ask and answer the questions.
2. Go over the answers with the class by calling on pairs to read the conversations out loud.

Answer Key

1. A: Excuse me. Is there a barbershop around here?
   B: Yes. There's a barbershop on Main Street, between the flower shop and the hotel.
2. A: Excuse me. Is there a gas station around here?
   B: Yes. There's a gas station on Hill Street, on the corner of Hill and Lake.
3. A: Excuse me. Is there a bank around here?
   B: Yes. There's a bank on Main Street, across from the police station.
4. A: Excuse me. Is there a movie theater around here?
   B: Yes. There's a movie theater on Star Avenue, next to the department store.
5. A: Excuse me. Is there a supermarket around here?
   B: Yes. There's a supermarket on Mason Street, on the corner of Mason and Dixon.
6. A: Excuse me. Is there a laundromat around here?
   B: Yes. There's a laundromat on Franklin Avenue, between the bookstore and the pet shop.
7. A: Excuse me. Is there a hotel around here?
   B: Yes. There's a hotel on First Street, across from the park.
8. A: Excuse me. Is there a drugstore around here?
   B: Yes. There's a drugstore on Central Avenue, next to the hospital.
9. A: Excuse me. Is there a restaurant around here?
   B: Yes. There's a restaurant on Lake Avenue, between the bank and the library.
10. A: Excuse me. Is there a post office around here?
    B: Yes. There's a post office on First Street, on the corner of First and Main.

Expansion Activity

Have students form pairs. First, have them work together to draw a simple map that has two streets running vertically and two streets running horizontally. Tell them to name the streets. Then have them each make a copy of the map. Next, have them sit back to back and take turns asking each other questions about the location of different buildings.

When one student gives a location, they both add it to the map. For example, the first partner asks: *Is there a bank around here?* The other partner decides on a location, says it, and they both draw it on the map. They continue asking questions, and add new buildings based on what is already on the map. After they ask eight questions, have them compare maps. The maps should be the same.

3. bank?

4. movie theater?

5. supermarket?

6. laundromat?

7. hotel?

8. drugstore?

9. restaurant?

10. post office?

COMMUNITY RESOURCES

▶ 🎧 *Look and listen. Then answer the question below each picture.*

1. Jane is cashing a check at Union Bank on Lake Avenue.

Where do you keep your money?

2. Mr. and Mrs. Baker are buying groceries at Junior's Market on Hill Street.

Where do you buy groceries?

3. Jack and Jill are studying at the library on Central Avenue.

Where do you study?

4. Nick is getting a haircut at Clancy's Barbershop on First Street.

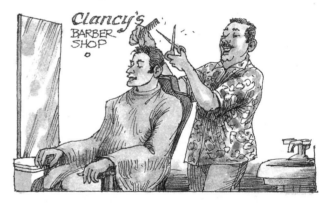

Where do you go for a haircut?

5. Suzi is mailing some letters at the post office on Main Street.

Where do you go to mail letters?

6. Carlos and Maria are exercising at Spike's Gym on Franklin Avenue.

Where do you exercise?

COMMUNITY RESOURCES

Page Summary

Grammar Review
Function Talking about using community resources

The Teacher's Notes for this activity continue on page T153.

Warm-up

Talk about activities that the students do, and how often they do them. Start by saying what you do, for example, *On Saturday, I buy groceries at (name of market). I exercise twice a week. I exercise on (Wednesday and Friday).* Ask individual students about their activities. After several responses, have students continue asking each other questions. The student who answers can choose who to ask the next question of.

Culture Notes

In illustration 1, the question is *Where do you keep your money?* Another way to ask this is *Where do you bank?* because this includes the variety of services available at a bank, such as ATM, savings, checking, and credit card transactions.

Grammar Note

- The expression *Where do you go for (something)* is widely used. It is a short form for *Where do you go to get (something)?* For example, *Where do you go for a haircut = Where do you go to get a haircut? Where do you go for ice cream = Where do you go to buy/eat ice cream?*
- The frequency expressions are generally used with simple present, not present progressive, to give the idea of a habit or routine: *I exercise three times a week.*

▶ ∩ Look and listen. Then answer the question below each picture.

1. Have students look at the illustrations and point at the different locations (*Union Bank, Junior's Market,* and so on) as you say them.
2. Play the recording (CD3, track 54) as students look and listen. Explain that first they will listen to what each person is doing. Then they will answer the questions below the pictures.
3. Do a quick comprehension check. Pick illustrations at random and ask what the person is doing. For example, ask, *What is Nick doing?* (He's getting a haircut.)
4. Have students form pairs. Tell them to take turns asking each other the questions. Encourage them to answer with true information.
5. Call on individual students to report to the class one thing they learned about their partner.

▶ PAIR WORK

1. Write the Frequency Expressions (in the box on page 153) on the board. Give examples or ask students for examples of things they do every day, every week, and so on.
2. Model the example in the book, taking Part A yourself and calling on different students to say each of the responses for Part B.
3. Have students form pairs. Tell them to take turns asking and answering the questions using true information.
4. To check understanding, do a chain question-answer activity with the class. Have Student 1 ask the first question of Student 2. Student 2 answers, and then asks the next question of Student 3. Tell students to ask the question of a new partner.

Answer Key
Answers will vary.

COMMUNITY RESOURCES

Expansion Activity 1

Have students form pairs. Ask them to use the Frequency Expressions to talk about their everyday activities and routines. For each expression in the box, have them make a sentence; for example, *I wake up at 6 o'clock every day. I do my laundry every week. I never go skiing.*

Expansion Activity 2

Have students talk to their classmates and use the information from Expansion Activity 1 to see if they can find three other classmates who do something exactly as often as they do. Set a time limit (10 minutes). Tell them to speak to as many people as they need to during that time. Tell them to return to their seats when they are finished (if students remain seated, have them raise their hands). Call on individual students to report to the class, for example, *Sonya and I go dancing every weekend.*

7. Becky and Jimmy are having lunch at the school cafeteria.

Where do you have lunch?

8. Donna is shopping for clothes at the Bargain Shop on First Street.

Where do you shop for clothes?

9. Bruno is washing his clothes at the laundromat on Dixon Avenue.

Where do you wash your clothes?

10. Daisy and Dallas are dancing at the Cowboy Saloon on Mason Street.

Where do you go dancing?

▶ **PAIR WORK** • *Ask and answer questions.*

go to the library

A: **How often do you go to the library?**

B: **I go to the library once a week.**

   OR **I go about three times a week.**

   OR **I go to the library every day.**

   OR **I never go to the library.**

1. read the newspaper
2. buy groceries
3. brush your teeth
4. exercise
5. get a haircut
6. take the bus
7. go downtown
8. shop for clothes
9. see your friends
10. go dancing

Frequency Expressions
every day
every week
every weekend
once a day/week/month
twice a day/week/month
three times a day/week/month
never

▶ **HEALTH PROBLEMS** • *Listen and repeat.*

1. a headache

2. a toothache

3. red eyes

4. a cold

5. a stomachache

6. chest pain

7. a sore throat

8. insomnia

▶ **PAIR WORK** • *Ask and answer questions about the health problems of these people.*

1. Grover
A: **Why is Grover taking aspirin?**
B: **He's taking aspirin because he has a headache.**

1. Why is Grover taking aspirin?

2. Why is Becky seeing the dentist?

3. Why is Jane using eye drops?

4. Why is Carlos taking vitamin C?

5. Why is Mabel taking antacid?

6. Why is Mr. Grand seeing the doctor?

7. Why is Suzi taking cough syrup?

8. Why is Ben drinking warm milk?

TOPIC • Health Problems

Page Summary

Grammar Review
Function Talking about health problems

Warm-up

Play "Simon Says" to go over the parts of the body. First review *point at*: Point at your head and say, *What am I doing? (You're pointing at your head.).* Remind students of the rules: If you include the phrase *Simon says* in your command, they do what you say. If you don't say *Simon says*, they do nothing. First check vocabulary by doing a round in which you say *Simon says* each time as you say and point to the different parts of your body. Say: *(Simon says) point to your head/arm/leg/stomach/teeth/throat/eyes* and so on. Then play a regular round in which you don't say *Simon says* each time.

Grammar Notes

- The rules regarding when to use *ache (stomachache)* and when to use *sore (sore throat)* are difficult to explain and beyond the scope of this lesson. At this level, it is enough to have students memorize the phrases.
- Health problems 3, 6, and 7, as they are presented here, don't take articles. For problem 3, if someone has irritation in only one eye the expression would be *a red eye*. For problem 6, the expression *chest pains* is also used.
- The conjunction *because* is used here to link what someone is doing and why *(He's taking aspirin. Why? Because he has a headache.)*

Culture Notes

- The expression *to see* a doctor or dentist = *to go to* a doctor or dentist. It can also be used in other contexts: *I need to see my teacher about my grade, I want to see a real estate agent about renting an apartment.*
- Many people suffer from insomnia, the inability to sleep soundly through the night. One home remedy is to drink a warm glass of milk. Different cultures have different solutions for this problem. Discuss with the students what they or others they know do to help them sleep.

- This lesson covers common remedies people use for health problems. Discuss with the students traditional or "folk" remedies that they or family members use for some of these problems, for example, chicken soup for a cold.

▶ PAIR WORK

1. Go over the examples in the book. Write on the board: *Grover is taking aspirin.* Ask, *Why?* Have the class respond chorally. Make sure students understand that to answer each question they should refer to the corresponding health problem at the top of the page.
2. Have students form pairs to ask and answer the questions.
3. Go over the answers with the class by calling on pairs to read the conversations out loud. Point out that we *use* eye drops, but *take* medicine.

Answer Key

1. He's taking aspirin because he has a headache.
2. She's seeing the dentist because she has a toothache.
3. She's using eye drops because she has red eyes.
4. He's taking vitamin C because he has a cold.
5. She's taking antacid because she has a stomachache.
6. He's seeing the doctor because he has chest pain.
7. She's taking cough syrup because she has a sore throat.
8. He's drinking warm milk because he has insomnia.

Expansion Activity

Have students form small groups. One person in each group pantomimes one of the health problems in the book. The rest of the group guesses: *You have (a headache).* The group should also give a command (advice) about what to do: *(Take aspirin).* (Review commands in Chapter 2 as needed.)

TOPIC • Health Remedies

Page Summary

Grammar Review
Function Talking about where health products and remedies are located in a store

Warm-up

Say a few health problems one at a time *(a stomachache, a sore throat)*, and call on students to tell you what to take *(antacid, cough syrup)*.

Culture Note

In the United States there are several choices for where to buy health remedies. There are two main categories of remedies: over-the-counter (OTC) and those that require a prescription from a doctor or dentist. Prescription medication must be bought at a pharmacy, whereas nonprescription health remedies, such as those mentioned on these pages, can be bought in drugstores, supermarkets, and discount stores. There are pharmacies inside of drugstores, some large supermarkets, and some large discount stores. A store whose name includes the word *pharmacy* usually carries a variety of drugstore items, such as toothpaste and shaving cream, and also has a licensed pharmacy for prescription medications. In this lesson, all of the medications are over-the-counter and are therefore located in the regular aisles of the store.

▶ ♫ *Listen. Listen and practice.*

1. Direct students' attention to the illustration. Set the scene: Mabel is at the drugstore because she has a stomach ache. Ask, *What does she want to buy? (antacid).*
2. Play the recording (CD3, track 56) as students listen.
3. Play the recording (CD3, track 57) again for students to listen and practice.
4. Divide the class into Groups A and B. Have the groups practice the conversation chorally, changing parts.

▶ **PAIR WORK**
1. Direct students' attention to the illustrations. Ask them to read each label. Call on individual students to say something about each medicine. It isn't necessary to make complete sentences, for example, *Pronto Cold Medicine—fast relief; Headache Relief—Extra Strength. Miracle mouthwash kills germs.*
2. Have students form pairs to have similar conversations about the items listed in the book. Before they begin, demonstrate how to gesture

toward the aisle as you say: *It's in aisle (1).* Also point out that eye drops and tooth brushes are plural and that they need to use *They're* instead of *It's.*

3. Go over the answers by calling on pairs to present each conversation to the class.

Answer Key

(a) aspirin: It's in aisle 2.	(d) eye drops: They're in aisle 3.
(b) cough syrup: It's in aisle 1.	(e) cold medicine: It's in aisle 1.
(c) mouthwash: It's in aisle 4.	(f) toothbrushes: They're in aisle 4.

Expansion Activity 1

Have students form pairs. Have each pair take six slips of paper and write down a health problem on each slip. Then have them fold the slips and exchange them with another pair of students (only so that students won't know the health problems they are going to talk about). Next, have students in each pair take turns choosing a slip and saying the health problem, for example, *I have a headache.* The partner says what to buy and where to find it. *You need aspirin. It's in aisle 2.*

Expansion Activity 2

Have students work in small groups to draw and write a label for a health remedy. You can assign a heath problem to each group or let the students decide. To help students get started (and for vocabulary development), present a few details about the labels on the page: *Pronto* means *fast*; therefore the medicine promises fast relief. *To blink* is to open and shut the eyes quickly; therefore, Dr. Blink eye wash will work in the "blink of an eye" to clean the eyes. A *miracle* drug is considered something that works wonderfully; *Miracle mouthwash* therefore must kill germs very quickly and effectively. Encourage students to use words and phrases from several labels in the book to draw their own labels, for example, *miracle headache relief* would promise to work very quickly and effectively. When groups are done, call on each group to present its label to the class.

TOPIC • Health Remedies

▶ 🎧 *Listen. Listen and practice.*

A: Excuse me. Where is the antacid?

B: It's in aisle 5.

A: Thank you.

B: You're welcome.

▶ **PAIR WORK** • *Have similar conversations about these items:* (a) aspirin (b) cough syrup (c) mouthwash (d) eye drops (e) cold medicine (f) toothbrushes

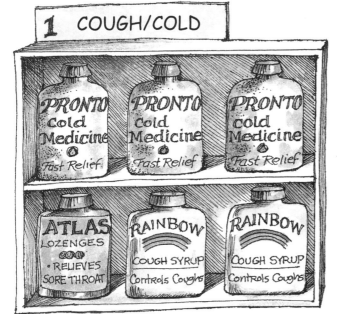

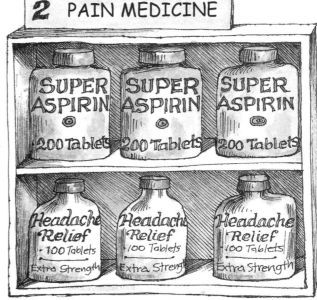

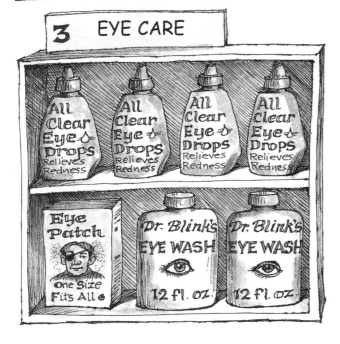

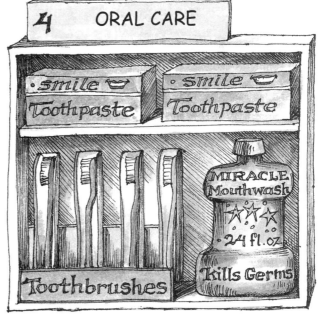

GRAND EXPECTATIONS

▶ 🎧 **PERSONAL INFORMATION** • *Read the profiles of Wendy and Fred.*

Name: __Wendy Walker__   Age: __28__
Occupation: __Police Officer__
Interests: __reading, listening to music, hiking, swimming, playing tennis__

Name: __Fred Fargo__   Age: __30__
Occupation: __Salesperson__
Interests: __birds, cartoons, video games, playing cards, having fun__

▶ 🎧 *About me.*

I am a happy, outgoing, energetic person who is a lot of fun. I enjoy life, people, good food and music. I am lucky to have a wonderful family and close friends. I live in the Los Angeles area. I love Southern California for its great weather, beautiful mountains and sandy beaches. I like to be outdoors as much as possible. I enjoy hiking, playing tennis and swimming. I'm adventurous, and I like to try new things.

▶ 🎧 *About me.*

I am a very interesting person. I have brown hair and brown eyes, and I have a nice smile. I'm a little shy, but everybody says I'm a cool guy. I'm really fun to be with. I like to stay home and play video games or watch TV. I also enjoy relaxing. Sometimes I go to the park and feed the birds. I give them bread crumbs. It's a blast to feed the birds, and it doesn't cost much. I think the best things in life are cheap.

▶ **QUESTIONS**

1. Where does Wendy live?
2. What does she enjoy doing?
3. Do you think Wendy is an interesting person? Why or why not?
4. Do you know any women like Wendy?

▶ **QUESTIONS**

1. What does Fred like to do?
2. Do you think Fred is an interesting person? Why or why not?
3. Do you think the best things in life are cheap, expensive or free?

Page Summary

Grammar Review
Function Talking about personal profiles
The Teacher's Notes for this activity continue on page T157.

NOTE

Prior to this lesson, ask students to bring a photo to class to use in their profiles. Alternatively, have students make a simple drawing of themselves to put in the profile.

Warm-up

Books are closed. Review the cartoon story in which Jason goes to Grand Expectations in order to get help finding a girlfriend. Remind students that Grand Expectations is a dating service. People write up a description of themselves when they register with the service. Ask students what information they think people include about themselves. Elicit their ideas and list them on the board.

Culture Note

In Fred's profile he uses a couple of expressions that might be unfamiliar to the students. *It's a blast* means *it's a lot of fun.* This expression can be used in many contexts; *It's a blast to snowboard. It's a blast surfing in Hawaii.* At the end he says, *I think the best things in life are cheap.* A common expression is *The best things in life are free.* This refers to the many things one can do in nature and elsewhere that are pleasurable but don't cost any money to do, for example, enjoying a beautiful sunset or sitting in a park.

▶ PERSONAL INFORMATION

1. Have students look at the illustration of Wendy Walker and then read the personal information about her at the top of the page.
2. Ask individual students comprehension questions, for example, *What is her name? How old is she? What does she do? What are her interests?* Have students answer in complete sentences.
3. Follow the same procedure for Fred Fargo. Ask the questions of different students.

▶ 🎧 *Read the profiles of Wendy and Fred.*

1. Play the recording (CD3, track 58) as students listen.
2. Play the recording (CD3, track 59) of Fred Fargo's profile as students listen.

▶ QUESTIONS

1. Ask the questions of individual students. Ask additional detail questions as well, for example, *What kind of person is Wendy? Does she have close friends? Why does Wendy like Southern California? Does she go outdoors often? How do you know? What does Fred look like? Is Fred shy? Is he fun to be with?*
2. Have students form pairs and discuss questions 3 and 4 for Wendy, and questions 2 and 3 for Fred.
3. Call on individual students to tell the class their answers to the questions they discussed.

▶ WRITING

Have students work alone to complete a personal profile for Great Expectations.

▶ PAIR WORK

1. Have students form pairs to talk about their interests.
2. Remind students to ask questions to get more information. Give students a few examples of follow-up questions to ask, for example, A: *I like reading.* B: *What kind of books do you read?* or *What is your favorite book?*

▶ COMPOSITION

1. Tell students to work alone to write a paragraph describing themselves. Encourage them to use the descriptions on page 156 as a model, but remind them not to copy lines directly from the profiles in the book.
2. Circulate and assist students as they write their paragraphs. Provide vocabulary as needed.

▶ PAIR WORK

1. Have students form pairs and exchange paragraphs.
2. Tell students to read what their partner wrote and to ask questions about anything that is unclear or that they would like to know more about.
3. Call on individual students to tell the class one interesting thing they learned about their partner. Tell the rest of the class to listen and find out who has similar interests.

Option: As a follow-up, tell students to talk to one other person in the class who has the same or a similar interest. Tell them to role-play an invitation to do something. If no one has the same interests, tell the student to invite someone to try something new.

Expansion Activity

Wendy says she is adventurous and likes to try new things. Tell students to imagine Wendy is coming to visit, and to imagine they are very adventurous. Before she comes, they each write a short letter telling her about the adventurous things they like to do. Model on the board how to write a casual letter with the greeting *Dear Wendy* and the closing *Sincerely yours, (first name only).* Tell them to each write at least three sentences in the body of the letter. When they are finished, have them form groups and take turns reading their letters out loud. As a follow-up, ask students if they came up with the same ideas of adventurous things to do.

▶ **WRITING** • *Imagine you are a member of Grand Expectations. Complete the profile with information about yourself.*

```
┌─────────────────────────────────────┐
│                                      │
│                                      │
│                                      │
│            Your Photo                │
│                                      │
│                                      │
│                                      │
└─────────────────────────────────────┘
```

Name: _____ Age: _____

Occupation: _____

Interests: _____

_____

▶ **PAIR WORK** • *Talk with your partner about your interests. Ask each other questions to get more information.*

▶ **COMPOSITION** • *Write a paragraph describing yourself. Use the description of Wendy Walker or Fred Fargo on page 156 as a model.*

About me.

_____

_____

_____

_____

_____

_____

_____

_____

_____

_____

_____

▶ **PAIR WORK** • *Read your partner's personal description and ask questions to get more information. Tell the class the most interesting thing you learned about your partner.*

VOCABULARY

NOUNS

Health problems
cold
cough
headache
insomnia
red eyes
sore throat
stomachache
toothache

Health remedies
antacid
aspirin
cold medicine
cough syrup
eye drops
eye wash
lozenges
mouthwash

Other
area
balcony
comb
dentist
dishwasher
dream
entertainment
farmhouse
feature

haircut
log cabin
nurse
parking lot
patio
swimming pool
teeth
third grade
vitamin

VERBS
hate
feed
keep
mail
say
teach

ADJECTIVES
adventurous
cheerful
close
cozy
different
energetic
fortunate

ideal
modern
old-fashioned
outgoing
peaceful
sunny

SUPERLATIVE
most expensive ≠ least expensive
most important ≠ least important

ADVERB
sometimes

EXPRESSIONS

Asking for and giving locations
Is there a bank around here?
Yes. There's one next to the hotel.
          …across from the park.

Talking about the weather
Beautiful day, isn't it?
     It's lovely.
In the summertime, when
the weather gets hot…

Giving opinions
It's okay.
It's a blast.
I think it's terrible.
I don't think so.

Talking about where people live
They live in the city.
     …by the sea.
     …in the mountains.
     …in the country.

Talking about routines
How often do you…?
     …every day.
     …every week.
     …every weekend.
     …once a day/week.
     …twice a day/week.
     …three times a day/week.

Talking about activities
I enjoy hiking.
     …swimming.
She likes to sing.
          …dance.

Asking permission
Is it okay if I sit here?

Other
This is my first time.
Me, too.

It doesn't cost much.
It's none of your business.

Are you serious?
I really mean it.

VOCABULARY

The games below provide additional opportunities to use the vocabulary, grammar, and expressions presented in the unit. Before students play any of the games, have them review the lists of words and circle any words they don't know. Then put students into small groups and have them review the circled words together. Circulate so you can help in case no one in the group knows a particular word.

Game 1: Concentration

Have students form pairs. Tell each pair to make 16 slips of paper. Have them divide the slips into two sets of eight each. Tell them to write the eight words under *Health problems* on the slips in one set, and the eight words under *Health remedies* on the slips in the other set. When they are finished, tell them to turn the slips facedown and spread them out between them. Students are now ready to play a matching game. One student starts by turning over two slips at random. The student reads the words out loud. If the slips match (one is the health problem and the other is the remedy), it is a match, and the student takes another turn. If they don't match, the student turns the slips facedown again, and the turn is over. Students continue until all the matches are made.

Game 2: Adjectives

Books are closed. Dictate the following words from Adjectives: *energetic, cheerful, cozy, old-fashioned, modern, ideal, sunny, peaceful, adventurous, most expensive*. Say each word twice, pausing for students to write. Have students open their books to check their spelling. Then have students close their books again. Tell them you will say one of the words (in random order), and they need to make up a sentence or question using the word. Tell them to raise their hands when they are ready to speak. Tell them you will only call on the first five students to raise their hands. Students get one point for each sentence or question they say in which they use the word correctly.

Game 3: Routines

Write the following list of activities on the board: *see a movie, eat in a restaurant, hang out with friends, go to the beach, listen to music, go to concerts, eat ice cream, go to the park, buy clothes, buy shoes, call a friend*. Have students form pairs and take turns asking each other how often they do these activities. When they are finished, ask them to sentences in which they summarize which of the activities on the board their partner does every day, once a week, and never.

PRONUNCIATION

Page Summary

▶A 🎧 *Listen and repeat.*

1. Have students look at the words. Tell them to pay attention to the two pronunciations of *th* as you play the recording (CD3, track 60).
2. Have students form pairs to practice reading the words out loud.

▶B 🎧 *Dictation*

1. Have students write the words in the blanks as you play the recording (CD3, track 61).
2. Read the sentences out loud as the students listen and check their work.
3. Check answers by calling on individual students to read their completed sentences.
4. Read each sentence to the class again, pausing for students to repeat.

Answer Key

1. We study together on Thursdays.
2. I think my mother is beautiful.
3. Thank you for the lovely flowers.
4. I get thirsty when the weather is hot.
5. My father is in good health.
6. There are thirty rooms in this hotel.
7. My brother is taking a bath.
8. Your teeth are over there.
9. Be careful with that thing.

▶C 🎧 *Pair Work*

1. Have students take turns saying the sentences in Part B.
2. Call on individual students to read the sentences out loud.

Option: Have students use a different gesture for each of the sounds as they read: raise their right hands for *think* and their left hands for *then*.

Expansion Activity

Books are closed. Have a spelling bee with the words in Part A. Pick a word at random and call on a student to spell it. Students get a point for each correct spelling.

PRONUNCIATION

▶ **A** 🎧 *Listen and repeat. Notice the two pronunciations of* **th**.

/θ/		/ð/	
think	bath	then	father
thank	mouth	that	mother
thirsty	health	there	together

▶ **B** 🎧 **DICTATION** • *Listen and complete the sentences.*

1. We study <u>together</u> on <u>Thursdays</u>.

2. I _____ my _____ is beautiful.

3. _____ you for _____ lovely flowers.

4. I get _____ when the _____ is hot.

5. My _____ is in good _____.

6. _____ are _____ rooms in ____ hotel.

7. My _____ is taking a _____.

8. Your _____ are over _____.

9. Be careful _____ _____ _____ !

▶ **C PAIR WORK** • *Take turns saying the sentences in Part B.*

TEST

1. a. Very good.   c. It's working.
   b. Yes, of course.   d. That's for sure.

2. a. delicious   c. over there
   b. expensive   d. right here

3. The boys _____ football now.
   a. plays   c. is playing
   b. playing   d. are playing

4. Sara is busy. She _____.
   a. is studying   c. study
   b. are studying   d. studies

5. Grover _____ Mexican food.
   a. love   c. loving
   b. loves   d. do love

6. Some people _____ every day.
   a. exercise   c. does exercise
   b. exercises   d. is exercising

7. Ellen _____ her job.
   a. no like   c. doesn't like
   b. don't like   d. likes not

8. Mr. Denby is unhappy when his
   students _____ their homework.
   a. do not   c. don't do
   b. not do   d. doesn't do

9. "Are Bob and Alice working today?"
   "_____."
   a. Yes, they are.
   b. No, they aren't.
   c. Yes, they do.
   d. No, they don't.

10. "Does Lulu like her new car?"
    "_____."
    a. Yes, she is.
    b. Yes, she do.
    c. Yes, she likes.
    d. Yes, she does.

TEST

_____ soup is good.

Whose oranges are _____?

11. a. This   c. These
     b. That   d. Those

12. a. this   c. these
     b. that   d. those

13. Oranges are my favorite _____.

     a. color   c. fruit
     b. vegetable   d. drink

14. We eat a big _____ every morning.

     a. food   c. lunch
     b. breakfast   d. dinner

15. "What do you do?"
    "_____"

     a. I'm busy.
     b. I'm fine, thank you.
     c. I'm doing my homework.
     d. I'm a mechanic.

16. "Is it okay if I use your computer?"
    "_____"

     a. Sure.
     b. You're welcome.
     c. Come on.
     d. That's right.

17. "_____ does Mike like his job?"
    "Because it's interesting."

     a. How   c. Why
     b. How much   d. When

18. "_____ do you exercise?"
    "Three times a week."

     a. How many   c. When
     b. How often   d. Where

Don't _____ that chicken!

Please _____ the phone.

19. a. wash   c. take
     b. buy   d. forget

20. a. hear   c. take
     b. answer   d. hold

TEST

21. a. Your   c. His
    b. My   d. Her

22. a. your   c. our
    b. my   d. their

23. I'm your friend. Listen to _____.
    a. I   c. you
    b. me   d. him

24. Mr. Grand is rich. Ask _____ for help.
    a. he   c. him
    b. her   d. me

25. We live ____ the city.
    a. in   c. at
    b. on   d. to

26. Are there many trees ____ your street?
    a. in   c. at
    b. on   d. to

27. _____ some apples on the table.
    a. It has   c. There is
    b. They're   d. There are

28. We don't have _____ bread.
    a. a   c. no
    b. any   d. some

29. a. Yes, there is.
    b. No, there isn't.
    c. Yes, there are.
    d. No, there aren't.

30. a. Yes, there is.
    b. No, there isn't.
    c. Yes, there are.
    d. No, there aren't.

TEST 2

Answer Key

1. b	11. a	21. d
2. c	12. d	22. c
3. d	13. c	23. b
4. a	14. b	24. c
5. b	15. d	25. a
6. a	16. a	26. b
7. c	17. c	27. d
8. c	18. b	28. b
9. b	19. c	29. a
10. d	20. b	30. d